To Chris and Marilyn,
as a mo————— ——————
friend,
March —— —

Chinese Amusement

Chinese Amusement

The Lively Plays of Li Yü

ERIC P. HENRY

1980
ARCHON BOOKS

Library of Congress Cataloging in Publication Data

Henry, Eric P   1943-
   Chinese amusement the lively plays of Li Yü
   Includes bibliographical references and index.
      1. Li, Yü, 1611–1680?—Criticism and interpretation.
I. Title.
PL2698.L52Z67   895.1'8409   80-17072
ISBN 0-208-01837-9

First published 1980 as an Archon Book,
an imprint of The Shoe String Press, Inc.,
Hamden, Connecticut 06514

To my friend and mentor Clara Claibourne Park

經師易求，人師難得

Contents

The laughter of comedy is impersonal and of unrivaled politeness, nearer a smile — often no more than a smile. It laughs through the mind, for the mind directs it; and it might be called the humor of the mind.

George Meredith, "An Essay on Comedy" (1877)

Preface and Acknowledgements

This book is based on a Ph.D. dissertation in Chinese literature that I wrote at Yale University.

For those who may find them useful, I have supplied Chinese characters for certain Chinese names, terms, and quotations in the Glossary, and I have likewise equipped the text with a set of notes containing much technical information; nevertheless, this book is not solely or even primarily intended for specialists. In fact it has been my whole aim and desire from the beginning to make this study an old-fashioned, unrigorous, nontechnical, nontheoretical, nonacademic, nonmysterious "English reader's companion" to the plays of Li Yü. If (as I fear is likely) I have not realized this ideal, the failure is due more to lack of ability than to perverse intent and I beg the reader's pardon and indulgence for it.

Since Li Yü's plays are still untranslated and thus accessible only to readers of Chinese, I have tried to make the play summaries at the end of this book leisurely enough to suggest a little of their original tastes and sensations. I have also taken care to supply enough quotation and scene recreation in the body of the book to make my remarks readily intelligible without prior reference to the plays.

Li Yü left interesting work of many types. It would be just as reasonable and rewarding to study him as an essayist, a drama theorist, a short-story writer, a garden designer, or a publisher-editor as it is to study him as a playwright. Here, however, I am directly concerned only with Li Yü's work as a playwright; and of the ten plays by Li Yü that are extant, I have chosen to deal at length only with four that are particularly representative.

I claim literary value for these works and study them for traditional reasons: they are ingenious and beautiful structures that (1) compel attention and delight in themselves and (2) allow the reader to grow in knowledge and sympathy by looking at the world from a point of view that is not his or her own. We are not seventeenth-century Chinese freethinkers and humorists; we can have no means of imagining how the world might have appeared to such a person if we do not have recourse to such things as literary remains.

Although the plays discussed in this book belong to a performed genre, I have intentionally neglected all those colorful appeals to ear and eye, such as music, costume, gesture, and acrobatics, that make such an immediate and striking impression on the viewer in any performance of Chinese drama and have instead treated the plays as purely literary texts. Techniques of performance are an absorbing and valuable study in themselves, but they are roughly the same for all plays within a given performance tradition. What make any particular play different from other plays are the thoughts, perceptions, and attitudes that it contains or implies, and it is with this cognitive content that I am concerned. To dwell on aspects of performance in a book of this sort would be like dwelling on physiology in a biography. The subject of a biography of course possesses a body, but what chiefly distinguishes him from other people is not the way his body works, but rather the sum of his thoughts and experiences.

I have not in every case been totally confident of the correctness of the interpretations I advance in this book, but I felt that in such cases of incomplete certainty it would be best to state what I believe to be true in a direct, incautious, and unencumbered manner, as this would best enable my views to be debated among others interested in the same subject. If, as a consequence of this debate, my views can be amended or replaced, I will be extremely gratified and will feel that my approach has achieved the desired result.

Among the many friends, teachers, and fellow students who took time from their pressing engagements to read and comment on portions of the manuscript, I particularly wish to extend my sincere thanks to Richard Strassberg, Stephen Owen, Conrad Lung, Christopher Stade, Helen Tartar, Clara Park, and P'ei-k'ai Cheng. Hans Frankel and Hugh Stimson contributed greatly to the accuracy of this book by compiling long lists of errata when reading one of the final drafts. Jeanne Ferris of The Shoe String Press caught many further errors and improved the style and sense of many sentences in the course of preparing the manuscript for publication. I am also deeply indebted to Chin Chia-hsi and Liang (née Liu) Ch'un-hua of the Stanford Center for Chinese Language Studies in Taipei for their patient and capable instruction in many matters pertaining to Chinese drama. I am especially grateful to Richard D. Yeung for consenting to adorn the dust jacket, Glossary and dedication page with his skillful calligraphy. I wish to thank Yin Yee for the typing of the second and third chapters and Cheng Kuang-yuan for assisting me with the interpretation of a play preface and the typing of chapter 4. I am indebted to my mother, Eleanor R. Henry, for suggesting the subtitle of this book, and to both my parents for their support and encouragement. My friend Francis Braunlich suggested the translation of the play title *Pi-mu yü* that appears in chapter 2 and elsewhere. My employers, Connecticut Ballet Inc., were kind enough to allow me a slightly irregular use of their reproduction facilities at a crucial stage in the manuscript preparation. I also wish to record my gratitude to Yale University for the award of a two-year prize fellowship in East Asian Studies without which this dissertation could not have been written. Finally I wish to thank my wife, Joan Garnett, for helping me with the manuscript when deadlines have loomed, and for having the good manners never to mention the odious truism that writing books about playwrights is not a highroad to prosperity.

Biographical Introduction

Li Yü was born in 1611 and died in 1680 or shortly thereafter.[1] He led a busy, turbulent, and productive life, during the course of which he became one of the principal literary figures of the early Ch'ing dynasty and one of the most versatile and inventive of all Chinese authors. He is a delight to read; his work possesses a special buoyancy, ease, and humor that assuage care and dissolve perplexity.

The variety of activities for which he is still remembered today is truly remarkable and their mere enumeration is sufficient to provide us with a lively and charming impression of the man. He is remembered (1) as the author of a book of informal essays entitled *A Random Lodge for My Idle Feelings* (Hsien ch'ing ou chi) in which three chapters of drama theory have attracted particularly wide attention;[2] (2) as the author of a number of plays, especially *The Kite's Mistake* (Feng-cheng wu) and *What Can You Do?* (Nai-ho t'ien), that abound in humor, incident, farce, and paradox;[3] (3) as the author of two collections of short stories in the Chinese vernacular, *Twelve Mansions* (Shih erh lou) and *Plays Without Sound* (Wu sheng hsi);[4] (4) as the reputed author of a cleverly devised erotic novel, *The Prayermat of Flesh* (Jou p'u-t'uan);[5] (5) as the author of the preface to *The Mustard Seed Garden Manual of Painting* (Chieh-tzu yüan hua chuan);[6] (6) as the landscape architect who designed "The Half-acre Garden" (Pan-mou yüan), one of the most beautiful garden estates of Peking;[7] and (7) as a theatrical impresario whose extravagant and irregular life-style as a roaming client of the wealthy diverted some and scandalized others.[8]

Like most intellectuals and writers of his time, Li Yü came from the Kiangsu-Chekiang region.[9] The son of a well-to-do family, he began his adult life in the enjoyment of a degree of comfort and security that might have hindered the subsequent emergence of his originality had he not been shaken loose from those circumstances in his mid-thirties by the Manchu conquest of the Kiangsu-Chekiang area.

xiii

Before that event, he did what many other young men of his means, interests, and abilities did: he traveled; studied; wrote poems and essays; paid filial attentions to his parents; made various attempts to pass the *chü-jen* or provincial examination; and, as conditions became more unsettled, tried his hand at the eremitic life on his family's estate at I-shan near Lan-ch'i, where, as he later recalled, he delighted in lying naked among lotuses where members of his family could not find him.[10] In 1644 and 1645, the deteriorating local situation compelled him to practice a less agreeable form of eremitism in an unspecified mountainous wilderness where he fled with his wife and daughter. Upon returning to his former haunts some time after the sacking of Yangchow and Nanking, he found that his townhouse, his library, his writings, and his country retreat had all been burnt to cinders by marauding soldiers.[11] He found temporary employment as a secretary in the office of a local subprefect, but was nevertheless forced to sell the family property at I-shan to make ends meet.

For the rest of his life he pursued a precarious and controversial but intermittently successful career as a free-lance printer, bookdealer, writer, garden architect, and theatrical manager, a mode of life that was perhaps facilitated not only by need, but by the circumstance that his father and mother could no longer be mortified by such behavior, having died in 1629 and 1642 respectively. For ten years (1648-57) he lived by West Lake in Hangchow, calling himself "the leaf-hatted old man on the lake" (Hu-shang Li-weng).[12] During this period he printed and sold books and composed social and ceremonial literature, such as epitaphs, inscriptions, and formal letters, in return for gifts.[13] Li Yü made many acquaintances with literary people during this period and was creatively active as well. One of his surviving plays, *The Jade Scratcher (Yü sao t'ou)*, and probably various others, were written at Hangchow[14] and it is likely that his two short story collections *Twelve Mansions* and *Plays Without Sound* were largely or wholly composed at this time as well.[15]

In 1657, Li Yü found his Hangchow publishing business threatened by the piratical activities of other printers, so he moved to Nanking, which remained his home for the next twenty years. This was the flood tide of Li Yü's career, the period of his greatest worldly success and the period in which his work and his life-style assumed the characteristic forms by which he is known to posterity. In 1660, when Li Yü was fifty-one, a long-awaited family event occurred: his first son was born, followed by three more sons within the next two years. This sudden appearance of offspring was matched by many new additions to the children of his imagination; he completed at least four (and probably many more) new plays during the ensuing decade— *The Paired Soles* (*Pi-mu yü*, 1661), *The Hen Seeks the Rooster* (*Huang ch'iu feng*, c. 1665), *The Careful Couple* (*Shen luan chiao*, c. 1667), and *The Amazing Reunion* (*Ch'iao t'uan-yüan*, 1668).[16] In 1666–67 he went on the first of a series of far-flung tours through various parts of China in which people of wealth and culture vied with each other in hosting and rewarding him. During the course of his first tour, which took him to Shensi and Kansu by way of Peking, he was presented with two young concubines surnamed Ch'iao and Wang, both of whom turned out to have great aptitude in singing and acting. They became the nucleus of a private female acting troupe that accompanied Li Yü on all of his subsequent professional journeys. Ch'iao generally played the female, and Wang the male, lead. From this time on Li Yü was able to observe the effect of a new scene as soon as it was written. His experience as a director may well have contributed to certain revisions of scenes by other authors that appear in his works, and to the unusually practical bent of the dramaturgical chapters in his essay-book *A Random Lodge for My Idle Feelings*, the preface of which is dated 1671.[17]

Though the proceeds from Li Yü's western tour were substantial, they were swiftly consumed by his debts, some of which were probably connected with a recently purchased hilltop home in Nanking that he called "The Mustard-seed Garden" (Chieh-tzu yüan) in allusion to the smallness of the property.[18] Li Yü adopted the name for his printing business as well and a number of editions bearing this imprimature, all finely executed, survive. Among them, the previously mentioned *Mustard Seed Garden Manual of Painting*, a collection of engraved reproductions with commentary prepared by Li Yü's son-in-law in 1679, is particularly well-known and has gone through a number of subsequent expansions and continuations.[19]

Li Yü went on long tours almost continuously from 1666 to 1672, but none of the later journeys were as financially successful as the one to Shensi had been. This mode of life was severely curtailed by the illness and death of Li Yü's two best actresses, Ch'iao and Wang, in 1672 and 1674 respectively. When Li Yü heard of the latter's death he was in Peking, where he had hoped to discover new sources of

patronage. A friend upon whom he had relied to provide him with
introductions died soon after his arrival, however, and none of the
acquaintances he made there were wealthy enough to help him
significantly.

On returning to Nanking he began to entertain the design of moving back to Hangchow, which he had left seventeen years previously,
but the move was difficult to accomplish due to his straitened circumstances and the size of his household which, with his wife and
concubines, his five sons, his two daughters, his various sons- and
daughters-in-law, his grandchildren, his maids and servants, his
musicians, and his printing employees, amounted to about forty people. In 1676 he was finally enabled to purchase a hill in Hangchow
and move there with his family through the aid of an official acquaintance and through the sale of all his Nanking possessions, including
his printing blocks.[20]

Shortly after arriving in Hangchow he suffered a succession of ill-
nesses and a fall down some stairs that confined him to bed
throughout most of the following year. With no money coming in
from his tours, the family lacked the means to engage a doctor, buy
medicines, or to repair the walls and roof of their dwelling. In the fall,
however, he recovered enough to go on a round of visits in north-
eastern Chekiang that enabled him, the following spring, to repair
his property and resume his printing activities. He passed the last two
years of his life improving his Hangchow garden Ts'eng-yüan, devising theatrical entertainments for friends, taking his sons to their *hsiu-
ts'ai* or licentiate examinations, and writing prefaces. The last of his
writings dates from the winter of 1679 and it is generally assumed
that he died shortly afterwards.[21]

I. The Medium: Drama, Story, and Comedy

    The growing drama has outgrown such toys
Of simulated stature, face and speech:
It also peradventure may outgrow
The simulation of the painted scene, . . .
And take for a worthier stage the soul itself,
Its shifting fancies and celestial lights,
With all its grand orchestral silences
To keep the pauses of its rhythmic sounds.
                E. B. Browning, *Aurora Leigh* (1857)

"As an exquisite embodiment of the poet's visions, and a realization of human intellectuality, gilding with refulgent light our dreamy moments, and laying open a new and magic world before the mental eye, the drama is gone, perfectly gone," said Mr. Curdle.
                Dickens, *Nicholas Nickleby* (1839)

In his essay "Thoughts on Comedy" (1798), Horace Walpole observed in passing that the Chinese were a highly ceremonious people ("even carmen make excuses to each other for stopping up the way") and concluded from this that their comedies could not be very striking. Despite appearances, the statement had nothing to do with China; it was a reflection of Walpole's anxiety that an "inundation of politeness" in England and on the continent had deprived the comic dramatist of his natural material by clothing man's passions and eccentricities in a decorous disguise.[1] The passage of time has simplified our recollection of the eighteenth century and suppressed

1

the sentimental comedy that was worrying Walpole when he made
these remarks, so we are apt to protest that the substitution of
ceremony for impulse in the conduct of social life results not in the
decline of comedy, but in the transition from a comedy based upon
psychology or ethics to a comedy based upon social convention: a
transition, in short, from a comedy of humors to a comedy of manners.[2] We have tended for so long, in fact, to associate the comic with
the comedy of manners that it is natural for us to fall prey to the opposite anxiety: that the gradual disappearance of the more rigid and
complicated forms of prescribed behavior in our social life leaves the
dramatist with a narrowed field of polite pretense, social embarrassment, and ironic repartee upon which to draw for comic purposes.[3] We might conclude that any people as devoted to ceremony as
the pre-Republican Chinese must have enjoyed a flourishing comic
tradition.

Both these reactions, however, err in viewing comedy simply as a
collection of humorous situations dependent for its vitality upon the
abundance with which such situations occur in the society portrayed.
Comedy is more than a matter of discovery and accumulation; it is a
matter of outlook and analysis. It is always to some degree an exposure and critique of the classifiable offenses against what the
dramatist and his audience would define as "good social behavior."[4]
Such offenses are present in every imaginable condition of society
and their skillful portrayal is bound to be funny and thought-
provoking.[5] What may be lacking is not the raw material of comedy,
but rather the spirit of skepticism, amusement, and devotion to
detached observation that must exist if the dramatist is to create a
viable comic system from the plethora of meaningfully funny
behavior that surrounds him.[6] Neither manners nor the absence of
manners is an obstacle to comedy; an attitude of fervent commitment
to either condition, however, can be fatal to it.

Comedy in traditional Chinese drama is in one sense very plentiful
and in another sense very rare. The innumerable long romantic plays
that were written in the Ming and early Ch'ing dynasties abound in
comic episodes of all kinds, but only a few of them are comic in their
main themes as well as in their episodes. The scattering of Chinese
plays that could be said to be comic in their totality includes some
splendid examples of the comedist's art, but none of them have
achieved great renown in China or elsewhere.[7] Therefore, when we

speak of comedy in the context of Chinese drama, we are talking about something that is not as visible and well-established in that dramatic tradition as it is in the western one. Traditional Chinese literati often had an acute sense of humor, but (perhaps for that reason) they never spent any appreciable amount of time discussing comedy as a category of drama.[8]

The term *comedy* and its derivatives can mean so many different things that it is necessary at this point to establish some categories in order to avoid confusion. Three broad distinctions of usage are readily discernible:

(1) Comedy as a literary form. In this sense the term refers to the type of plot structure found in the plays of Menander, Plautus, and Terence (called "new comedy" in contrast to the "old comedy" of Aristophanes).[9] A presentable young man and an agreeable young woman fall in love and at length overcome the resistances of circumstance, villains, rivals, and churlish elders to their happy union. Their efforts are typically aided by clever slaves or servants, love tokens, disguises, and the recovery of long-lost family secrets. This type of plot structure ordinarily persists unchanged throughout many styles of comedy, which we distinguish by such terms as romantic comedy, satiric comedy, the comedy of manners, farce, sentimental comedy, and so on. Intimations of it may even be perceived in Aristophanic or old comedy, which has a different structure. There is no necessary connection between comic structure and prevailing mood. A play or a novel may have nothing to do with gaiety or laughter and yet be a comedy in this structural sense. *Measure for Measure* and *Little Dorrit* are structurally comic regardless of the gravity of their themes. Chinese romantic dramas of the Ming and Ch'ing dynasties are usually serious and occasionally somber in outlook, but they are nevertheless comedies in the structural sense. Their young lovers win through; they gain each other and they gain social acceptance. Wrongs are righted, sufferings assuaged, and families reunited. The same is true of the Chinese popular romance or *ts'ai tzu chia-jen* novel, which derives its structure from the stage.[10]

(2) Comedy as a literary outlook. Comedy in this sense is the point of view that defines the ideal man as a conforming member of a community. It is opposed to the tragic point of view, which assumes that the ideal man can or should be spiritually independent of the prudential rules of ordinary human society. Tragedy celebrates our impulse

to rise above our condition; comedy deflates the presumption that must accompany such an impulse and implicitly advises us never to forget our condition.[11] The comic point of view may or may not be present in pieces that are comic in structure. Typically it is associated with comedy that inclines toward realism and critical observation rather than with comedy that inclines toward romance. Though often associated with comic structure, the comic point of view may flourish in works that do not have that structure, such as *The Alchemist* (Ben Jonson) or *The Scholars* (*Ju-lin wai-shih*; Wu Ching-tzu.) Though often associated with humor and laughter, it may be intensely present in works that are not particularly laughter-provoking, such as the novels of Jane Austen and Henry James. Conversely, a gag told for a laugh may be funny without being comic in this sense. Chinese romantic dramas are comic in structure, but only a few are comic in this second sense. The principal plays of Li Yü, including the ones dealt with in this book, are among those few.

(3) Comedy as a type of literary content. Comedy in this sense refers to humor or jocularity and is the popular, nonspecialized sense of the word. It can occur alone (as in the performance of a stand-up comedian) or in conjunction with either or both of the first two types of comedy. As I mentioned earlier, it occurs episodically in all Chinese drama. Clowns are among the standard role-types of the Chinese stage and the villains (another role-type) often behave as comically as the clowns. It is also very plentiful in Li Yü, whose work abounds in every kind of amusement, from the most delicate shade of irony to the coarsest belly laugh.

It might be objected that the above meanings of the term comedy are often conjoined and are indeed so closely associated as to imply each other. That is perfectly true, and that is precisely why the above distinctions are necessary. Semantic misunderstanding is only a serious danger when the meanings denoted by the same term are so closely related that the fact of faulty communication may pass undetected.

When I refer to Li Yü (or any other author) as a comedist, it will be sense two (comedy as a literary outlook) that I primarily intend. Sense one is not restrictive enough. In that sense, every writer of Chinese romantic drama (or of romantic comedy in the west) would be a comedist. Sense three, on the other hand, is too reductive. There is no need to apply the term *comedist* to a writer whose primary concern is to devise laughs, when the term humorist will do as well.

Li Yü is probably the most well-known of the Chinese playwrights who wrote sustained comedy, and his interest to us derives in some measure from his membership in such a small literary category. It is natural, even if our curiosity cannot in the end be satisfied, to wonder what thoughts or experiences might have caused him to desire to write such an unusual type of play. It is also natural to wonder what comedy might be like in a culture that owes nothing to Greece or Rome. Before we discuss how Li Yü goes about writing comedy, however, it is necessary to say something about the medium in which he wrote it.

English forces us to say that Li Yü wrote "plays," but these works are quite unlike anything that that word is apt to suggest to the uninitiated western reader. The Chinese term for the genre is *ch'uan-ch'i,* an expression that etymologically means "to transmit the strange" and that was originally applied not to plays, but to a type of classical-prose short story, often dealing with the supernatural, that first appeared in the T'ang dynasty. The earlier meaning survives along with the later one in current speech, but the occasional confusion to which this gives rise can be avoided in English by using the terms "*ch'uan-ch'i* tale" and "*ch'uan-ch'i* play."

Ch'uan-ch'i plays are dramatic in format; they consist of song lyrics, poems, and prose speeches that the reader is to imagine performed by a cast of actors on a stage. They are usually divided into thirty or more acts *(ch'u)* of varying length and complexity. An average *ch'u* is longer than an average Shakespearean scene but shorter than a Shakespearean act. It is not uncommon for *ch'uan-ch'i* plays to have forty or fifty such acts. The *Peony Pavilion (Mu-tan t'ing),* one of the best-known, has fifty-five. *Ch'uan-ch'i* plays are today almost never performed in their entirety; they are too long. The usual practice in *ch'uan-ch'i* revivals is to stage famous single acts, not necessarily drawn from the same work. This practice seems to have been common even in the Ming and early Ch'ing dynasties, when the *ch'uan-ch'i* play was the dominant dramatic form[12] It is a form that aims at comprehensiveness, like a novel or a wall tapestry. Cyril Birch aptly characterizes them as "undulating cavalcades."[13] It is also a form that, in its later and more literary manifestations, was intended as much for reading as for performance.[14]

I must mention parenthetically that *ch'uan-ch'i* plays differ markedly in this respect from another Chinese dramatic form, the *tsa-chü*. Both forms began as popular entertainments in the late Sung and ended as pastimes of the cultured elite in the mid-Ch'ing. The *tsa-chü*, however, became a dominant form about a century before the *ch'uan-ch'i* play achieved that status. They are short (usually four or four and a half acts) and focused (only one character may have arias). In the Yüan dynasty, the period of their greatest vitality, they were written for performance, not perusal. Texts of Yüan *tsa-chü* apparently were preserved only as a belated afterthought.[15] The *tsa-chü* is narrower in scope than a typical western play; the *ch'uan-ch'i* play much broader.

When we think of the *ch'uan-ch'i* play as a form, we have to imagine something at once more novelistic than a play and more ritualistic than a novel. There are no particular limitations of time, place, or focus. Months or years may elapse between acts; the location may change from a luxurious private courtyard in one act to a rude military encampment thousands of miles distant in the next, or to an enchanted island or afterworld located nowhere in particular. A change of location may be accompanied by a change to a new set of characters whose relation to the other sets of characters need not become clear until some later point. New characters may in fact be introduced whenever convenient, even, if need be, in the final act. There is often a subplot that parodies or parallels the main plot.

The characters in *ch'uan-ch'i* drama have an internal life of thought and sensibility that is rendered as explicitly and continuously as their external life of action and speech. This interior perspective is principally built up through the ubiquitous aria lyrics, and is contributed to as well by entrance and exit poems and freely used asides. *Ch'uan-ch'i* plays develop through a continuous alternation of action and reflection. Each slight change in the dramatic situation leads to a lyric mood-portrait.

So nearly does this form of drama approximate narrative literature that we may even from time to time discern in some of its details intimations of a detached, moralizing narrator's voice. A stage manager-cum-author comments on the play in the first act and at the close of the work, and the characters themselves are free to stand back and take a detached view of the action (even, at times, discussing the play as a play) in the closing lyrics of each act. Less commonly, and in a more oblique fashion, they may also detach themselves from the action in their entrance and exit poems.

In all these respects, the *ch'uan-ch'i* play is a form of immense freedom and expansiveness; if there is a clock ticking in the background, it ticks so feebly and at such long intervals that stretches of *ch'uan-ch'i* drama may be read (just as stretches of life may be lived) as if it were not progressing or coming to an end. In these respects, the *ch'uan-ch'i* play might be compared to the roomiest and most "interior" of western literary forms: the novel. The tendency of the novel, however, is to refine away or conceal whatever is artificial in its own structure, to encourage in the reader the illusion that he is being shown life exactly as it is, undistorted by any literary convention or structural necessity. The tendency of *ch'uan-ch'i* drama at first appears to be exactly opposite; it impresses us as a form that insists on the perfection of its rituality and abstraction. The type of admiration it appears designed to elicit is not "How lifelike!" or "How true!" but rather "How ingenious!" or "How delicate!"

It is important to realize, however, to what extent this perception of *ch'uan-ch'i* drama is a function of unfamiliarity. The more one reads *ch'uan-ch'i* drama, the less one notices its conventions. An experienced reader in the genre looks through the conventions at the subject matter as through a pane of glass. Also, there is considerable variation among *ch'uan-ch'i* playwrights with respect to abstraction versus realism. There is an "adorned" tradition (*wen-tz'u p'ai*) that stresses refinement and allusiveness. There is also a naturalistic tradition (*pen-se p'ai*) that stresses intelligibility and vigorous directness. Li Yü was both in theory and practice an enthusiastic upholder of the second tradition. Nevertheless, a newcomer to the genre is apt to be more impressed by the elaborateness of its conventions than by its dedication to naturalism

In the world of *ch'uan-ch'i* drama, every character belongs to one of a variety of standard theatrical role-types such as clown, villain, leading man, and so on. The characters are identified in the texts not by their own names, but by the names of their role-types, which are immediately identifiable on stage through strongly marked conventions of makeup and apparel. There are consequently no ambiguous people in *ch'uan-ch'i* drama and no major revelations of personality; a character's theatrical identity tells us at once what behavior traits to expect from him. The initial division of humanity into types does not preclude subtlety of portrayal, but it does establish boundaries within which subtlety may be exercised. Delicacy and sensibility, for example, are traits that in general may be highly developed only in the leading man and the leading lady (the *sheng* and the *tan*). The supporting roles (the *hsiao-sheng* and the *hsiao-tan*) will be characterized by honesty, loyalty, decency, and so forth, but not by advanced sensibility. Earthiness and humor are the prerogative of clowns and villains (*ch'ou* and *ching*). These distinctions belong to the grammar of the form.

Ch'uan-ch'i plays possess grammars of gesture and event as well as a grammar of personality. Stage directions rarely depart from brief formulae such as "very astonished," "laughing," "weeping," "bowing," or "heaving a sigh," states and actions that are represented on stage by various elaborate gestures clearly intended as signs rather than imitations. The free use of signs to stand for actions and emotional states is not as antimimetic a practice as one might at first suppose; rather it can be regarded as an intensification of a tendency found in all levels of the culture. Ch'uan-ch'i plays are elaborately stylized, but so was the life that they reflect. Of course what an outsider perceives as ritual may be so much a part of the unconscious routine of the insider that he does not notice it at all.

Ch'uan-ch'i plays owe something of their novelistic breadth to their quite unnovelistic stylization of action. The agreement to use nonimitative signs allows the *ch'uan-ch'i* playwright to imagine scenes with the freedom of a storyteller; he need not be deterred by difficulties of realistic enactment on the stage. This is all the more true of literary *ch'uan-ch'i* plays written more for reading than for performance. Documents may be composed or perused on the (frequently imaginary) stage in foreshortened time; journeys whether on foot, on horseback, by boat, or by sedan chair may occur (or be supposed to occur) onstage; full-scale battles may take place before the eyes of the (supposed) spectators, and so on.

The only limitations to a *ch'uan-ch'i* playwright's storytelling freedom were ones that derived from his inherited habits of narrative and dramatic imagination. These limitations were all the more effective for being unconscious and habitual, and were sufficient to impart a remarkable degree of generic resemblance to the plots of *ch'uan-ch'i* plays. Most *ch'uan-ch'i* plays use a traditional, or at least a preexisting, story, but even those that use a new story belong to, or depend upon, some traditional type of narrative. The distinguishing features of these narrative types are many, and they collectively constitute the grammar of events referred to above.

Here it will only be necessary to describe the most generally prac-
tised of these narrative types, for which I will borrow the term
"romantic comedy."[16] This type comprises well over half of the total
ch'uan-ch'i corpus; almost all of the dozen or so most famous ch'uan-
ch'i plays belong to it; and all of the plays of Li Yü belong to it, or
derive from it, or react against it.[17]

Chinese romantic comedies are concerned with quests for love and
social standing. The first act consists of introductory verses, including an outline of the story to be enacted. These are sung by a
stage manager who acts as the author's persona.[18] The second episode
introduces the male protagonist. He is a young man of great but
unrecognized abilities, not yet married and looking for an ideal mate.
He is poor and without connections; often, in fact, an orphan.[19] The
third episode introduces the female protagonist, who is refined and
literate. She may be (a) the daughter of a (usually distinguished) official family, or (b) a famous courtesan whose favors are sought by all
the young men of the region (usually the Kiangsu-Chekiang region,
also known as "the land of Wu"). If a courtesan, she is often a well-
born woman who has been separated from her family through some
misfortune. The following several episodes include a portrayal of the
initial contact between the romantic principals. This is always
discreet and delicate; typically it is accomplished through an
exchange of poems. The female protagonist admires the male protagonist and suffers lyrically and volubly from his absence, but she remains inaccessible, due either to the prestige and decorum of her
family or, if she is a courtesan, to the greed of her professional "step-
mother," who must be paid an immense sum of money if she is to
relinquish such a valuable property. The lovers' fidelity to each other
is usually pledged and symbolized by a gift, such as a fan or bracelet,
which later may serve as a means of (true or mistaken) recognition.
Ch'uan-ch'i plays often take their titles from this love token.

Two types of villains generally arise during the course of the narrative. The first is a powerful vulgarian (often a wealthy merchant;
sometimes a wicked official) bent on making the female protagonist
his concubine. The second is an ambitious bandit or rebellious
general who desires to overthrow the dynasty and become the new
Son of Heaven. The social disruption created by his military activities
often causes the romantic leads to become separated from each other

or from their families and gives rise to many occasions of suffering or adventure. The rebel, traitor, or invader is opposed by a virtuous and loyal general who is acquainted, or becomes acquainted, with the protagonist. At some point in the story, the protagonist travels to the capital and takes the highest or metropolitan examination, which he passes brilliantly, usually coming out first. This often causes the great officials of the capital (typically including the prime minister) to seek him as a son-in-law. He usually turns down these offers out of loyalty to the female protagonist and frequently incurs the hatred of a high official through his refusals.[20] The official retaliates by involving him in difficulties, such as having him sent on a dangerous or undesirable assignment. The protagonist displays ingenuity or fortitude in surviving these difficulties and often gains imperial favor by contributing (typically through the suggestion of a military tactic) to the defeat of the rebellion or invasion that was threatening the dynasty.

In the meantime the female protagonist cleverly or heroically frustrates the designs of the vulgarian who desires her as a concubine. Often she is driven to attempt suicide, usually by drowning, from which she is fortuitously rescued, often by nuns, priests, spirits, or wise and good people with supernatural knowledge. Her rescuers enable her to commence a second, anonymous existence unknown to her family, her persecutor, or her betrothed. Often, neither the male nor the female protagonist realizes that the other is still alive. In such cases, parents or parent-surrogates force them to marry, neither party realizing till the last moment that their prospective spouse is actually his (her) long-lost betrothed. Whether through this or some other process, the protagonists eventually triumph over their enemies and over parental opposition and marry amid general approval and rejoicing. Or alternatively, if the world's difficulties prove insuperable, their souls may meet and settle down to continuous bliss in an afterlife.

Though *ch'uan-ch'i* plays are expansive in time and involve many sets of characters, they do not in general convey an impression of diffuseness or improvisation; rather, one is impressed at the thoroughness with which the material of most plays is made to serve the interests of unity and pattern. This is a little surprising, as traditional Chinese drama critics (many of whom were also playwrights) appear from their writings to have been much more concerned with technical details of lyric writing than with problems of overall dramatic construction.[21] But unity is perhaps something that transcends theories. A principle of unity, whatever local and temporary guise it may assume, and regardless of the frequency with which it is violated, can in general be distinguished in any artistic genre, since it is in itself one of the preconditions for the existence of a genre. As C. S. Lewis puts it in his *Allegory of Love*,

> Unity of interest is not "classical"; it is not foreign to any art that has ever existed or ever can exist in the world. Unity in diversity if possible—failing that, mere unity, as a second best—these are the norms for all human work, given, not by the ancients, but by the nature of consciousness itself. When schools of criticism or poetry break this rule, this rule breaks them.[22]

Of course it is not unknown for a *ch'uan-ch'i* play to consist of a random string of adventures involving a central figure or of two or more narrative strands having little relation to each other, and occasionally a traditional critic will complain about "diffuseness" (*man-yen fa-chieh*),[23] but such plays are not typical of the genre as a whole. Representative *ch'uan-ch'i* plays (those that are praised, remembered, and read) and the majority of obscure examples as well tend to be conspicuously well-made. Characters are symmetrically opposed, segments of narrative parallel each other, coincidence is freely used to construct patterns, stories are arranged so that love scenes and ensemble scenes occur at rhythmic intervals, climaxes are carefully prepared for and cleverly delayed. The stories are usually derived rather than invented. They are drawn from history, legend, biography, and prose fiction, and are then adapted sufficiently to provide occasion for obligatory features of the genre such as happy endings, battle scenes, clowning, and, above all, lyric poetry.

Such are the general characteristics of *ch'uan-ch'i* drama. This is the tradition to which Li Yü's work belongs and of which it is an organic development. But Li Yü did as much to alter the nature of the genre as he did to carry it on. While breaking none of the codifiable conventions of *ch'uan-ch'i* drama, he evinces a sharply distinctive sensibility, supported in his theoretical writing by certain consciously and combatively maintained ideas on how *ch'uan-ch'i* plays should be composed. A just description of his work must therefore differ somewhat, in respect of emphasis and content, from a description of the genre to which it belongs.

The main technical source of this difference is the predominance in his work of narrative, as opposed to lyric, elements. Li Yü is a writer who thinks through story. He makes his points through arrangements of events. Of the various literary functions of narrative in *ch'uan-ch'i* drama, the following are unusually prominent in Li Yü's work:

(1) It is a source of surprise and wonder. To Li Yü, the fundamental requirement of drama was novelty. He felt that, in order to be artistically successful, a *ch'uan-ch'i* play must deal with a type of situation or relationship untouched in any earlier play. He supports this idea in his *Random Lodge for My Idle Feelings* by appealing to the etymological meaning of the term *ch'uan-ch'i*: "to transmit the marvelous."[24]

(2) It appeals to the rational faculty through logical intricacy. Li Yü's plays are rich in narrative complication.

(3) It is an object of abstract contemplation which, when perceived all at once, like a bridge or cathedral, pleases through balance, economy, or wholeness.

(4) It is a means of exploring a theme or intellectual problem. Each development of the plot brings the characters into a situation which illustrates a fresh aspect of a gradually developing thematic concern, so that by the end of the sequence one has a sense of intellectual, as well as emotional and esthetic, repletion.

Li Yü did not, of course, invent the art of narrative in *ch'uan-ch'i* drama, but he brought that art to a new degree of prominence and centrality. The functions of narrative mentioned above had not previously been so highly developed. It was a possibility that had always been latent in the form, however. The spaces to be filled in *ch'uan-ch'i* drama are vast; they invite narrative. The common (and, in dramatic genres, unprecedented) occurrence of the word *chi*, "record, history, narrative," in titles of *ch'uan-ch'i* plays, as in *Tale of the Lute* (*P'i-p'a chi*) or *Tale of Wan-sha* (*Wan-sha chi*), is itself an indication of the new prominence of narrative in this genre. The much briefer *tsa-chü* of the Yüan dynasty could be dominated by a single lyric mood, or even by a single situation throughout its four and a half acts; it could in short be written as a dramatized lyric poem. In the *ch'uan-ch'i* play, with its thirty or more acts, this is impossible. But even in this greatly expanded form, Chinese drama continues to exemplify a typical cultural preference for static as opposed to dynamic structure. The great spaces are supported more by textural contrast than by suspense. Suspense, or the urgent desire to know what will happen next, cannot in any case be a dominant concern in a genre that depends for the most part upon well-known traditional stories. Even in Li Yü, who avoids traditional stories, it is not an important attribute of narrative. Audiences usually knew well what was to be portrayed from the outset; if they were in any doubt, their curiosity was (in theory at least) satisfied at once by a plot summary sung by the stage manager in the first act. They did not come to participate in the hopes and fears of imaginary characters on the stage so much as to admire the masterly portrayal of well-known roles. One imagines them arriving or leaving or conversing with their neighbors while the play was in progress, pausing to listen when attracted by an unusually fine bit of singing, clowning, or military acrobatics.

In traditional *ch'uan-ch'i* drama the attributes of narrative mentioned above (wonder, complication, wholeness, and thematic exploration) tend to be fulfilled as much by the song lyrics as by the narrative. When the narrative material is famous, it cannot freely be altered to exemplify a problem or express a point of view; and in any case, the main interest of the traditional dramatist was elsewhere. Imagery was the fluid element; the meaning of a narrative was controlled by the poetry in which it was clothed.

In Li Yü's work, the song lyrics are not as central to the total experience of a play as in most *ch'uan-ch'i* plays. The stories of many plays, including some of the most famous, appear to exist for the sake of the lyrics; the lyrics, at any rate, are their most memorable aspect. When a reader recalls *The Peony Pavilion*, he is apt to think first of the sensuous, convoluted poetry of the garden episode. The situation underlying the poetry in that episode is simple and essentially undramatic: a sheltered girl is awakened to the world of passion by her first experience of nature. It is the overpowering urgency and lyricism of the poetry, not the situation, that makes the episode memorable.

In Li Yü's *ch'uan-ch'i* plays, the lyrics are fluent, pleasing, clever, and objective; they are neither extremely passionate nor extremely delicate. Of his work, it is truer to say that the poetry exists for the situations than that the situations exist for the poetry. In Li Yü, the principal episodes are never the ones in which a character soliloquizes upon a mood. Such moments are transitional, not climactic, in his work.[25] The principal episodes are the ones in which essentially dramatic confrontations occur, such as act 13 in *The Kite's Mistake*, in which a solemn idealist comes to a love rendezvous and struggles to control his amazement and dismay when the object of his dreams proves to be an illiterate vulgarian; or act 15 in *The Paired Soles*, in which a young actress adopts the persona of a *ch'uan-ch'i* character in order to heap scorn and abuse on a wealthy persecutor who sits watching her perform. The conflicting demands of social convention and personal motivation in these episodes are endlessly complex. The artistic emphasis is in fact the opposite of that exemplified in the *Peony Pavilion* episode. The poetry is simple. It exists for the sake of the situation, which is complex.[26]

Li Yü's fascination with dramatic situations leads him to make extensive use of prose as a medium of dramatic exchange. In Chinese drama there is a greater contrast between poetry (meaning, primarily, the song lyrics) and prose (meaning dramatic imitations of vernacular speech) than is common in English. The poetry tends to be more "poetic"—more gorgeous, allusive, and adorned—than English poetry, while the prose tends to be simpler and more rigidly confined to the functional and mundane than English prose. There is always a sense of immense contrast in passing from one to the other. In traditional *ch'uan-ch'i* drama, prose tends to be subordinate to poetry (though not to the same extent as in Yüan *tsa-chü*); its function is to provide the song lyrics with introductions and transitions in the manner of recitative in Italian opera. In Li Yü the relation of prose to song lyrics is nearly reversed. The prose passages are long and carefully constructed, meant to engage the attention independently. The function of the song lyrics is to sum up or illustrate the prose passages. They restate in bold colors and simple outlines a feeling or situation that the preceding prose passage has explored in modulated hues and careful twists of line. In Li Yü's work, then, the function of poetry is more often rhetorical than poetic. It is used to bring essentially prosaic sentiments to the greatest possible degree of extravagance and exaggeration. Thus the sentiment "I am determined to reject invitations to come out of retirement" becomes in Li Yü's song lyric language "I'm sorry I can't raze the mountain and split apart the Chung-nan shortcut, or borrow an axe to fell the tree Duke Shao sat under." (Chung-nan is the name of a mountain range near the former capital Ch'ang-an where literati hoping for a shortcut to preferment were wont to pose as hermits. Duke Shao is a legendary figure mentioned in poem sixteen of *The Book of Songs*. He was so popular a ruler that, after his departure, his people revered the pear tree he used to sit under, refusing to let it be cut down.)[27]

Both the tendencies mentioned above—the interest in dramatic interaction and the development of prose as a dramatic medium—contribute to an aspect of Li Yü's work that could be characterized as realistic or empirical. He is fascinated by the casual and the commonplace; or, more precisely, by the incongruities that arise from the clash of commonplace experience with the ideal romantic world of *ch'uan-ch'i* tradition. He likes to undermine the dignity of his romantic characters by including base or comic traits in their makeup; by setting them against a background of petty dissension, derision, or calculation; or by placing them in disorienting situations that reveal the natural person beneath the social exterior. Thus, the hero of *The Amazing Reunion* has scholarly tastes and ambitions but is brought up by a cloth pedlar and must himself submit to a test of competence in that trade in order to gain a bride.[28] The lovers in *The Paired Soles* endure a great deal of ribald horseplay at a rustic wedding ceremony (a shepherd boy dances around the groom and threatens to emasculate him with his teeth unless the bride drinks another glass of wine)[29] and the literate and refined heroine of *The Kite's Mistake* is first portrayed against the background of a vulgar family squabble between her father's concubines.[30] In his *Random Lodge for My Idle Feelings*, Li Yü insists that the proper concern of drama is with everyday reality:

> Writers of *ch'uan-ch'i* plays should seek their material only from that which the ear and eye perceive; they should not seek it in that which is neither seen or heard. This is true not only of plays and song lyrics but of all literature in all ages. Those who wrote of human feelings and material reality have been transmitted to posterity, while those who ventured into the fantastic and the monstrous are now no longer read. Among the Five Classics and the Four Books, the chronicle of Tso, the Conversations of the States, The Historical Annals, the Han History, and the great masters of the T'ang and Sung, is there a single one that does not speak of human feelings? Is there a single one that is unconcerned with material reality? Today, as in the past, they are transmitted and recited in every home. Is

there anyone who dismisses these books because their subject matter is commonplace and simple? All that remains today of the ghost stories of Ch'i Hsieh is its title. Later generations never saw its contents. Is this not a most clear and striking demonstration of the fact that the common and the simple endure, while the strange and the fabulous disappear?[31]

Li Yü, then, tends toward realism in his philosophy of literature, in his management of dialogue, and in his choice of subject matter. It would be a serious mistake, however, to suppose that all the characteristics of his work can be explained by a postulated esthetic of realism. The ch'uan-ch'i play, as we have observed before, is a form that tends to insist on the perfection of its own rituality and abstraction. In certain respects Li Yü tends to exaggerate rather than to diminish this insistence. His plots, for example, are cleverly and somewhat exhibitionistically contrived. Unlike most ch'uan-ch'i playwrights he doesn't turn preexisting stories into plays; he invents new stories. One of the ways he uses his elected freedom to tell a new story is to heighten the element of abstract design in narrative itself. His stories aspire to a condition of perfect artificiality, a condition in which each narrative passage is paralleled or opposed by some other narrative passage within the same structure. Li Yü's narrative parallelism usually serves to bring out some moral or intellectual point. In The Careful Couple, for example, the protagonist and his friend each take a singing girl as a concubine so that two different approaches to love may be illustrated. In some cases, however, his narrative parallelism simply subserves a taste for elegant completeness. An example of the latter is The Mirage Tower, in which two traditional tales about love affairs between a mortal and a water princess are cleverly combined. It is the only extant play by Li Yü that is based on traditional narrative material. Li Yü's use of the material in that unique instance is typical of his creative sensibility. He "thickens" the two old stories through the development of internal parallelism.

Li Yü's love of patterns is as evident in his management of episodes as in his construction of stories. It might in fact be said to be too intrusively evident on this level. Ritualized, quasi-mechanical schemes of representation appear to have constituted a peculiarly irresistible temptation to his imagination; he never misses an opportunity to construct such a scheme. They are to him what comic tags were to

Dickens, or half-cadences with flourishes to Mozart. When there is a conflict between clarity and any other artistic value in the presentation of a situation, it is always clarity that he chooses. This defines both a peculiar strength and a peculiar limitation of his work. He turns complex or chaotic situations into orderly pageants. In *The Amazing Reunion*, the wealthy but heirless Yin Hsiao-lou suffers incessant harassment from people offering their own sons to him for adoption in order to gain a share of his wealth. To represent this situation on stage, Li Yü has two figures, a relative and a neighbor respectively, arrive at Hsiao-lou's house, each with a son and a servant. Each visitor advances his proposal in an orderly, formulaic, exaggeratedly symmetrical fashion. A lively quarrel then develops between the two parties, illustrating the opposite, naturalistic side of Li Yü's genius.[32] Another example is act 18, "Arduous Selection" (*Chien p'ei*) of *The Kite's Mistake*, in which Han Shih-hsün has just won first place in the metropolitan examination and tours the city streets to appraise the beauties who are now eager to be married to him. Four women are in turn led by matchmakers to balconies overlooking the street; Shih-hsün appraises and rejects each in turn. A religious ritual could not be more insistently formal. It is like the description of the temples of Mars and Venus in Chaucer's "Knight's Tale."

The use of static patterns is in accord with the spirit and methodology of *ch'uan-ch'i* drama. Rituals are used to represent complex interactions as promenades about the stage are used to represent long journeys. The unusual abundance of such patterns in Li Yü is due in part to his unusual preoccupation with interactions as opposed to moods; there is more in his work to be ritualized than in the work of most *ch'uan-ch'i* playwrights. It is also due to the innate bent of his mind: his love of ratiocination, his fascination with systems and arrangements.

The same spirit is evident in the construction of his prose dialogue passages. Like the characters of G. B. Shaw, the actors in Li Yü's plays are prone to turn into skillful dialecticians the moment they have a point of view to express or a scheme to defend. At such points they speak schematically, as if they had an outline in their minds. An example is the opening of act fourteen in *The Paired Soles*, in which the actress Liu Miao-ku soliloquizes about her relationship to the actor T'an Ch'u-yü, to whom she is secretly engaged:

Other actors fear being onstage and enjoy being offstage. Onstage, they have to expend effort; offstage, they can shirk work as much as they wish. He and I, however, are the opposite of the others; we enjoy being onstage and fear being offstage. Offstage, we must avoid envy and suspicion; onstage we can be a husband and wife as we wish. The moment we are onstage, he treats me as his real wife and I treat him as my real husband. There is not a line we recite that doesn't pierce to the heart and slice to the bone. Other people think they are watching a play, but what he and I do is actually a reality. When plays consist of real things and the actors derive unwearying pleasure from them, how can they avoid attaining to the utmost perfection? That's why the reputation of our Jade Sprout Troupe has been gaining fragrance every day.[33]

Another often-used device in Li Yü's dialogues is the "elicited exposition," in which one character tries to guess what is in the mind of another. Sometimes the device is used to prolong a state of dramatic irony, as in act 14, "Oppression through Profit" (Li pi), of The Paired Soles, in which Liu Miao-ku, the female protagonist, tries repeatedly to guess the contents of a large, heavy chest that has just been delivered to her mother. The spectator/reader knows that the chest contains Liu Miao-ku's purchase price of a thousand gold pieces; her mother has sold her as a concubine to a rich merchant, the vulgarian-villain of the piece. More characteristically, the device is used simply to point up the ingenuity or novelty of someone's brilliant scheme. The first character poses his idea in the form of a riddle, so that, after a delay and a number of wrong guesses, he may reveal it at last with a special flourish. An example occurs in act 22, "A Wicked Scheme" (Chüeh chi), of the same play, which portrays a conversation between a bandit chief and his military advisor. The scheme elicited by questioning involves hiring an impostor to pose as a famous general in order to surrender imperial forces to the bandits.

In the following four chapters I shall enter in detail into four of Li Yü's worlds of thought, experience, and imagination. Of these four plays, the first two are closer to the romantic nature of traditional ch'uan-ch'i drama whereas the last two exemplify the genre after full comic metamorphosis. Even in the first two plays, however, we will meet with a variety of characters and attitudes that could exist with comfort in comedy.

II. Life as Impersonation: *The Paired Soles*

Li Yü has a despicable nature. He is good at playing up to people and at circulating among the gentry. He is fond of writing plays and stories that are extremely lewd and filthy. He always has three or four prostitutes under his thumb. When pleasure-seekers visit him, these will sing behind a curtain; or sometimes he has them carry goblets and pour wine, chatting with people as they do so to entice them into paying liberally for their entertainment. Such behavior is truly filthy and unworthy of genteel society. I met him just once and afterwards avoided him.

> Yüan Yü-ling, *Notes from No-ju Mountain Hermitage* (c. 1670)

. . . popular Stage-plays are sinful, heathenish, lewd, ungodly Spectacles, and most pernicious corruptions; condemned in all ages, as intolerable Mischiefs to Churches, to Republics, to the manners, minds and souls of men.

> William Prynne, *Histrio-Mastix* (1632)

The Paired Soles is a fairy tale about actors in which Li Yü uses his humble and semidisgraced adopted trade as a medium through which to view the shifting relationships of status and virtue in the world.[1] The play is concerned throughout with the opposed values of name (*ming*) and substance (*shih*), appearance and reality; and as it progresses, it gradually leads us to associate the first value (name or appearance) with the obvious, material things of the world

19

and the second value (substance or reality) with its invisible and unnameable essences. The play's elaborate convolutions of plot, suggesting the delicately tortuous exaggerations of a jade carving, reflect not only a delight in plastic manipulation, but an evident desire to view these contrasting values from every possible point of view. Narrative complexity is here the outcome of thematic simplicity, an obsession with a single intellectual concern.

As is typical of Li Yü's *ch'uan-ch'i* plays, *The Paired Soles* is firmly planted in a structural paradox: its actors portray actors. Li Yü ensures that this paradox is never far from our minds. The conventional distance between an actor's identity as an actor and his identity as a character within a drama is a variable quantity in this work; the author delights in his freedom to expand and contract that conventional distance, like an inquisitive youngster fiddling with the controls of a new machine. The bantering *ch'ü* (aria) with which the play opens establishes the keynote at once:

> A slow year has come around; our engagements are sporadic.
> I've dug up old plays and asked after new ones, looking
> everywhere for signs of novelty.
> Plays within plays are a thing you don't generally see;
> You can look and look for one and still just waste your labor.
>
> When actors act a story about actors,
> Their essential nature isn't lost, isn't lost.
> A leading man and a leading lady make a fine romantic couple,
> ready at hand.
>
> Let the clappers lightly sound;
> Let the tinted veils slowly dance.
> This play is different from all others:
> The leading man is a faithful lover;
> The leading lady is a chaste wife.
> They represent the kind of life we actors lead.
>
> Thank you, thank you;
> With voice and face we'll each repay your kindness.[2]

This opening *ch'ü* gives offhand expression to two types of humorous, teasing indifference to received values ("defiance" would be too strong a word). The authorial presence represented by the stage manager assumes the role of a theatrical impresario here; he is unequivocally interested in profits, a merchant dealing in novelties. Flaunting his commercialism, he invites a response of (mildly) disdainful amusement. But the concluding verses of the *ch'ü* contain a sly challenge to that disdain. The faithfulness and chastity of this leading couple, we are told, is a notable novelty among *ch'uan-ch'i* plays, a novelty which derives from the unusual milieu they represent. The implication that actors are more faithful and chaste than members of great official families (the class ordinarily represented in leading roles) is so sudden and quiet as to deprive the reader of the opportunity to react before the moment is past; it is a surprise thrust. Having inserted the oblique challenge, the speaker at once reassumes his professional manner, ending the *ch'ü* with a conventional expression of humble gratitude.

The *Paired Soles* is not a polemic (not even a disguised one) in defense of actors. The discreditable side of the profession is portrayed in detail, and with gusto. But the corruption of actors is seen as but one aspect of a world that teems with greed, hypocrisy, and commercialism. The work does not permit readers to draw moral conclusions concerning particular social classes. It only permits us to draw the moral, if we wish, that one must not hasten to judge reality by appearances.

Four figures in the drama, a spirit, an official turned hermit, a scholar turned actor, and an actress, embody perfect goodness and spirituality. No two of these characters are of equal station; they stand in a vertical relationship to each other in social standing and wisdom. The three lower figures are all involved in varieties of impersonation. The official and the scholar each act as a regent for the next higher figure in the chain. The concluding *ch'ü* in the introductory act draws attention to the moral completeness of these four figures, and predisposes the reader to pay particular attention to their roles in the drama:

> In being faithful, T'an Ch'u-yü [the scholar] was faithful to
> the marrow.
> In following honesty, Liu Miao-ku [the actress] followed it
> into water.[3]

In coming to the rescue, P'ing-lang-hou [the spirit] made a
double rescue.
In aiding others, Mo Yü-weng [the official] aided them to the
hilt.[4]

The goodness of the three human figures is of an explicitly spiritual
and supernatural character, as it is validated by the miraculous interventions of the spirit P'ing-lang-hou.

The villainous characters have no supernatural representative in
the play because they are identified with matter as opposed to
spirituality, with animality as opposed to humanity. Their evil proceeds not so much from a determined will to enact evil, as from a
natural inability to discern the more delicate human values. There is
something innocent and buffoonlike in their misbehavior. They are
embodiments of the untransformed natural world as interpreted by
the crudest of natural faculties. Their fantastic representative is a
creature who stands lower, not higher, than man in the chain of
being. He is Shan Ta-wang (Great Prince of the Mountains), the
military villain of the piece. He is a man-beast with the face of a tiger,
whose military strength derives in part from his connections with the
animal kingdom; tigers, bears, rhinoceroses, and elephants serve as
his assault troops.[5] The threat to the empire posed by his animal
revolt parallels the threat to the leading couple's marriage vows posed
by the rampant commercialism of Ch'ien Wan-kuan and Liu Chiang-
hsien.

Goodness is identified with nature (in its benign, bountiful aspect),
rusticity, simplicity, poverty, and obscurity. It is a secret, hidden,
evanescent thing, perceptible only to those who themselves possess
the spark. Thus, in the second act, the male protagonist T'an Ch'u-
yü is portrayed as a man ill-treated by polite society because, reduced
to poverty by the early death of his parents, he lacks the gross,
material emblems of distinction. Too proud to endure the scorn of his
fickle neighbors and friends, he has become a wandering scholar who
supports himself by writing lyrics for actors. Too poor to marry, he is
at the same time totally uninterested in marrying wealth. "Money,"
he reflects, "is nothing to the true beauty and the true genius; that is
why the most difficult-to-obtain things in the world are called
'priceless.'" He seeks to select a mate, and to be selected himself, on
the basis of naked personal distinction.[6]

These opening sentiments bear a strong family resemblance to those of all protagonists of romantic *ch'uan-ch'i*; it is routine for these figures to be poor and unrecognized and to yearn for an ideal mate. There is nevertheless an original flavor in this opening that relates directly to the dominant thematic concerns of the play. It is to be found in the directness and explicitness with which wealth (appearance or reputation) is contrasted with personal distinction (substance or reality) as a basis for the formation of judgments, and in the energy with which the protagonist rejects any acquiescence to conventional social role playing.

Like T'an Ch'u-yü, the female protagonist Liu Miao-ku is a person whose true value goes unnoticed by the world. The once-in-a-generation beauty extolled by Ch'u-yü's friends in act 2 is not Miao-ku, who is girlish and immature, still wearing the pigtail of childhood, but her sensationally beautiful and worldly mother, Liu Chiang-hsien. Ch'u-yü's admiration for Miao-ku's beauty is a foible; it is peculiar and uncommunicable. In act 4, "An Unusual Taste" (*Pieh-shang*), Ch'u-yü is brought by a friend to the performing area, where he sees the actresses for the first time as they file past him to the stage. He tries to open his friend's eyes to the great superiority of the daughter's beauty to the mother's, but soon realizes that his persuasions can do nothing to remedy his friend's basic lack of sensibility. His friend will never perceive Miao-ku the way he does. He therefore pretends to acquiesce in his friend's point of view and silently accompanies him to the performance.

The mother's beauty is presumably of the obvious, spectacular type that appeals to average theatre spectators, a group of whom are portrayed in act 2, engaged in ribald horseplay at the close of a performance. This passage presents us with one type of judgment on the theatre as a social influence: it is a source of occasions in which ordinary social distinctions and ordinary rules of social decorum are gleefully ignored by the generality of the public. Rich and poor, male and female, "with no curtains to seclude them," mingle promiscuously, jostling one another and making an uproar. Ch'u-yü's reaction to this aspect of the acting trade is one of unhesitating distaste. "Whatever good points the play may have had, these men and women behave very vulgarly."[7]

The sort of immorality portrayed in act 2, however, is mild indeed compared to that which forms the subject of the following act,

"Forming a Troupe" (*Lien pan*). Here, Liu Chiang-hsien instructs her daughter in the art of turning an acting career to commercial advantage. The act begins with an effect of yawning contrast, for the preceding act concludes with the lyrics of Ch'u-yü's friends in praise of Chiang-hsien's unearthly beauty. In act 3 the miraculous Chiang-hsien at once reveals herself to be a monster of selfishness, calculation, and materialism; traits which she develops in ever-deepening detail as the act progresses. Her unearthliness is all a facade, an illusion created to entrap rich admirers.

Introducing hereself, Chiang-hsien announces that she owes her outstanding financial success in the acting profession to her looks, her stage presence, her memory, and her skill in handling amorous spectators, whom she sometimes cheats out of half their life's savings. Her fourteen-year-old daughter Miao-ku has even greater natural abilities; she has her appear so she can begin instructing her in the art of making a fortune as an actress for, as she informs her, "money-making tricks are not set forth in play scripts."[8] The instruction that follows goes far to explain the disgraced position of actors in Chinese society. In Chiang-hsien's conception, the actress, as much as the courtesan, "exchanges feigned love for genuine money and favors" and her daughter is to "think of the embroidered coverlets as an extension of the stage."[9] Her instruction giving is generically related to those scenes (a fairly regular feature of *ch'uan-ch'i* plays and novels concerning courtesans) in which a brothel mistress instructs a fresh captive in the technical refinements of the profession.[10] The actress differs from the courtesan in that she is less prone to dispense real sexual favors. Chiang-hsien tries to overcome her daughter's horror of the profession by assuring her that her concessions to admirers need not be real; if she will base all her actions on the "three secrets of our trade," she will retain both her reputation and her chastity." The three secrets are "allow them to look but not to eat," "agree to the name, but not the reality," and "permit the scheming but not the gaining."[11] Miao-ku protests vigorously against the practice of so much deception:

> Stratagems and stratagems! Snare upon snare!
> You'll make the plotter herself afraid for others!
> What evil have the victims done to suffer such entanglement,
> That I should thus deceitfully spread nets of love, capturing
>   bewildered souls?[12]

To these objections Chiang-hsien has two (mutually contradictory) answers: men are no more straightforward with actresses than actresses are with men, but turn cold the moment you let them "lower their members" (i.e., satisfy their desire); and it is not true that the actress's promises of sexual favors are always deceitful. There are times when an actress should consent to fulfill her promises, but only when a large sum of money is to be gained. She is not to waste more than word-of-mouth love on small spenders.[13]

Miao-ku at length consents to work as an actress insofar as she can do so with no loss of her real (as opposed to her apparent) virtue. Simply ignoring her mother's more vicious suggestions, she offers to study "any good Confucian play dealing with loyalty, filiality, virtue, and righteousness," but absolutely refuses to "study plays made of lust-provoking lyrics that ruin one's sense of shame." She is nevertheless uneasy about relinquishing the appearance of virtue:

> Though they count for nothing more than empty reputation,
> I care nevertheless for conventional rules of behavior.
> What I fear is that male and female, muddy and clear, will melt and mingle.
> When people neglect thjeir empty reputations, it leads to offense in matters of substance.[14]

In this act, both mother and daughter phrase their different concerns in such a way that the dominant thematic concern of the play—the relationship of true states to apparent states—is again brought to the foreground. The best wisdom of the mother is to keep appearance and reality forever distinct; the self one should attempt to cultivate is a coolly efficient and self-centered entity, a thing that waits for prey behind attractive facades. The daughter can scarcely imagine such a division. Her great anxiety is that in abandoning the appearance of virtue she may abandon an essential means of knowing virtue, and thus succumb by imperceptible degrees to habits and values that she finds repugnant. She therefore reaches instinctively for a *modus vivendi* that will allow her not to violate in public the values that she holds in private.

T'an Ch'u-yü undergoes a comparable crisis in act 6, in which he struggles to subdue his self-regard sufficiently to "enact the virtue of faithfulness in love" by becoming a member of Miao-ku's acting troupe. The humiliation he hesitates to endure is all the more exquisite in that the role for which he must apply is that of "big painted face" (*ta hua mien*), or military villain. Like Miao-ku, he hopes to avoid the full consequences of his decision to become a performer. He might not have to go all the way; he might secure a promise of marriage from Miao-ku before they are through learning their first play.[15] Once in the troupe, he endeavors to preserve a measure of his self-respect through refusing to put aside his scholar's cap, though in other respects he dresses as an actor.[16]

Miao-ku's father Liu Wen-ch'ing, though a retiring, ineffectual figure, represents a significant intermediate position in the drama's dialectic of values, a position midway between the purely acquisitive and the purely sincere. More than any other figure in the play, he cares about the artistic and technical perfection of the actors' performances. His first entrance couplet indicates this aspect of his nature and incidentally places the desire for artistic perfection among the more elevated human values:

> I inquire everywhere into techniques of the stage
> In order to put together an elegant company.
> I am grieved that the plays of heaven
> Will not deign to be paired with the world's.[17]

Profit, the incessant theme of his wife's conversation, is almost never a theme of Liu Wen-ch'ing's speeches (though in the opening aria of act 7 he sings that he cares more for wealth than for his family's reputation). His concerns are as much those of a craftsman as those of a merchant. He wants the name for his newly formed troupe of youthful actors to be a fitting one, and he has definite ideas concerning the skills required to fill the missing role of "military villain."[18] He hires a well-known drama teacher to instruct his recruits and is emphatic about preserving strict social and artistic discipline among them.[19]

The discipline of an actor's existence in fact comes as an astonishing revelation to Ch'u-yü. This is an area in which reputation and reality are totally at variance. Throughout *The Paired Soles* we are shown outsiders who speak of the acting world as a place of shameful abandon in which old and young, male and female, living and working at close quarters, are free to mingle carelessly, without ceremony and without restraint.[20] It is evident that Ch'u-yü disapproves of any marked indifference to decorum, but having fallen in love, he is inconsistently enchanted with the prospect, promised by this supposed existence, of being close to Miao-ku:

> Going to warmth and softness is like returning to one's childhood home.
> I yearn more for the walls of the troupe director than for the gates of the imperial palace.[21]

Coming to her first rehearsal, Miao-ku worries about the durability of "the wall between the sexes":

> Day after day the dikes will be crumbled, the defenses destroyed;
> How can I bear such exposure? How can I obstruct those furtive gazes?[22]

But neither the hopes of Ch'u-yü nor the fears of Miao-ku are quite realistic. Almost the first thing Ch'u-yü encounters upon entering the troupe is the strange figure of Erh-lang-shen, a patron spirit of actors. The new recruits are all required to bow and offer sacrifices to his image and to promise obedience to his rules. Described as the Confucius, the Buddha, and the Lao-tzu of the acting profession, Erh-lang-shen shows no trace of the compassion of those founding teachers, but punishes slips of behavior with the utmost watchfulness and severity. What he mostly dislikes, according to the freshly engaged drama teacher, are improper or lascivious behavior among troupe members, the use of old actors to play young parts, and of male actors to play female parts. He inflicts great and small misfortunes upon any actor who offends against order and propriety.[23] The director gives each recruit an assigned place to sit in rehearsals and threatens them with corporal punishment for leaning or whispering.[24] Ch'u-yü finds, after being in the troupe for a month, that its members' behavior is governed even more strictly than in a family. He is able to communicate with Miao-ku only with eyes and eyebrows and is tortured by the constant aggravation of his longing which her nearness excites.[25] Thus the art which nourishes the spectators' dreams of romantic abandon is shown to require a strict renunciation of romance on the part of its practitioners.

Though the theatrical world is inconveniently arranged for the pursuit of love affairs, it is not so perfectly organized as to prevent all expression of the other natural passions. Fear, envy, and laziness enjoy a secret but flourishing existence. A richly amusing portrait of the internal dynamics of the acting troupe emerges from the events (none of which are superfluous to the developing story) portrayed in act 10, "Promoted to the Principal Role" (*Kai sheng*). The first thing we learn about the actors (other than Ch'u-yü and Miao-ku) is that they have no particular vocation for literature or the stage:

> Rather than read the *Songs* or *Documents*, we turned to acting.
> It was only to steal some leisure, and because we loved to fool
>   around.
> Who could have known that we all would get the rod!
> That the cane would never be absent from our heads![26]

These actors stand for the lower aspects of nature in their comic unruliness and spontaneity. Too simple to be harmfully or designedly malevolent, they nevertheless need the restraint of external discipline in order to behave properly. They are not equal in incompetence. The two actors playing secondary male roles (the *wai* and the *mo*) are able to memorize their parts, albeit slowly and painfully. The villain (*ching*) and the leading man (played by a clown, *ch'ou*) are incapable of remembering anything and must be prompted by Ch'u-yü and Miao-ku when singing before the drama instructor if they are to avoid beatings. Ch'u-yü allows himself to be persuaded to give surreptitious aid to the actor in the villain's role, but Miao-ku refuses to do anything to help the leading man out of his difficulties because he is so poorly adapted to his role-type. She cannot stand the thought of being paired, even in imagination, with such a buffoon. Ch'u-yü, likewise, does not hesitate to show him up by singing perfectly the aria he fails to remember.[27] Li Yü's ideal society, it appears, will tolerate a villain or an idiot if he conforms to his natural role, but turns on him without pity if he presumes to take credit for qualities (such as magnanimity, dignity, or seriousness) that are above him.

The clown in the role of leading man is the most limited in intellect, the most mismatched, and the most humiliated of the four actors, so it is he who attempts to lead an insurrection against Ch'u-yü as soon as the singing instructor leaves them alone, but the other actors fail to support him.[28] The *wai* knows the actors need the threat of authority to behave properly and so quells the brawl (and provides an instance of the drama's principal theme) by mimicking offstage the voice of the returning drama master.[29] When the true source of authority is absent, a subordinate may maintain order in his own sphere through impersonation.

Though Ch'u-yü and Miao-ku are prevented from speaking to each other by the proximity of the other actors, their much greater skill in the use of language provides them with a means of undetected communication. Ch'u-yü's love message is so recondite that it is safe against discovery by the others, but Miao-ku grasps its significance in a couple of glances. Pretending to practise an aria, she sings a reply, the conventional stage language of which protects it from the notice of all except Ch'u-kü, who grasps all her meanings without delay.[30] Spiritual distinction can be recognized only by those who themselves possess distinction. This is admittedly an assumption that may be found anywhere in *ch'uan-ch'i* drama. Skill in recondite allusion is the usual means of recognition and attraction among heroes and heroines of the Chinese stage. Here, the assumption is brought to life through the crucial role it is made to play in a complex dramatic situation and through its relation to a larger structure of meaning. The lovers' subtle intellect is one aspect of the intangible, inexpressible truth or reality which Li Yü attempts throughout to distinguish from all its worldly imitations and disguises.

True virtue is gained by the abandonment of the appearance of virtue. Ch'u-yü demonstrates his authenticity by his indifference to the opinions of polite society as embodied first in the material snobbishness of neighbors and prospective fathers-in-law, and second in the general admiration of theatre goers for the glamor-queen Chianghsien. Since Chiang-hsien is herself one of the major representatives of the inauthentic, acquisitive spirit, it is no very forced manipulation of the terms of the play to regard the two fashionable admirations—for wealth and position and for a glamorous impersonator—as images of each other. Ch'u-yü's indifference to Chiang-hsien's beauty and his admiration for the subdued, immature harmony of Miao-ku's features corresponds to his rejection of material values. It is his renunciation of the polite world, his submission to the status of a paint-smeared performer of villains' roles, that demonstrates his authenticity as a lover to Miao-ku: "For my sake you gratuitously

subdued your ambition, languished and turned pale. You bore suffering and injustice to the full."[31]

The same paradoxical rule applies to the method he employs to
achieve promotion to the position of leading man. As Miao-ku advises him (in the guise of rehearsing an aria): "The means to union lie
in separation."[32] If he wishes to be advanced, he must announce an
intention to leave.

When the director and manager ask him why he wishes to leave,
Ch'u-yü tells them he is dissatisfied with the role of military villain
and advances reasons for his attitude that recall Miao-ku's scruples
concerning the acting trade in general. He wants the roles he plays to
be suitable to his conception of his personal dignity. Clowns',
villains', females' and old men's roles are out of the question. Not
even a supporting male role will suit him.

> Supporting male roles in drama are always either relying on
> others to accomplish things or else helping others to become
> known. You never see them establishing their own fortunes
> through their own efforts. And that also is inconsistent with my
> character.[33]

He does not stop at his request for the position of leading man,
which is quickly granted, but, in an uncharacteristic access of self-
assertion, demands personal privileges not granted the other actors,
hints boldly at his esteem for the manager's daughter, and gives vent
to a towering—even arrogant—sense of his own worth.

> There is one more thing I would like to say. There is no one
> who is not aware of the reputation of T'an Ch'u-yü. There is no
> one who does not recognize the features of T'an Ch'u-yü. My
> entering your troupe and acting on the stage is like Hsiang Yü
> playing the flute or Han Hsin begging for food; it is nothing
> more than an expedient of poverty. There have been sages of
> bygone times who have hidden themselves among actors and
> musicians. Onlookers naturally made allowances for them.[34]

Ch'u-yü's manner is so intimidating that the director is reduced to
comic expressions of servility:

> The lowly master can't face down his high disciple;

From now on I agree to yield in everything—
I give you absolute permission to indulge your every whim.
As long as the repute of our company isn't injured,
What harm is there in taking lessons from a follower?[35]

Ch'u-yü's burst of truculence is a thematic preparation for what follows, for the next act, "Empty Intimidation" (*Hu-wei*),[36] portrays a vulgar, conceited, blustering local money bags to whom bullying is a way of life. His name, Ch'ien Wan-kuan, means "ten thousand strings of cash." We have already been shown an instance of insatiable acquisitiveness hiding behind feigned appearances in Miao-ku's mother, Liu Chiang-hsien. The portrait of Wan-kuan shows the same spirit at work in a different sphere. Significantly, there is an old relationship between the two: Wan-kuan is one of the wealthy admirers who have helped make Chiang-hsien rich. Like Chiang-hsien, he deals in empty appearances, but his aim is to frighten rather than to entice.

Describing his rise to prominence in his introductory soliloquy, he recalls that his first move was to purchase a post as a district magistrate's assistant in a prosperous area. The opportunities for graft in this position allowed him to become wealthy in three years. Rather than risk denunciation and exposure by continuing to hold official positions, he then retired to a rural area, where he has since used his status as a gentry-member to intimidate the local people.[37]

The episode that follows is an example of his system. Three local chiefs of *pao-chia* (community council) organizations come to him with a request. Their organizations are about to be inspected by a group of visiting district magistrates. They have collected a gift for the inspecting magistrates but feel they are not of sufficient status to deal with them personally; they could not successfully placate them if they should happen to desire a larger gift.

This is a moneymaking opportunity for Wan-kuan. He begins by coldly and rudely rejecting their request and accusing them of treating him with disrespect. His houseboy then reminds him that his visitors all owe him money on delinquent accounts. Wan-kuan threatens to have the visiting magistrates sentence them to beatings:

I'm of a mind right now to send you before the deputy magistrate and have him interrogate you in person. I'm sorry I can't break your doglike tendons, let alone take care of a little matter like that. [sings] You miserable cave-skulkers are nice and plump! Perfect material for the officials' rods! After the beatings you'll pay the money; don't think they'll let you off afterwards![38]

The chiefs are awed and submissive:

[sing] Your power is vast as the ocean. We'll settle our accounts of course. Even if we have no money, we'll pawn our wives and children.[39]

Having exacted promises of payment, Wan-kuan consents to greet the magistrates and promises to placate them in case any irregularities in the community council groups are revealed. Privately, he resolves to pretend to the magistrates that the gift and the banquet are fruits of his own largesse, and resolves to keep half of the gift for himself as his rightful profit in the transaction ("I did not originate the custom; everyone does it.").[40]

Ch'ien Wan-kuan betrays his inauthenticity throughout the act by his gratuitous rudeness to his visitors and by a ludicrous concern with the figure he cuts in others' eyes. Devoid of delicacy or respect in his relations with the world, he is forever detecting deficiencies of respect in the world's behavior to him. He declines, at first, to convey the gift because his gentry-member's calling card "is not something to be lightly used on just any occasion." When the council chiefs protest that, being peasants, they would never dare to use such a calling card themselves and that he, as a gentry-member, is the only person in the area who can do so, Wan-kuan asks why they habitually treat him with contempt if gentry-members are so important. When they protest that they have the utmost respect for him, he asks why they don't pay their accounts if they respect him so much. After consenting to their request, he tells them that he expects more deference in the future and takes them to task for addressing him only as "Mr. Ch'ien" (Ch'ien-yeh) instead of the more honorific "Lord Ch'ien" (Ch'ien lao-yeh). He has them repeat the desired form several times to facilitate remembrance.[41]

He has no sense of modesty or propriety. He complains of weariness[42] and bad digestion[43] before his inferiors. When Liu Chiang-hsien's acting troupe is mentioned, he indulges in sexual braggadocio in front of them as well, recalling his former relationship with the actress.[44] When his houseboy tells him that Chiang-hsien has a beautiful daughter who is also an actress, he immediately transfers his sexual anticipation to the daughter, more pleased than displeased at the flavor of incestuous generational confusion this involves. It is a novel accomplishment, a new demonstration of his power:

> Houseboy: I've heard of sisters sharing a husband, But never a mother and a daughter thus paired.
> Wan-kuan: The bridegroom shall be none other than the father; a single figure shall fulfill both roles.[45]

The thick irony of the exit couplet intoned by the circumspect, deferential council chiefs is a far funnier and more telling comment upon Wan-kuan than any direct statement could have been:

> We never knew before that rural gentry were virtuous,
> And only today did we learn that a wealthy man is to be respected.[46]

The following act, "Luxurious Hiding" (*Fei tun*), stands in direct contrast to the one just discussed. Every value and every personality trait that we see in act 11 is inverted in act 12. As act 11 portrays the most extreme imaginable degree of inauthenticity, act 12 portrays the most extreme imaginable degree of authenticity. Act 11 shows a man striving to amass and retain as many forms of power and signs of prestige as he can in order to impress himself and others with his worth, his substantiality. Act 12 shows a man determined to cast away every possession, title, or personal trait that could possibly distinguish him from anyone else in the eyes of others, a man dedicated to total anonymity and obscurity.

Mu-jung Chieh, the central figure in this act, has already appeared in act 5, "Dealing with Bandits" (*Pan tsei*), and act 8, "Bandits Issue Forth" (*K'ou fa*). In act 5 he was introduced as a wise and virtuous military governor in charge of an unsettled area, who chafes at the burdens and dangers of his official career, but who remains at his post, partly from a sense of duty and partly because his many requests for retirement have been denied. He has a close, confiding relationship with his wife and is naturally pious. He prays to heaven for the wisdom to save his person and his reputation in the dangerous military situation with which he is faced.[47] Act 5 directly precedes the act in which Ch'u-yü wrestles with his reluctance to become an actor and, as is so often the case in Li Yü (and other *ch'uan-ch'i* playwrights) there is a reason for this juxtaposition. Mu-jung Chieh's acceptance of danger and moral ambivalence in order to put an end to the bandits is parallel to Ch'u-yü's acceptance of the indignity of an actor's existence in order to unite himself with a rare beauty. To an authentic person, a person of finely adjusted sensibility, the life of a great official is repugnant in the same way that the life of an actor is repugnant. Both existences are involved with falseness; both are images, it might be said, of "the world" in the traditional and unfavorable western sense.

In act 8, Mu-jung Chieh gives further evidence of his spiritual elevation when, remembering his wife's entreaty to shed as little blood as possible, he refrains from pursuing and slaughtering the routed bandits.[48] It is only in act 12, however, that Mu-jung comes fully into his own and emerges clearly as the chief representative of a way of life that is opposed in every respect to that of the acquisitive characters. It is at the beginning of this act that his long-awaited opportunity to retire occurs. Word comes that his request has been granted by the court. He fears, however, that the permission may be revoked as soon as the court hears of his recent military success. To forestall this eventuality, he is determined to withdraw into obscurity as swiftly, thoroughly, and irreversibly as he can. This is to be no ordinary retirement. Instead of returning to his ancestral home he will travel to a remote wilderness unknown even to himself, where he, his wife, and two servants will build a thatched dwelling, enjoy the "pine wind and creeper moon," subsist on "greens and mushroom soup," and finish out their natural span of years.[49] He will wear the rain cloak and conical hat of the laboring class; a mandarin's winged cap and round collar would signify a lingering disposition to distinguish degrees of rank, to possess an identity.[50] In his haste to fly from all human acquaintance, he pushes his way through crowds of local people anxious to detain him and clamorous for souvenirs. Instead of boarding the large boat appropriate to his station that awaits him and his entourage at the dock, he boards (by secret prearrangement) a light fishing boat with his wife and servants, leaving his entourage behind. His wife, who has also yearned for retirement, rejoices that she does not have to pack for their return; she brings only a few sets of casual clothing.[51] As the act progresses, all the accoutrements of their past life are cast away one by one. As soon as they are underway, Mu-jung chants a funeral ode to his mandarin's cap before consigning it to the current:

> I now must sacrifice to my black felt hat with no wine or
>   savories,
> Relying merely on empty phrases to act the part of golden
>   goblets and precious wine.
> I owe you many thanks for your pretended nobility and feigned
>   glory,
> Your driving out of poverty, your chasing away of baseness.
> But you brewed miseries and brought on complications as well.
> I never relied on your prestige to amass gold and silver;
> If I am ungrateful to those two spread wings of yours,
> It is because they resemble claws dancing and fangs gaping.
> Today I do not betray my duty or forget your past regard, repay-
>   ing favor with resentment.
> It is because your nature is to contend among the winds and
>   waves of the central plain
> That I consign you to the cold vastness like drifting duckweed.[52]

The tone of this farewell is not righteous or ascetic; it is not the tone of a person attempting otherworldliness through violent suppression of those elements in his own nature of which he disapproves, but that of a man who, having given the things of the world their due regard, finds he can abandon them without inner division and without regret. His consignment of his official status to the stream is a sign of his wholeness and authenticity, a sign that no wisp of an inclination to return is hidden anywhere in his mind. In this respect, he represents a more advanced state of detachment from the world than T'an Ch'u-yü, who will not on any account relinquish an item so vital to his self-esteem as his scholar's cap. It is true that the acting milieu from which the cap distinguishes him is as much an aspect of the "world" as the world of official service, but so is the scholarly status to which he clings in preference. His is the typical, and perhaps proper, attitude of a young man untried by experience. Mu-jung knows that "only we who have worn [this cap] till it is tattered complain of its misery."

Mu-jung's wife sings an elegy to the embroidered phoenix on her own elegant hat before throwing it into the water to "follow after" her husband's cap:

> My person is already promised to the gulls and egrets,
> So my head cannot be crowned with phoenixes.
> How many plain-capped girls never saw you come?
> How many lazy plyers of the loom yearn for your descent?
> How many bucket-pouring maidens can't wait for you to come
>   release them?
> It is not that I was unlucky to have enjoyed your company;
> It is just that casting things away is a better means of avoiding
>   disaster than snatching them up.[53]

Mu-jung discards his name along with his emblems of rank ("first-class people don't even reveal their courtesy-names; that is why there are so many anonymous figures in the dynastic histories") and announces that he will henceforth be known as "fisherman Mo" (Mo Yü-weng). As for his servant, his title will be changed from "attendant" (yüan-tzu) to "fishing boy" (yü-t'ung). Mu-jung's wife renounces the title "madame" (fu-jen) and desires to be known henceforth as "mum" (niang-tzu).[54] As each relic of their former existence is cast away, the spirits of the four rise, and their sense of free and joyous communion with nature is expressed in ever more buoyant arias. Even the servant responds to the new surroundings. Formerly his anxieties as a doorman and messenger at the yamen kept him away from wine; now he drinks to his capacity, a change which Mu-jung observes with wonder and satisfaction.[55]

As they draw closer to nature, they also draw closer to the immaterial world and to a sense of participation in the purposes of heaven. Omens guaranteeing the bounty and fertility of nature are swiftly granted them, as if in approval of their new relation to it. Mu-jung hooks a sea perch with his first line; the serving couple net a turtle with their first cast.[56]

When Mu-jung learns that he has drifted unawares to Yen-ling in Chekiang, a place where Yen Kuang (courtesy name Tzu-ling), a famous recluse of the eastern Han, used to fish with pole and line, he is overwhelmed with a sense of numinous coincidence:

> I tie my fishing boat by the side of the green water,
> Build my thatched dwelling on an azure mountain,
> And hide together with the recluse of the fishing jetty.
> I did not come here stubbornly following an old example, as if
>   copying the silhouette of a gourd;
> Who could have known that the past and present would un-
>   consciously clasp hands?
> A thousand years apart, we suddenly collided;
> I am not entering the mountains and forests after all, but form-
>   ing another faction.
> The sounds of trees help along the dissemination of fame;
> Because the mountains are high and the rivers long,
> They cast two past and present idlers into peace together.[57]

Mu-jung's elation is so intense that he feels he has already joined the ranks of immortals. Nothing is as it was before. His return to simplicity transforms every act:

> This wine goes down the throat as if returning home, then
>   drops to the lower entrails,
> Not like the stuff that choked the throat, then wouldn't leave
>   the pit.
> Yesterday's sorrows still undispersed, it brewed still further
>   sorrow.
> Today before three cups are down, a hundred affairs are
>   forgotten.[58]

The pastoralism in *The Paired Soles* is not (as is often the case in Chinese plays and poems) a tepid mark of culture, but a spontaneous outrush of joy and relief.[59] The intensity with which the benign pastoral emotions are expressed here more than balances the robustness with which the vanity and greed of Ch'ien Wan-kuan is portrayed. It is a commonplace of Western criticism to observe what a high and difficult feat it is for an author to endow his good characters with as much energy and interest as his wicked ones. Here the problem does not even emerge. The reader does not have to exert himself to invest Li Yü's ideal alternative to the world of affairs with vitality;

it is already fully alive before his eyes.

The sense of unfeigned enjoyment that emerges in this act is enhanced by a sense of the perdurability of that enjoyment. In his act-concluding quatrain, Mu-jung fears that the exquisite sense of freedom from time and necessity that he now delights in may be no more durable after all than any other natural feeling:

> The sad burdens of ten years are cast away in an instant.
> We fear only that this evening's magic mood is nothing more in
>   the end than human gaiety;
> That we are powerless to keep the dreams from turning back.
> Or the bitter tastes from coming forth again.[60]

As if in fulfillment of Mu-jung's forebodings, the following act, "Throwing Money Around" (Hui-chin), does in fact return to Ch'ien Wan-kuan and to the world of power and pretence that he stands for. The pastoral act therefore stands in isolation. It is a lyrical idyll surrounded by discordant ugliness. This isolation impels the reader to attend to its thematic role. It stands as a paradisiacal alternative to the familiar world of ambition and affairs; for true, as opposed to false, identity. No tendril of narrative as yet connects this world with the main world. It floats in a region by itself, as heaven floats. It is found only through the abandonment of all ideas of destination. Ch'u-yü and Miao-ku will in fact reach this world and be nurtured by it, but only after passing through death and magical restoration to life. They will get there not through their own efforts, but through the guidance of an aquatic army obeying the directives of a spirit.[61] As soles, they will be devoid of the faculty of self-regarding, plan-devising awareness throughout their conducted journey there.[62] It is a world that is unknown and unimaginable in their existence as actors.

Acts 13, 14, and 15 are distinctly "this-worldly" in flavor. They portray the sequence of events leading to the lovers' public suicides. Act 13 is devoted to the clever, gradual, tenacious persuasions through which Wan-kuan induces his old paramour Chiang-hsien to sell her daughter to him for a thousand silver taels. Chiang-hsien comes to the interview knowing that Wan-kuan is after her daughter, but she knows from experience that Miao-ku will have nothing to do with admirers. In lyrics that continue the theme of impersonation and that add imaginative substance to the incestuous nature of Wan-kuan's lust, she offers to take her daughter's place:

> The child declines the lover's meeting, so the mother serves as
> the companion to your joys and smiles.
> The riverside willow must perforce fill in for that face like a
> flower.
> Let your body befriend the dry and hard, but let your heart
> imagine soft suppleness.
> I am not, after all, an herb without a root, or a precious flower
> without a base.
> Looks and voice are hard to reproduce.
> If you want to see the pearl shell, ask the womb that bore it.
> Though one is old and one is tender, their substance isn't far
> apart.[63]

Wan-kuan gradually induces Chiang-hsien to accept the idea of
outright sale by playing on her financial anxieties ("a daughter so un-
cooperative will ruin you if you keep her"), exciting her lust for profits
(you'll be able to use the purchase price to buy ten actresses to replace
her, each of whom will bring you a fortune"), and offering sops to her
conscience ("since she refuses to associate with spectators, she plainly
has her heart set on marriage; you will be doing her a great favor").[64]
This act, like the preceding pastoral act, ends on a note of anxiety.
Just as Mu-jung fears to lose his world-renouncing joy, Wan-kuan
fears to lose his purchased paradise and is anxious to press payment
on Chiang-hsien at once:

> I'm just afraid that without money to nail it down,
> The marriage contract won't be firm.[65]

The play's thematic preoccupation with the relationship of appearances with realities surfaces repeatedly in the course of the
following act, "Coerced by Profit" (*Li-pi*), in which Miao-ku learns of
her purchase and plans her public suicide. It appears in the opening
soliloquy in which Miao-ku ponders the paradox of her relationship
with Ch'u-yü; offstage they are forever acting a part; only on stage are
they free to stop acting and to behave as their hearts prompt them.[66]
It appears as well in the lines marking the exit of Wan-kuan's servants, who have just deposited the chest of silver:

Servants: The silver pieces he sent you are very numerous,
But the people exchanged for them are very few.
Chiang-hsien: The numerous items are only dead pieces of
money,
But the scarce item is a living treasure.[67]

The chest, remaining in view as a mute symbol of the exchange,
becomes the center of the following episode, in which Chiang-hsien
makes her daughter try to guess what is in it. Theatrical parapher-
nalia is what first comes to her mind, but it isn't purple robes, or
tassels, or lyrics for arias, or embroidered clothing. A more sinister
thought then occurs to her which, though incorrect, foreshadows the
nature of the exchange:

Miao-ku: Then I've guessed it. (sings) The words linger on my
tongue; I fear that when I try to speak I won't be able to.
Chiang-hsien (speaks): If you've guessed it, why can't you say it,
for heaven's sake?
Miao-ku: (sings) Could it be that within half an hour a thousand gold pieces changed the bright sun for a spring evening
and due to this you gained a profit of a thousand gold pieces?[68]

When Chiang-hsien reveals the facts of the transaction, Maio-ku
exhibits the customary resourcefulness in argument of Li Yü's characters in her efforts to persuade her mother of the legitimacy of her
secret betrothal to Ch'u-yü. For a young scholar to become an actor
in their troupe and then to insist on playing the leading male role was
plainly a proposal of marriage. Her parents' acquiescence to these actions was plainly an acceptance of his proposal. The go-between was
the placard her father made, advertising for a recruit. The spectators
are the witnesses:

The thousand eyes of those who watched the plays were all wide
open.
Who wouldn't say we were phoenixes paired by heaven?
What lack is there of firm witnesses to the marriage?[69]

As elsewhere in the play, the peculiar purity of spirit associated
with Miao-ku is connected with her tender age. The confrontation is

one of innocence versus experience. In scolding her daughter, Chiang-hsien refers repeatedly to her childishness and to her failure to come to terms with reality. She is "too bashful to clasp the phoenix before her eyes" and instead "insists on imitating the mandarin ducks in a painting" who can never bring their heads together.

But Miao-ku cannot be made to accept the unreality of her imaginary marriage. Marriage, she insists, is "the one thing that cannot be mimicked on the stage." Since she has "enacted falsehoods," she is determined to "turn them into realities."[70]

The act that follows, "Accompanied in Death" (*Chieh wang*) is a dramatic and structural tour de force in which the worlds of appearance and reality are brought into the sharpest and most dramatic degree imaginable of juxtaposition. It is the play's central act, both from the point of view of physical location and of its relation to the theme. It is "the act for which all the other acts in the play exist."[71] The play which Miao-ku chooses as a vehicle for her public suicide, *The Thorn Hairpin* (*Ching-ch'ai chi*; late Yüan or early Ming) is one of the earliest and most well-known plays in the romantic *ch'uan-ch'i* corpus. It is the archetype of many later plays in which the heroine tries to drown herself in order to avoid a forced marriage. It is also the play from which, later on, the lovers choose an act to effect a change of heart in Miao-ku's mother. This repeated reference to a literary archetype is yet another embodiment of the theme of imitation. *The Thorn Hairpin* is the ghostly play standing above or behind the actual play, just as various human and supernatural figures (such as P'ing-lang-hou, Mu-jung Chieh and the drama instructor) serve at various times as ghostly (because hidden or absent) patterns for the imitations of their inferiors.

Ch'ien Wan-kuan's behavior in this act conforms brilliantly to the expectations we have developed from his previous appearances. Swaggering into the performing area before the temple, he imagines that everyone present must secretly be resenting him. He must constantly remind himself that others see and envy his happiness, as this is the only way he can make his happiness seem real to himself:

I've cast away a fortune to purchase a lovely fawn.
I'm the only one who can have beautiful women at will,
A thousand eyes are staring, envious of my happy fortune.
There is no need to fear a lack of spectators.[72]

As before, he is insecure about his status; he is worried that people aren't giving him enough respect:

> (pointing to Miao-ku and Ch'u-yü) She is not the same anymore as she was before. She is my wife now. You should all stand further away. Don't crowd around like that; it's unseemly.[73]

Miao-ku acts her part with such composure that no one is aware of her unwillingness to marry Ch'ien. Even T'an Ch'u-yü is deceived. When she tries to reassure him just before performing, his angry retort is unconsciously ironic: "I'm a blind man! I'm not able to see you!" [74]

Miao-ku then performs her version of the death soliloquy of Ch'ien Yü-lien from act 26 (T'ou chiang) of The Thorn Hairpin. Her soliloquy is more than twice as long as the original and contains a greater proportion of speech as opposed to song lyrics.[75] The only portions of the original preserved without change are Yü-lien's opening and closing arias. The speech and arias in between are almost entirely new, and give Miao-ku an opportunity to address words of searing reproach to Ch'ien Wan-kuan and her mother, and words of comfort and farewell to Ch'u-yü. One change in particular is very typical of Li Yü's dramaturgy: in the original soliloquy, the heroine embraces a stone to ensure her submersion in the river. In the revision, she embraces the stone and then has a second thought. She wants to vent her anger against her persecutor before dying, so in order to have a focal point for her rage, she replaces the stone on the ground, letting it stand for the Thorn Hairpin villain Sun Ju-ch'üan. She proposes to scold the stone continuously until it nods its head in acknowledgement. Only then will she stop. This is one of several instances in which Li Yü makes use of a mutely expressive symbolic object on the stage, another example in the same play being the money chest referred to previously.

Her scolding, which concentrates on her persecutor's mediocrity and on the probable lapses of his own wife, is a masterpiece of insulting invective, but Ch'ien Wan-kuan does not see its application to himself. He is as insensible to the real import of her words as is the stone. In the crowning irony of the act, he nods his head and shouts:

> Well scolded! Well scolded! Those situations have never appeared in a play before. The revisions are really marvelous![76]

Here, perhaps, we have Li yü's sardonic comment on the potentialities of drama as a means of moral awakening. With grim, rigidly controlled humor, Miao-kü takes Wan-kuan's shouts of praise as the inanimate response she has been waiting for:

> Since the stone nodded its head, I have no choice but to cease my scolding. Now I had better embrace the stone and seek a way out of the world.[77]

The double suicide accomplishes what words could not; it arouses the moral sense of the audience and puts Wan-kuan in danger. He runs away from the scene of the performance, a fugitive from an aroused crowd eager to drag him before a magistrate. The act concludes with the comments of the moved and astonished spectators:

> (sung in unison) We call on the magistrate to wash away this injustice
> And publicly announce the marvelous deeds of the faithful wife and husband.
> The play they performed was actually the reality;
> They really gave up their lives in acting the plunge into the river.
> *The Thorn Hairpin* will be yet more famous after this.[78]

With this act, the first broad movement of the play, encompassing the destruction of the lovers by the "false" world of money and power, is completed. The remaining seventeen acts, like the second panel of a diptych, portray a complementary narrative movement: the rescue and restoration of the lovers by the "real" world of invisible ideals. The complementary movement begins with a direct portrayal of the other world. Act 16, "A Spirit's Protection" (*Shen hu*), introduces the "lordly commander of the waves" (P'ing-lang-hou), a mighty being to whom the oceans and continents of earth are no more than "a spoonful of water and a scattering of dust."[79] He is shown making the rounds of his local shrines to receive birthday offerings and supplications. His relationship to his suppliants is the ideal relationship of superior to inferior, of which Ch'ien Wan-kuan's relationship to the community council chiefs, portrayed in act 11, was a clumsy imitation or parody. The supernatural commander of watery nature is above all else a moral spirit; he cares nothing for the tangible and visible components of the sacrifices and prayers offered him. Only the inner sincerity and respect of the celebrants gains his respect and favor.

Visits to three shrines are enacted. At the first the ceremony is barbarous and crude, accompanied by an exotic local instrument, the "drumhorn" (ku-chiao), but the sincerity of the celebrants (and thus the sacrifice itself) is perfect. The spirit comments that these rude people are "close to the simplicity of the sage-kings of high antiquity."[80] The second, more orthodox, ceremony pleases him less because it is perfunctorily executed and the celebrants' request for magical restoration of life is something that lies not in his own, but in heaven's, jurisdiction.[81] It is at the third shrine that he hears of the couple who have drowned themselves out of mutual fidelity. It is because he is moved at the grandeur of their spiritual authenticity—"the smallness of their dust-treading steps surpasses the vastness of my tower-leaping strides"[82]—that he directs his legions of shrimps, snails, crabs, and turtles to carry out the miraculous transformation and journey through which they are restored to life. He closes the act in self-justification for presuming to intervene: the deaths, after all, occurred in his own watery domain, and in a ceremony offered to him at his own shrine.[83]

The next act, "Collecting Profits" (Cheng li), is an outstanding example of Li Yü's ability to transform an uncircumventable segment of narrative into a highly polished illustration of his theme. The narrative function of the act is to portray the further adventures of Ch'ien Wan-kuan and Liu Chiang-hsien after the suicide of the lovers. Out of this storytelling necessity is constructed a spirited satiric study of greed as a universal social principle.

The positive values of the supernatural and pastoral worlds are shown here in a diabolical inversion in which all the blacks become whites and all the whites blacks. As the previous act portrayed a supernatural bureaucrat discharging his duties, this act portrays a worldly bureaucrat, the local assistant magistrate, discharging his. Like so many other figures in the drama, he is engaged in imitation of an absent and (to him) ideal superior. In his act-opening soliloquy, he is lost in helpless admiration of the moneymaking skill of his boss, the new chief magistrate. This magistrate is a perfect marvel of hawklike attention to detail; he squeezes all the profit from a case before his underlings can make a single move. He himself, the assistant magistrate, has made a mere five thousand cash in his three years in office, but his boss has cleaned out the district in only half a year.

The news that Ch'ien Wan-kuan is in trouble for forcing two people to kill themselves fills him with glee, for he hates Wan-kuan for appropriating half the funds collected in the region for his own group of officials (cf. act 11). Even more pleasing is the fact that his boss is out of town visiting a superior. This time he should be able to pocket the profit from the case before his boss hears of it. He sends his runners off to extort money from Wan-kuan (they are to avoid explicit threats; all they have to do is to act as if they are in earnest about prosecuting the case).[84]

This introduction states the theme of the act. The theme is then taken up by one character after another (as in a musical development), until we find ourselves contemplating a veritable whirlwind of selfish interests. At the still center of the whirlwind there lies, of course, a large disputed sum of money: the thousand taels that were to have purchased Chiang-hsien's daughter.

Before the runners can get to Wan-kuan, Chiang-hsien appears. She is determined to hang on to the thousand taels if she can and is on her way to denounce Wan-kuan to the magistrate ("it was for money that I sold my daughter yesterday and it is for money that I denounce my lover today").

The community council chiefs whom Wan-kuan used to bully then appear. They are also going to the magistrate with formal accusations.

Wan-kuan next bustles on stage, followed by a servant with (another) money chest. He is still insensible to the nature of his guilt ("All because of one wrong move, my wanting to hear them perform *The Thorn Hairpin*, I'm suddenly accused of causing those two deaths."). He hurries after Chiang-hsien and the council chiefs, plucking their sleeves, begging them to drop the matter in return for a cash gift. The chiefs are willing to be bought off, as they stand to gain more that way than by going to a magistrate. Chiang-hsien, however, resists the offer. Wan-kuan persuades them all to join him in a neighboring tavern to discuss the matter.[85]

The two *yamen* runners, who have secretly observed all this, now fear that they will lose the profit in the case, since the concerned parties appear ready to come to a private agreement. They therefore lie in wait outside the tavern and arrest Chiang-hsien and the citizens when they emerge (Wan-kuan remains behind to pay the bill) for "attempting to negotiate a case involving human life among themselves." Brought before the assistant magistrate, they are forced to turn over three hundred taels of hush money that they received in the tavern.[86]

The runners then go to work on Wan-kuan. Threatened in his home by the runners, he tries unsuccessfully to bluster his way out of the situation, then placates them with a scheme for getting rich, by means of which he can get back at Chiang-hsien for having been ready to denounce him. They are to have to assistant magistrate force Chiang-hsien to return the thousand taels betrothal money. He (Wan-kuan) will then turn the whole sum over to the *yamen* for them to divide among themselves. This leads ultimately to a sublimely outrageous judicial verdict which will remind Dickens readers of the trial scene in *Pickwick*:

> Assistant magistrate: Mme. Liu's daughter simply missed her footing and fell into the water; it was no fault of Mr. Ch'ien's. Since she now has no daughter to give him as a bride, she must return the betrothal gift to him.
>
> Liu Chiang-hsien: Do you think the young man who drowned missed his footing as well?
>
> Assistant magistrate: The young man wanted to rescue Chiang-hsien's daughter and missed his footing. It was no one's fault.[87]

Even now, with the fate of the thousand taels apparently disposed of, the jockeying for profit is not yet done. In the sudden silence of the *yamen* after the protesting Chiang-hsien is hustled out, the runners congratulate the assistant magistrate on his good fortune and hint respectfully that he might share a bit of it with them. Hoping for a silver ingot apiece, they are outraged when he at length offers them much less, with the suggestion that they "buy tobacco with it." They therefore repeatedly decline the gift, saying they "would not dare" to accept it.[88]

And now the final masterstroke in this little comedy of greed occurs; the piece held in reserve from the opening of the game is brought out. A messenger from the absent chief magistrate appears, demanding (to the great glee of the cheated runners) that the apprehended booty be turned over to him, together with a full report on the case. The assistant magistrate doesn't even get to keep the three hundred taels hush money collected earlier; even in this detail, his chief's eyes have seen further and faster than his. This fine comic act is thus brought to a sudden, energetic, and happily logical conclusion, with an effect like a thunderclap or a house of cards collapsing. The runners have the last word:

> First runner: It's a good thing we didn't accept those rewards.
> Second runner: We just missed having to cough up that
> tobacco.[89]

The structural relationship of this act to the others is as cunningly thought out as is its internal mechanics. Just as, in the first half of the play, the first pastoral act (act 12) enjoys an isolated position that causes it to stand out aginst a background of selfish worldly passion, so in the second half this last and most devastatingly satirical of the "worldly" acts is surrounded by opposite matter; its farcical nastiness contrasts absolutely with the unforced altruism of the supernatural and pastoral acts that precede and follow it. A new norm has been asserted. It is now the "worldly" world rather than the pastoral world which is the exception, the dreamlike aberration.

In "Return to Life" (*Hui-sheng*) and "Rustic Wedding" (*Ts'un-chin*) the portrayal of the pastoral alternative, begun in act 12, is completed; and new, clarifying touches are added to the developing set of contrasts between proper and improper refinement, suitable and unsuitable vulgarity. Accompanying the discussion of actors and acting, and of the relationship between the apparent and the substantial, there runs throughout the drama a subdued but not quite ignorable strain of ribaldry, of bawdy sexual frankness. The play's implicit judgements upon these episodes can no more easily be summed up than can its judgements upon actors and acting. There are occasions when we are meant to regard a character's ribald behavior as a personal imperfection, a sign of inner coarseness and blindness, and other occasions when we are meant to regard such behavior as an incarnation of the invisible truth behind all facades. The boundary between the apparent and the substantial is a line that cuts straight through the domain of sex as it does through all human affairs. Or, phrased differently, the elements of human behavior are not meaningful in isolation; they are empty counters capable of carrying any number of different meanings depending on the peculiar genesis of each occurrence.

Thus, Ch'u-yü is not amused at the baldly suggestive banter or the barely disguised sexual groping of the returning playgoers in act 2. Chiang-hsien's offhand frankness in discussing sex is no more agreeable than her hard commercialism or her unashamed dishonesty. Ch'ien Wan-kuan's delight at the thought of cohabiting with both mother and daughter is part of the general grotesquerie of his behavior. And yet in act 10 Miao-ku, surely one of the play's repositories of positive values, explicitly welcomes the chance, afforded by the actors' quarrel, to come into physical contact with Ch'u-yü:

> I'll make as if I'm trying to pull Master T'an away. I'll grab hold of his hand and be able to feel his flesh pressing against mine . . . (She grasps Ch'u-yü's hand and they woo each other with hand-clasps)[90]

When, in act 18, the lovers, now changed into flatfish, are drawn from the water, their sexual attraction is so undisguised as to be (comically) indecent and disturbing:

> Servant's wife: They lie together just like a long knife. Their heads and tails sway back and forth together. They are making love in front of our faces! How can I look at them without feeling envious! (sings) My envy is hard to bear! I'm jealous of the male and female protuberances and concavities, their artfully united organs. (speaks) I can't look at them; all I want to do is split them apart. (She tries hard to split them apart and fails.) Oh! (sings) Surely you're not going to stay pressed together all day long without ever becoming separate and alone! (she points to the fish and turns to her husband, speaking) You useless cuckold! Just look at those fish! (sings) Who else could match your shamelessness! When we are under the covers together with the milky way between us, you turn over where you lie in order to run away from pleasure!
> Servant: It's hard to look at that species of fish. Let's cover them up with our rain-clothes ...[91]

As fish, Miao-ku and Ch'u-yü are temporarily devoid of human consciousness; all Miao-ku can later remember of her underwater journey is that "it was as if I grew larger and were floating away without drowning at all."[92] We may therefore suppose that their sexual union as fish is perfectly unselfconscious and thus free of any real impropriety. However grotesque in appearance (note that we are again involved in judging appearances), their piscine union is an innocent natural sign of their spiritual union.

Li Yü's doctrine of propriety becomes semiexplicit in the course of the rustic wedding banquet portrayed in act 19. Every detail of this scene is calculated to impress us with the extreme innocence and authenticity of the rustic participants, their freedom from all sham. The first three guests are an old woodcutter, an old farmer, and an old orchard-tender. The gifts they bring are things they have produced themselves in their different lines of work (money is unknown in paradise): the woodcutter brings half a pole-load of kindling "to warm the lovemaking wine"; the farmer brings three catties of wine "to make the bride and groom drunk"; and the orchard-tender brings a basket of fruit "to help the couple down their wine." Having heard that a wedding was afoot and desiring an excuse to get drunk and enjoy themselves, they have come uninvited, but the host Mu-jung Chieh was on the point of inviting them anyway[93] (in paradise people do not need words to divine one another's desires any more than they need money to supply one another's wants).

But the most authentic of all the guests has yet to arrive. Mu-jung Chieh worries that he hasn't yet found wind-instrument players or a master of ceremonies. As if in answer to his thought, that central figure in all pastoral idylls, the shepherd boy (*mu-t'ung*), enters playing his flute. He is the quintessence of that "insubstantial substantiality" which is the underlying theme of all the situations of the play; he is the model whereof the other rustic types are but imperfect imitations. Unlike the three old men, who are sedate and respectful, the shepherd boy is flamboyant, spirited, unpredictable. He lacks the outward status that years and steady productivity in a particular line of work can give, and his wedding gift is not tangible as are those of the three old men. These three challenge his right to contribute to the festivities (truth resides in the humblest and unlikeliest of forms and is invisible to those who lack the spark themselves; cf. the contempt which Ch'u-yü's poverty excites in his neighbors, act 2). They are baffled when he maintains that he has brought "a gift superior to all the others: my mouth," and are unimpressed when they learn that he means to contribute his flute-playing. (The shepherd boy's position here is analogous to that of commercial artists, such as Li Yü, who claim a right to tangible rewards in return for intangible contributions. In act 27, actors are referred to as "the spongers of the underworld.")[94] They too can play the flute. What they really need is a master of ceremonies, a function he undertakes to fulfill with complete self-assurance.[95]

It is the shepherd boy who is the most ribald in the ribald horseplay that concludes the banquet. The old woodcutter apologizes to Ch'u-yü for their rude local custom of "helping the groom" and "encouraging the bride" to get drunk. The three old men each induce the bride to drink a cup by threatening Ch'u-yü with beatings, etc., if she does not. The shepherd boy climaxes the process by presenting the bride with a particularly large cup of wine, dancing menacingly around the groom, and threatening to bite off his "important member" if the bride fails to drink it. Miao-ku's alarmed compliance is of course followed by a charming confusion. The guests soon afterwards depart, leaving the wise and beneficent Mu-jung Chieh to say a few more words to Ch'u-yü. In apologizing to Ch'u-yü for the rough behavior of the departed guests, Mu-jung apologizes as well for the occurrence of such a scene in a *ch'uan-ch'i* (and in so doing assumes a touch of the absent, "ghostly" author's identity):

> Brother T'an, when you two were on the stage, you acted the roles of man and wife all the time, but it was all according to formal conventions of the stage; there was never anything resembling the way this woodcutter, farmer, and orchard-tender saw you off to the marital bedroom or the way in which this shepherd boy encouraged your performance of the rites. Though a bit rustic and vulgar, it has its own interest. You've got to admit at least that it's not like anything you've seen before.[96]

Ch'u-yü's response puts beyond doubt the valuation the reader is expected to make. The sensibilities that recoiled in offense from urban bawdiness are refreshed and enlivened by pastoral bawdiness:

Not only is it very different; it is also very refined. I feel I have been honored beyond my deserts, and I am more grateful than I can say.[97]

A final round of impersonations brings the action of the play to a conclusion. Liu Chiang-hsien is awakened to shame through being made to impersonate the grieving male protagonist in *The Thorn Hairpin.*[98] Mu-jung Chieh gives hidden aid to Ch'u-yü through assuming the identity of the benevolent spirit P'ing-lang-hou.[99] A hired imposter brings temporary success to the bandit rebels by impersonating the famous Mu-jung Chieh.[100] Ch'u-yü defeats the bandits through strict adherence to the advice of his "silent general," invisible to all.[101] Finally, in the last act, Mu-jung Chieh impersonates his impersonator in order to trick the bandit chief into confession.[102]

The "highest" of these impersonations—the highest in the scale of being and the most sincere in intention—is the one in which Mu-jung Chieh attaches the name of P'ing-lang-hou to the little instruction book he writes for Ch'u-yü. It is appropriate that he should be the figure that impersonates the spirit, as he is the wisest, the most experienced, and the most hidden, of all the figures in the drama. When his wife protests that in using the spirit's name he will deprive himself of all credit for his deed, he responds that that is not the way to look at it; the credit may not in reality be his to claim, and his use of the spirit's name may be more than a subterfuge:

How do we know that our idea didn't come from the spirit's inspiration! Perhaps he led us to do this from some invisible region. In this world I am borrowing a spirit's name. In that world he is borrowing a mortal's hand.[103]

In bidding farewell to Ch'u-yü shortly afterwards he urges him never to surrender to a merely worldly point of view.

Listen to all the spirit tells you on this journey, and tell all your troubles to the unearthly wizard; don't suppose that the other world half exists and half does not.[104]

The perfect parody of Mu-jung's high and altruistic impersonation is the hired imposter's impersonation of Mu-jung in act 23, "Feigned

Hiding" (*Wei yin*). In this character we have a stock butt of derision in traditional Chinese culture: the would-be statesman who angles for promotion through a showy display of indifference to worldly advancement.[105] He enters carrying a fishing pole in his left hand and a bag in his right containing an official's felt cap and round collar (here, of course, we are meant to recall the scene in which Mu-jung and his wife demonstrate a genuine renunciation of ambition by casting their hats into the water.) In his entrance couplet he provides an example of a standard moral shuffle of the opportunist: he justifies his base motives by denying the possibility of the existence of high motives. The low protects and perpetuates its lowness by proclaiming all highness to be illusion:

> You never meet real hermits in this world, so there's no harm in a mountain bandit pretending to be a mountain dweller.[106]

He attempts to compose his features into "the stern, imposing look of a lofty individual who has renounced the world," and settles down to fish and await his discoverers:

> (sings) Hoping that people will know my surname
> I pretend to conceal my given name.
> This is the true tradition of "gentlemen in hiding."
> It is called "hiding the form but letting the shadow be seen."
> The fisherman's song offers its sounds for sale;
> The goatskin cloak aims to dazzle the beholder.
> If you want to converse with one of heaven's rare stars,
> A horse and carriage will suffice to get you there.
> My black felt hat is ready at my side
> And so is my blue scholar's gown.[107]

But the natural world gets even with the imposter for his violation of its laws by involving him in a situation of fantastic and ribald indignity. The region is too wild and rugged for a sedan chair; the best conveyance his discoverers can supply is a stretcherlike affair made of long dried vines to which the person to be carried is harnessed, straddling the vines. The imposter consents to this arrangement with offensively showy magnanimity (which we are to contrast with Mu-jung's determination to travel in a fisherman's boat), and is shortly the victim of a practical joke of nature:

"Though your shoulder-stretcher is a vile thing, your intentions are good. I'll just have to pretend I'm riding a child's bamboo horse.

(sings) Though the dried vines are soft, they feel hard when you straddle them, hard when you straddle them.

They rub like iron on one's amorous handle, one's amorous handle.

It's almost enough to break off the life of a married woman.

Stop chattering and stop for awhile!

(The bearers quicken their pace.)

When I tell them to stop, they just grow more unruly.

This child's bamboo horse is much too passionate![108]

The imposter's action allows the drama to conclude with a final *coup de théâtre*, the scene, "A Scary Reunion" (*Hai chü*), in which Ch'u-yü comes within a hairsbreadth of condemning his benefactor to death for committing crimes against the state. On the conceptual level the act illustrates the unfortunate consequences of unworthy (i.e., interested) impersonation: it brings the worthy models themselves into disrepute; it deprives the world of its points of reference and brings about a situation in which justice itself mistakes justice for iniquity.

In a splendidly characteristic and dramatic gesture, Mu-jung again displays in this final act his indifference to any values but the unworldly one of truth. Believing Ch'u-yü to be deliberately and ungratefully perpetrating a falsehood, he remains furious and aloof through most of the inquiry. Only when it at last becomes apparent to him that Ch'u-yü's conviction of his guilt is sincere, that he has not been cynically engaged in trumping up a criminal charge, does this aloofness vanish:

(greatly astonished) Good heavens! This means you were not purposely trying to injure me . . . I beg you to clear this matter up. If you don't, my life is only a small matter; but how can I endure the endless infamy that will follow? Before I was unwilling to bend my knee to you, but now I have no choice; I must play the part of a criminal kneeling in court, listening to the magistrate's questioning. (He kneels.)[109]

After truth is established and ceremonies of mutual esteem and gratitude have been performed, a last confrontation of worldly and otherworldly values takes place. Ch'u-yü wants to do more for his benefactor than to write memorials and announcements clearing his name. He wants to recommend him for further government service. As on several previous occasions, Mu-jung vigorously rejects this proposal ("Even three fierce armies could not strip off my hermit's rain-clothes made of steel.")[110] Now, however, he goes further and exerts his persuasive powers to the utmost in urging Ch'u-yü to perform the opposite action: to leave the worldly arena in which he has just had the good fortune to distinguish himself and join him in the anonymous depths of the hills and streams. The comparison of life to the stage has been the great theme (or, more precisely, the great vehicle of the theme, which is the relationship of truth and appearance) of all that has gone before, but until this point it has remained a comparison which is largely implicit. It is now brought into the open and made the basis of a handsome piece of valedictory rhetoric:

> Mu-jung: I have a few persuasions to retirement to urge upon you. Though they might sound harsh to your ear, I nevertheless want to speak about them this once. Whenever a person enjoys success, he should think ahead to the time when he will suffer failure. On the stage, for example, there are no drums and cymbals that sound continuously from beginning to end. There is a leading man and a leading lady, but there is a villain and a clown as well. If there are moments of joy and merriment, there are moments of sadness, too. The villains and clowns are merely the opposites of the leading men and leading ladies; the sadness is merely the result of the merriment. The road of public office is peopled mostly by villains and clowns, and in the world of officialdom it is easy to come by sadness. Those who fully comprehend the principles of things invariably put away the cymbals and silence the drums in situations of joy and merriment; that way they cannot arrive at situations of sadness. "Remove your sash and put away your cap" [i.e., retire from government service]. You cannot but engrave these few ungrateful words on your heart. (Ch'u-yü and Miao-ku incline their heads.)
>
> Ch'u-yü: These words of yours are like blows on my head

from a stick, like tolling bells that scatter my dreams. When I
hear them my whole body becomes covered with sweat.
When you return home this time, sir, please build a few
thatched rooms on either side of your honored dwelling.
When I have completed this appointment, I will immediately
remove my official's ribbon and retire to the mountains to
live a secluded life with you.[111]

The last in-character aria sung by Mu-jung and his wife celebrates a
devotion to obscurity so thorough that even the usual emblems of a
withdrawn, pastoral life are seen as worldly snares:

> We're wrong to walk in danger for no reason, wrong to walk in
> danger for no reason.
> It is as if immortals loaded with blessings should come to peer at
> ghosts.
> Go, go, go. Fly from the clear wind and hide from the bright
> moon.
> Bid farewell to happy things; repent your former error.
> Lessen, lessen, lessen. Lessen the plain, unseasoned rice; strip off
> the rough clothing.
> Break, break, break. Break the broad-leaved hat; let there only
> be our skin.
> Angle, angle, angle. Angle with the fishing line, but don't cast it
> toward the road.
> Fear, fear, fear. Fear the tail of an idle person entering Peach-
> spring paradise.
> Choose, choose, choose. Choose a unique and still-secluded
> fishing pier of stone.[112]

Thus the drama ends in the lyrical evocation of a pastoralism so
intense and pure as to make conventional pastoralism seem but a
faded image of the original; an evocation of a simplicity beyond all
imaginable simplicities, an obscurity beyond all imaginable
obscurities. This is the tonic chord, the resolution to which all the
events of the play have tended.

The quality that most stands out in the play as a whole is the immense dexterity and intelligence displayed in the invention and
disposition of its narrative segments. Li Yü was never more

thoroughly the master fabulist, never more happily absorbed in his craft, than he is in this play. There are few parallels to Li Yü's story-making art to be found elsewhere, because few authors speak so much through narrative in a long work intended for adults. *Little Dorrit*, perhaps, displays a similar tenacity in pursuing a single conception—the idea of life as imprisonment—in all its great and little episodes, but the story itself is less autonomous, less visible and perfect, as a vehicle of meaning. One remembers characters and situations in *Little Dorrit* while forgetting much of the machinery of wills and concealed misdeeds through which they are related. But if you forget what happens in *The Paired Soles*, you have forgotten the play.

An additional point must be made about Li Yü's art of story construction, and that is that it is not something that can be fully savored in isolation from its function. The thing that causes the skill to come into being, that imparts value to it, that causes us to notice and admire it, is something that is distinct from the skill itself. An activity attains full vitality and perfection only when it ceases to be regarded as an end in itself, but is pursued as a means to a further end. The ability of a musician's fingers to execute swift and precise movements is gained because it is a scarcely noticed by-product of an attempt to realize another thing that has nothing to do with muscular coordination: an imagined relationship of sounds. The point at which a student of mathematics will most probably become fluent in trigonometry is not when he approaches the subject directly by doing distance problems, but when, in the course of studying calculus, he uses it as an incidental means of deriving answers to problems that transcend trigonometry. A person does not become fluent in a foreign language when studying the language itself, but when circumstances later force him to use the language as a means of conducting his affairs.

So with Li Yü's peculiar dexterity in the construction of stories. It is a dexterity that results from a deeper preoccupation, a desire to grasp and communicate something which is not the story, but which can only be envisioned and embodied by means of the story. The way that can be spoken of is not the true way. A thoroughgoing philosophical materialist, one who rigorously adheres to the principle that "a gentlemen does not concern himself with ghosts,"[113] could have no motive (other than a pointless delight in complexity) for constructing the sort of many-tiered and honeycombed stories that are his specialty. His stories depend for their effect upon the assumptions (which are of course antipathetic to the general trend of modern thought) that (1) existence has a transcendental meaning and that (2) the meaning can be got at, can be partially glimpsed, through analogy. Each ingenious inversion, each parallel situation in the story, is a hint pointing to a larger hidden unity of meaning in existence, of which the story itself is an imperfect imitation. Li Yü tells stories because his assumptions about life are those of a moralist and a mystic.

Again and again in *The Paired Soles* we notice the accents of a man who is carried away by his argument, who is lost in the excitement of a vision that greatly transcends the inert symbols with which he labors to make it clear. One feels that the stage manager-author is saying no more than what is already abundantly apparent when, at the close of the play, he says of the play's lyrics that he has "woven his heart's feelings into them without limit." The concluding quatrain very properly (yet with becoming casualness and modesty) refers to the didactic element in the play, its tendency to teach and enlighten:

> In recent times, virtue and duty have been a bit disordered
> And everyone fastens blame upon the stage for portraying lust.
> I thought I'd use the stage to uphold virtue and duty
> So that he who ties the bell on, will have supplied a way to
> remove it.[114]

The Paired Soles is filled with elements that occur in other *ch'uan-ch'i* as well. Its scenes are so varied that it might indeed be said to be richer in convention than a conventional play. Indigent protagonists, cruel mothers-in-law, bullying landlords, uncouth rebels, wise and loyal generals, uninhibited shepherd boys, and even scholars who disguise themselves as actors, are the very stuff of Chinese drama. In each such case, however, a slight but definite shift in emphasis or alignment warns us that, in its new surroundings, the convention points away from the familiar world of entertainment to regions unknown. The stones are old but the building is new.

III. Life as Sincerity:
The Amazing Reunion

In the Four Books there are two sentences that say:

Wealth nourishes the house;
Virtue nourishes the person.

Readers have never been able to understand the meaning of this word "nourish." It doesn't necessarily mean to rebuild a house in such a way that it looks sparkling new. The thing referred to above as being "nourished" was a dwelling with an abandoned garden. Even a few thatch-covered rooms can have a prosperous look as long as a wealthy person lives there. This is brought about by changing economic conditions. It possesses what it apparently lacks. If we suppose that this "nourish" means what it does in the expression "to nourish a house," then it means to refurbish, to decorate, etc. But if we take "nourish" to mean what it does in "to nourish the person" [i.e., to nourish character], we must reverse ourselves and imagine an entirely different process before we can allow ourselves to use such an expression. How can anyone bear to confuse uprightness and sincerity with a showy parade of moral precepts learned from books?
Li Yü, "The House Where I was Born," *Twelve Mansions*[1]

. . . he almost felt . . . that he had two heads; one was calm, careless, and efficient; the other saw the danger like a deadly map, was wise, careful, and useless.
G. K. Chesterton, *The Ball and the Cross* (1910)

59

The word *reunion (t'uan-yüan)* in the title of the play we are now to consider is, among other things, a technical term used in discussions of *ch'uan-ch'i* drama. Etymologically, it means something like "gathering or collecting into a ball." It refers to that point in the plot of a *ch'uan-ch'i* near the conclusion of the play, in which the husbands, wives, parents, and children who have previously been unhappily separated from each other are (whether through divine or human agency) brought back together and enabled to resume or initiate a happy existence free of further threats and misfortunes. The skill with which the dramatist brings about this *t'uan-yüan* or reunion is a freqeunt subject of discourse in Chinese drama criticism. The *t'uan-yüan* can be criticized, for example, for occurring too suddenly or too late, for involving patent impossibilities, for offending the reader's sense of justice or fitness, and the like. It is one of the points in the structure of a *ch'uan-ch'i* play in which high tact or ingenuity is often displayed or demanded; in dramatists who, like Li Yü, are inclined to a flashy display of dexterity and originality in the creation of plots, the *t'uan-yüan* can be the occasion for an impressive explosion of painstakingly prepared narrative fireworks.

The title of the play, then, is in one sense an advertisement of the ingenuity with which the reunion will be brought off; and the implied boast is in this case more than fulfilled, for nothing could be more astonishingly ingenious (or exquisitely artificial) than the manner in which Li Yü makes his story lead to the three successive climaxes of acts 31 through 33. The word *amazing* in the translated title is in fact an unavoidable compromise, a groping attempt to match the range of a Chinese word *(ch'iao)*, the basic meaning of which is not "amazing" but "ingenious." But the meaning "ingenious" cannot in this instance be retained in English translation without creating a possibility of serious misunderstanding, and the reason for this leads us to a further implication of the play's title.

In Chinese literature, the quality of *ch'iao* or ingenuity is something that is commonly attributed not only to human beings, but to the "shaper of events," whether conceived of anthropomorphically as "the creator" *(tsao-hua)* or simply as the force of destiny. Events which we would call "astoundingly coincidental" are said in Chinese to be "ingenious" because they reflect the ingenuity of the power that brought them to pass. Thus Li Yü really means two things by the expression "ingenious reunion." First and foremost, he means "a set of

miraculously coincidental events brought to pass by the creator."
Secondarily, he means "a masterly conclusion to a play devised by a
clever playwright." This double attitude is expressed in a perfectly
open (and yet delightfully ironic) manner in a narrator's aside in a
short story by Li Yü ("The House Where I Was Born," *Twelve Mansions*) that tells the same story as our play. The aside occurs in the
midst of the concluding phase of the story, the part that corresponds
with the reunion of the play:

> It was sheer good luck that the old woman and the young
> woman ended in the same boat and struck up an acquaintance
> with each other. If the young women had been sold first and the
> old ones later, Yin Hsiao-lou and his wife could not have been
> reunited. Even if the old ones had been sold first and the young
> ones later and Yao Chi [Yao K'o-ch'eng] had bought a different
> old woman and the old woman he actually bought had been
> sold to a different man, then Yao Chi and his wife could never
> have been reunited. Who could have known that the ingenuity
> [*ch'iao*] of God would turn out to be a hundred times that of
> mortals! It's just as if he brought them together with the inten-
> tion of providing someone with perfect material for some idle
> piece of fiction. Who knows how much thought he must have
> expended in taking those two couples, uniting them and then
> parting them, parting them and then uniting them! Yes, this af-
> fair could indeed be considered marvelous in the extreme and
> thoroughly ingenious [*ch'iao*] as well! But who could have
> suspected that there was still another miraculous and ingenious
> [*ch'iao*] circumstance in this case, which, though it had already
> been brought about, had not as yet been detected . . .²

Li Yü is obviously pulling the reader's leg here and having great fun
while he is at it, but it must not be supposed that his amusement is so
one-sided as that of a modern, or even a Confucian, sceptic. Li Yü
laughs at many things, but it does not occur to him to laugh at the
casual, popular spiritualism of his time. He is on the contrary quite at
home with it; at home, that is, in the suggestively shadowed and
modulated mental atmosphere in which mysticism and rationality,
analogy and deduction, are equally active and mutually supportive.
Again and again in his work, regardless whether the tone of the

passage in question be serious or gay, teasing or straightforward, one comes across the idea that human and supernatural agencies are equally and harmoniously responsible for the accidents of our existence. It does not occur to him that the assumption requires a defense. Thus at the conclusion of *The Amazing Reunion*, the characters sing:

> When people lose each other, heaven makes them meet again
> If there is a gap or rent in heaven, men will safeguard it, have no
> fear.
> Neither heaven nor man can be discounted.[3]

The Amazing Reunion, then, shows how a group of characters are reunited in a way that we would call "amazing" (considered as a natural event) and "ingenious" (considered as a product of conscious artifice). But, as the lines quoted above indicate, this reunion is not to be conceived as resulting from external agencies alone. The ingenuity of the (supernatural) creator and the skill of the playwright are both indispensable, but the personal qualities that condition the choices of the reunited characters are equally indispensable. The miraculously fortunate outcome of their adventures depends upon the fact that they are most uncommon people, that their actions are consistently informed with a moral and intellectual insight of an altogether transcendent order. The unconventional (and yet logical and considered) actions with which they respond to their dilemmas are so far beyond the comprehension of the ordinary man as to give them the appearance of fools or madmen, but this foolishness of theirs is at length shown to be the only true practicality. This is the third significance of the word *ch'iao* as it is used in the title of the play. The reunion is "amazing" or "ingenious" because it is conditioned by such madly sane behavior.

This behavior owes its bizarre quality to an extreme excess of a traditional virtue. Yin Hsiao-lou and Yao K'o-ch'eng are thought to be dangerous eccentrics because they behave as if they were ignorant of the universality of egotism and distrust. In moments of crucial decision they act with a wildly hypertrophied sincerity, a sincerity so insistent and pure as to resemble madness, while the normal characters to whom they are contrasted are in varying degrees deficient in this virtue. The word *theme* may be used to denote either a storytelling theme or a conceptual theme. The quality of sincerity as it affects human relations is the conceptual theme of *The Amazing Reunion*, for it is the principal philosophic concern that arises from the storytelling theme of a son's reunion with a pair of forgotten parents.

It is important to our discussion, however, to understand what the term *sincerity* denotes in a traditional Chinese context. In Chinese one cannot, like Fyodor Karamazov, say, "he prefers to have more nobility than sincerity in his words, but I prefer in mine to have more sincerity than nobility . . ."[4] In Chinese, an evil thought or an evil action cannot in general be described as "sincere," nor can an act that falls short of perfect moral solidity and harmoniousness be said to be perfectly sincere. The word (*ch'eng*) means not only "to be free of dissimulation," but (like the Latin *sincerus* and, in previous centuries, the English "sincere") "to be clean, pure, sound; not falsified or perverted in any way."[5]

The Chinese concept is extensively developed in two Confucian texts that have enjoyed canonical status since the end of the Southern Sung dynasty. Six chapters are devoted to sincerity in the *Chung-yung* or *Doctrine of the Mean* (the close of chapter 20 through the beginning of chapter 26), and two much-quoted passages in the *Ta-hsueh* or *Great Learning* (in sections 4 and 5 of the text and chapter 6 of the commentary) directly concern sincerity.

In these passages, we are told that sincerity can only be an attribute of someone who has "extended his knowledge to the utmost" through "the investigation of things"[6] and has by this means come to an "understanding of goodness."[7] Sincerity, and the preparatory labor that allows it to come into being, is to be understood as an act of "self-completion."[8] Though sincerity is attained only through arduous and unremitting moral and intellectual effort,[9] all strain disappears once the state is realized. The sincere man is able to make perfect choices without effort and without reflection:

> Sincerity is the way of Heaven. The attainment of sincerity is the way of men. He who possesses sincerity is he who, without an effort, hits what is right, and apprehends a thing without the exercise of thought. The sage is he who naturally and easily embodies the way. He who attains to sincerity is he who chooses what is good and firmly holds it fast.[10]

From the above, we see that to say in Chinese that a person is perfectly sincere is to imply a great deal more about that person's moral attainments than is implied by the weakened equivalent usage now current in the west. It implies that all of the person's faculties—intellect, desire, conscience, will, and faculty of action—are effortlessly and harmoniously integrated. Sincerity in this sense will be attained rarely and with the utmost difficulty. One does not wonder that the process of becoming sincere, rather than sincerity itself, should be characterized in the *Chung-yung* as the way of man. Anyone so unusual as to exemplify the quality itself might, like Yin Hsiao-lou and Yao K'o-ch'eng, appear mad or foolish to ordinary people.

It should not go unnoticed that this comprehensive and indeed mystical concept of sincerity is an idea that involves yet another version of "amazing or ingenious reunion." The reunion referred to in the play's title is of course purely practical and concrete; it is not intended to signify anything more rarefied than the reunion of a group of characters. To deny this would be to do violence to the idiom in which the play is written. But to fail to allegorize, to fail to notice immaterial patterns of significance thrown up by the material stuff of the play, is (while respecting the idiom) to do violence to the spirit in which the play was written. It is not necessarily an exercise in sophistry, therefore, to notice that the reunion of characters celebrated in the play has a shadowy parallel within the psyche of the sincere person, especially when we consider that the happy outcome of the story is explicitly attributed to the main characters' capacity for spontaneously disinterested behavior. The physical reunion with which the play concludes is the external material image and outcome of a set of internal reunions that have already taken place. The *Chung-yung* defines sincerity as self-completion, but it goes on to say that the operation of sincerity does not end with the completion of self; it extends as well to the completion of external things.[11] Ceaselessness is in fact one of the outstanding attributes of entire sincerity:

> Not ceasing, it continues long. Continuing long, it evidences itself.
> Evidencing itself, it reaches far. Reaching far, it becomes large and substantial.[12]

In addition to having a potentially unlimited power to transform people, things, and events, the sincere person has an intuitive understanding so sharp and delicate that, like a spirit, he is able to foreknow good and evil events.[13] It is entirely in accord with the Confucian conception of sincerity that the rare individual who, like Yao K'o-ch'eng, is capable of perfectly disinterested action should also be able to direct his steps unerringly to a lost and forgotten father. It is like a repetition of an act already performed.

The operation of sincerity is not only studied in the principal actions of the play. The theme is shown in many different lights and is made to appear in small details as well as in the central episodes. In order to follow these adventures of thought in detail, however, it is necessary to make some preliminary observations concerning a set of characteristics peculiar to this play that create the special environment in which Li Yü's philosophy of sincerity unfolds.

To say that *The Amazing Reunion* has a highly individual flavor is to say no more than we expect. The typical mark of a play by Li Yü is an exuberant, even reckless, eccentricity of concept. Its basic situation, its organizing idea, is (with but one or two exceptions) characterized by some prominent feature that sets it apart from all other *ch'uan-ch'i* plays. But this prominent feature is introduced not through an arbitrary invasion of the form from without, but through organic development or logical extension of the form from within. It results not from the mechanical application of some novelty that has no relation to the usual world of *ch'uan-ch'i* drama (as, for example, replacing the usual two-character act headings with quotations from Mencius),[14] but from a systematic enlargement and concentration upon some element that is already inherent in the form, accompanied by a corresponding diminution and subordination of other inherent elements (as in nature the different mammalian specializations result from variations in the development and mutual relationships of organs common to the whole class). Nearly all *ch'uan-ch'i* plays, for example, depend to some extent upon the narrative device of disguise, and the form is itself an instance of impersonation. We have already observed that in *The Paired Soles* Li Yü seizes upon this universal structural element of drama and uses it as a theme, an instrument of meaning. The play not only *employs* impersonation, but is *about* impersonation, in the sense that it is philosophically concerned with it. That which in most *ch'uan-ch'i* plays serves an entirely corporeal function is there endowed with a sort of consciousness. The body, while remaining a body, becomes an idea as well.

The same type of relationship to the form is evident in *The Amazing Reunion*. To say that all *ch'uan-ch'i* plays involve the establishment of human relationships is to say no more than that they all possess the kind of narrative structure that is associated with comedy. The form requires that a group of good characters, initially powerless and isolated, gradually succeed in establishing an assortment of stable kinship bonds that insure their future prosperity and happiness. If the drive that makes them do this were not present, the story could not move forward. Without this drive, there could in fact be no stories of any kind whatever. But the bond-making activity is rarely what a *ch'uan-ch'i* play is about; it is rather the thing that makes the play go. It is not where the focus of attention is; it is rather the thing that allows a focus of attention to exist. It forms part of that assumed matrix of human activity and concern that supplies the physical support, as it were, for an extended development of the mood or preoccupation that is to domionate the whole (as the idea of gratitude dominates *The Tale of the Lute* [*P'i-p'a chi*] or the idea of passion dominates *The Peony Pavilion* [*Mu-tan t'ing*]).

In *The Amazing Reunion*, this element of the background is made to occupy a position in the foreground. It is isolated, examined from a hundred aspects, placed in a hall of mirrors. The process begins in the second act, "Questions Asked in a Dream" (*Meng hsün*), with an audacious transposition of emphasis. All *ch'uan-ch'i* plays involve the formation of relationships, but not all types of relationships are of equal prominence. It is in the very nature of the form that the central relationship should be that of husband and wife. Just as in western comedy, it is ordinarily the formation of this relationship that constitutes the principal movement of the plot and that initiates the train of adjustments that bring all the other types of new relationships into being.

The relentless structural centrality of the romantic relationship (rather than the political, the filial, the brotherly, and the amicable relationships) in *ch'uan-ch'i* drama is at first sight a strange phenomenon, for this relationship is not the one which traditional Chinese philosophy and morality stress most heavily. The relationship of prince and minister and of father and son are of incomparably greater dignity and prestige. These two relationships, and not that of husband and wife, stand at the center of Chinese ethical thought. In popular novels about heroic bandits in the tradition of *The Water Margin* (*Shui-hu chuan*), there are countless instances of the fact that, in the popular estimation, the claims of a wife cannot even compete with the claims of a friend. It is the mark of a hero that he will abandon his wife at once if loyalty to her conflicts with his duty to a comarde-in-arms. Chinese critics are themselves at a loss to explain the dominance of the sexual relationship in *ch'uan-ch'i* drama and are inclined to attribute an allegorical significance to romantic subject matter. If a commentator admires a particular *ch'uan-ch'i* play, he is apt to observe that the loyalty to each other of the hero and the heroine is an image of what the relationship of a prince and a minister should be like. The playwright, he maintains, has borrowed something humble in order to shadow forth something great. He is thus relieved of the embarrassment of praising a celebration of insubordinate eros.

The first great novelty that confronts us in *The Amazing Reunion* is that its central relationship is not that of husband and wife, but that of father and son. This is such a striking deviation from standard practice that the anonymous commentators, forgetting allegory, devote most of their paragraph of "general criticism" (*tsung-lun*) at the end of the play to expressions of amazement that Li Yü should be able to base a *ch'uan-ch'i* play upon a nonsexual relationship and yet so engage the interest of the reader.[15]

In accomplishing this transposition of emphasis, however, Li Yü does not violate the canons of the form. He does not extirpate the romantic element in the play; he does not even make any formal alteration in its mode of presentation (i.e., the hero is introduced in act 2 and the heroine in act 3). The romantic element exists and is even (as we shall see) developed with a certain delicate care and originality, but it is greatly overshadowed by Yao K'o-ch'eng's quest for a father and by his father's quest for a son. K'o-ch'eng's self-introduction in act 2 is centered on his yearning for a set of parents and his feeling of nostalgia for an imperfectly remembered childhood home. The romantic theme is reduced in this act to its unavoidable essentials, being entirely disposed of in two brief remarks, the first occurring near the beginning, and the second near the conclusion, of the act. In the first, he mentions that he is unable to be accepted anywhere as a son-in-law because he has no family and no money; in the second passage, he tells us that he has been struck by the beauty of the daughter of his neighbor to the east, but has had to keep out of her way to avoid suspicion.[16]

The filial quest theme is on the other hand invested with all the natural attractiveness, all the intrinsic wonder and poetry, that is ordinarily characteristic of the romantic quest. It is the mysterious and prophetic dream, to which the greater portion of the second act is devoted, that accomplishes this. All the things that are presented in the dream—the unsolved question of the house's location, its air of incipient occupancy, the testy evasiveness of the old neighbor, and the moving familiarity of the toys in the chest—combine powerfully to create a state of imaginative hunger in the reader, a sense of being but a hairsbreadth away from the solution of a significant mystery.

In most *ch'uan-ch'i* plays it is the search for a mate that occasions the most serious breaches of correct social behavior: the smuggled letters, the disguised entries, the violated walls, the ignominious expedients, the equivocal explanations, and so on. In this play, however, the lovers exchange their vows with the greatest imaginable degree of respect for propriety; they refrain even from meeting or speaking to each other. [17] It is rather the father and son who, in their quest for each other, exceed all bounds of conventional restraint.

The thematically central act of the play is the one (number 10, "Breaking Up a Disturbance," *Chieh-fen*) in which Yin Hsiao-lou stolidly invites and calmly endures the scorn of all the world's smart and proper people by offering himself for sale—an apparently penniless, unskilled old man—to any passerby who wants a father; and in which Yao K'o-ch'eng, with as great a show of indifference, offends the propriety of the world even more drastically by taking the crazy offer seriously.[18] The other actions of the play very largely tend to echo this principal action of Yin Hsiao-lou and Yao K'o-ch'eng. Most of the characters spend most of their time seeking parents or seeking children. Significantly, we never learn the given name of the heroine; she may not even possess one. To K'o-ch'eng, as to us, she is simply Miss Ts'ao (Ts'ao-shih), the adopted daughter of Yao Tung-shan (alias Ts'ao Yü-yü).

The romantic and erotic images that usually predominate in *ch'uan-ch'i* drama—the nesting phoenixes, the paired mandarin ducks, the trembling flowers, and the audacious bees—are not noticeably present in *The Amazing Reunion*. Instead, its lyrics are dominated by images of birth and nurturing ("the vine warms the germinating melon in its embrace"),[19] by expressions of cosmic nostalgia or loneliness ("Heaven has set loose a withered old contemplative; all his destinies have come to nothing. What need is there to imitate the Buddha? The western heaven is already here."),[20] and by elegiac laments over separations and devastations produced by time and war. ("You ask after the well-being of a chick whose nest is overturned; don't you hear the branch in the cold wind sigh for her?")[21]

This transposition of emphasis from the romantic to the filial relationship, reinforced by such imagery, contributes decisively to the importance of the idea of relationship making in *The Amazing Reunion*. The unusual emphasis in itself invites the reader's attention and reexamination; it prevents him from taking the basic situations of the play for granted. And the type of relationship celebrated is more exclusively a *relationship* and less a fulfillment of a fantasy or instinct than that which dominates romantic and erotic *ch'uan-ch'i* plays.

But there is another factor (already touched on above) that raises the relationship-making process to a position of signal prominence in the play. That factor is the crazy and astonishing (and yet, in the circumstances, utterly logical and motivated) means by which Yin Hsiao-lou seeks a son.

Fatherhood and sonhood are matters in which there is ordinarily no element of choice. The awe and primacy of the relationship in some measure derive from that absence of choice, from the fact that it is a relationship mysteriously conferred upon man by a confluence of forces—nature, heredity, and custom—over which he has no personal control. The marital relation is less primal than the filial relation (and easier to use as a subject for plays) because it is something that can be conditioned by human preference. Because it is something upon which humans may operate, as well as something which operates upon humans, it is more comprehensible and more amenable to alteration and subordination than the filial relationship. Comprehensibility breeds contempt.

What Yin Hsiao-lou does in going to a place where he is unknown, in pretending to be penniless, and in offering himself for purchase as a father, is to increase the element of filial choice from zero to one hundred percent. This has two consequences, one structural and one philosophic. The structural consequence is that the relationship of the protagonist to his prospective father is now very like the relationship that he usually bears to the principal female role. He is now in a position to scheme and suffer to gain a father just as he usually schemes and suffers to gain a mate.

The philosophic consequence is that a quite unexpected awe and dignity is conferred upon the filial relationship itself. It might appear that to make fathership depend upon a commercial transaction (and a paltry one at that) is to reduce the concept of fatherhood to a level of complete frivolity. The paradox of the situation is that it is only by means of this total frivolity that the relationship can attain to total seriousness. The only actions that can be proven to be totally sincere are those which are totally gratuitous. The only actions that can be proven to be totally gratuitous are those which are not conditioned by any external necessity. But actions that have no relation to external necessity are precisely those actions that are vulnerable to the censure of frivolity. It is therefore impossible to be an idealist without at the same time being a clown. He is the most sincere who is the most frivolous.

Li Yü gives full play to the humor inherent in the unconventional behavior of Hsiao-lou and K'o-ch'eng, but at the same time he does not wish the reader to dismiss lightly the more serious implications of their adventures. As the narrator in "The House Where I Was Born" remarks,

> I beg to offer this advice to the people of our age: not everyone will be able to take Yao Chi [Yao K'o-ch'eng] as a model and purchase people to be their fathers and mothers; but neither should anyone take Yao Chi as an example of what to avoid and place the widow, the childless, and the orphan outside of his concern.[22]

This identification of playfulness with sincerity (in its full Confucian sense) is, as we shall shortly see, an explicitly upheld principle in this play and is embodied in another major action, one that involves Ts'ao-shih rather than Hsiao-lou and K'o-ch'eng.

The means employed by Ts'ao-shih to avoid rape while being held captive by the bandits parallels the means employed by Hsiao-lou to avoid allying himself with an opportunistic son, and calls into play the same highly developed capacity for indifference to public opinion that characterizes the two men. Applying an extract from croton oil beans to her skin, she first disfigures herself in a way that mimics leprosy and then conceals some additional beans in her sleeve so as to have a means of inflicting discomfort and disease on would-be ravishers.[23] Her plan is designed to insure that anyone pursuing her only from a motive of sexual enjoyment will automatically lose his ardor (just as fortune seekers will automatically be cool to the proposal that they pay for the privilege of adoption by a penniless man).

In their concluding aria, the hero and the heroine look back on their past deeds and celebrate the wisdom of their foolishness:

> The way I saved my virtue was strange, yet amusing;
> The way I bought my parents, though clever, seemed foolish.
> A buffoonlike young man and a joking young woman—
> In making clowns of ourselves, we turned the bolt of heaven.[24]

This "wisdom of foolishness" cannot be attained by following examples or adhering to principles:

> For repose and health, don't imitate the crazy scholars.
> Before undertaking any task, consult an augury book.
> Aimless footsteps are the hardest to track.
> Above Yao and Shun there was no Yao and no Shun.[25]

The Amazing Reunion, then, is a play about the wisdom of making crazy, arbitrary decisions. That these decisions seemed bizarre enough to the work's contemporary, indigenous audience may easily be inferred from the remark of the commentators at the point in the next-to-last-act ("The Original Dream," *Yüan meng*) when it is at last revealed that K'o-ch'eng's arbitrarily chosen parents are in fact his natural parents. "When one has read to this point," they say, "it at last appears that the desires of all the characters obeyed a broad harmony of purpose. One realizes that the purchase of a father and the acknowledgement of a mother was caused by the nature of heaven; they were in fact not monstrous events at all."[26]

The discoveries of blood relationship that reveal the characters' "broad harmony of purpose" are a significant part of the thought inherent in the play, but it is precisely in the "unnaturalness" of the principal events (in their as yet mysterious, unrationalized state) that the peculiar charm and the peculiar challenge of the work lies. The treatment of these events implies a blend of amusement and wish fulfillment. "What a humane, rational, and amusing world it would be," one senses the author musing, "if people would take the work of heaven into their own hands and become each others' relatives." As K'o-ch'eng observes at the close of act 10 ("Quelling a Disturbance," *Chieh fen*):

> When a good man has no heirs, he can easily arrange to get
>   one.
> What's the use of having Mr. Heaven take charge?
> When a Po Tao meets a Ting Lan,
> The two will soon forget their pent-up sorrow.[27]

Elsewhere, in the concluding aria of act 14 ("Discussing Return," *Yen kuei*), it is observed that the "marvelous attachment" of Hsiao-lou and K'o-ch'eng does not conform to "the traditional five relation-ships of the world."[28]

In passages such as these there is a tendency of thought which, if pushed further, might result in an intentionally absurd (yet sub-liminally sincere) utopian proposal; a proposal, say, that the creation of artificial extended families be officially encouraged as a solution to the problems of isolated and resourceless people (a situation that the similarly humane and jocular Kurt Vonnegut describes in his novel *Slapstick*). In Li Yü, however, the proposal remains in the incipient, unformulated stage. This may in part be due to a deep-grained assumption that solutions to personal problems should have a per-sonal character and should be of personal origin. It may also reflect a conviction that people are in general incapable of trusting one another. They have a habit of prudence that is ineradicable.

The establishment of heaven depends upon a rare immaturity of spirit. K'o-ch'eng, trying to sooth Mme. Yin's astonishment at his wish to regard her as his mother, assures her that his heart "is as free from guile or sarcasm as a newborn infant's."[29] When the idea is im-itated by people who cannot understand its spirit, it is immediately debased, as is shown in the parodic tavern episode (in act 11, "Buying a Father," *Mai fu*) in which a servant (acting on orders from a group of antagonistic onlookers) poses as a person who wants Hsiao-lou to adopt him.[30] Any idea so contrary to custom will always be perceived by the vulgar as unnatural, and therefore unwholesome, no matter how humane or sensible it may actually be. As one of the crowd of mockers observes,

> This affair just now [K'o-ch'eng's purchase of Hsiao-lou] was extremely odd and contrary to natural principles. The other day I heard someone say there was a man who gave birth to a child and a woman who grew a beard. And now a thing like this happens before our eyes as well! These recent events are all inauspicious omens. The Ming dynasty will lose its mandate without a doubt.[31]

The foil to Yin Hsiao-lou is Yao Tung-shan (alias Ts'ao Yü-yü), the adoptive father of the heroine Ts'ao-shih. As Yin Hsiao-lou is preeminently the character who makes reckless and naive decisions that turn out to be right, so Yao Tung-shan is preeminently the character who makes prudent and shrewd decisions that turn out to be wrong. Portrayed as a generous, courageous, and capable man, he is not in any sense a *bad* character. He is merely a consistently (and comically) *mistaken* character.

As many parallels as possible are worked into the situations and aims of the two characters, so that the implied contrast between them can scarcely be missed even by the ideally inattentive reader. Like Yin Hsiao-lou, Yao Tung-shan is a man of property and rank whose only son died in childhood. Like Yin Hsiao-lou, he wishes to adopt Yao K'o-ch'eng as his son. Like Yin Hsiao-lou, he subjects his prospective son to tests of character. Like Yin Hsiao-lou, he leaves his home and lives incognito, pretending to be a commoner. In the play these resemblances are not set forth schematically as they are here, but emerge piecemeal from the evolving circumstances of the play. It is only when the reader has read as far as the final act, involving the clash of wills between Hsiao-lou and Tung-shan, that he is able to contemplate the full range of their similarities and differences. It is only then that he realizes how meticulously this set of contrasts has been prepared.

The crucial difference between the two is that Hsiao-lou acts from a desire for truth or authenticity whereas Tung-shan acts from a desire for security. As it turns out, the heavens are disposed to grant the first desire and to pour scorn on the second. When the play opens,

Tung-shan has fled from his home in Szechwan and has assumed a new identity as an itinerant herb doctor in Hukuang in the hope that he will thus be able to escape the destructive fury of the bandits then marauding throughout the countryside. As a consequence of his efforts, his home in Hukuang is plundered, his adopted daughter is taken captive, and he and his wife have no choice but to undertake a long and dangerous journey back to his home province, which turns out to have remained relatively secure. Yin Hsiao-lou, by contrast, leaves home to find something rather than to avoid something, and his search is at length rewarded. His wife, it is true, is taken captive by bandits, but then he never proposed to avoid disaster; he only proposed to find a son.

Again, the test imposed upon Yao K'o-ch'eng by Yao Tung-shan is primarily a test of hardihood and competence. His idea is that if he can gain a son who is good at dealing with practical matters, keeping a steady head in tight situations, and so on, he and his family will be *safer* (in view of the unsettled times) than if they ally themselves with a bookish young scholar, however promising a match he might be under ordinary circumstances. K'o-ch'eng shows he is as practical and reliable as Tung-shan could wish, but because of the delay and separation occasioned by the test, Tung-shan loses touch with his prospective son and daughter-in-law before he can bring them together. Yin Hsiao-lou, by contrast, is primarily interested not in testing K'o-ch'eng's competence, but in testing his sincerity. His idea is that if he can gain a son who has a genuine regard for his parents, he and his wife will be *happier*, and he does in consequence gain K'o-ch'eng's wholehearted allegiance. Tung-shan expresses his desire to adopt K'o-ch'eng in such a gruff and oblique way that K'o-ch'eng misunderstands his intent. When he receives a message from Tung-shan to the effect that "your use of the expression 'son-in-law' is extremely inappropriate," he naturally assumes that this expresses a desire to keep him out of the family rather than to take him into it. Hsiao-lou's offer of fathership stands for the opposite extreme. It is so direct and guileless as to appear mad. It is nevertheless the approach that works. Nothing is more sophisticated than naivety.

There is one instance in which Hsiao-lou departs from guilelessness: his failure to give K'o-ch'eng his true name and address; but this one lapse of his serves ultimately to reinforce the high value that is placed throughout upon childlike sincerity, for it results in the one serious miscarriage in his plans—he and K'o-ch'eng lose touch and for a time have no way of locating each other. In act 23 ("Suffering Separation," *Shang li*), the sincere man's regret and self-loathing over a moral lapse is vividly depicted:

> Speaking of it, my mouth rants feverishly;
> Thinking of it, my heart saws like a file.
> There is a tongue in my throat; it hasn't been cut out by anyone;
> Why did I chatter like a silly woman, telling falsehoods and sowing deception?
> Instead I concealed the facts and that germ of concealment grew into disaster.
> And now, even if my tongue were at the sky's end,
> It could not spout forth a thousand flowers.
> That a mere gold image should play such devilish tricks,
> A sealed mouth give rise to tidal waves!
> Doesn't this show that people's souls make even more foolish blunders?
> It is all because I have the unhappy destiny to face perpetually to the left;
> And even if I exhaust my wits, I cannot alter fate.
> How can I know anything of him now?
> I want to send my soul to him,
> But I fear my dreaming words would be deceptions too![32]

It appears likely that *The Amazing Reunion* came relatively late in Li Yü's development. Its preface is dated 1668, which is about thirteen years before his death. In the introductory verses to the play, Li Yü apologizes for the defects of eight earlier plays (unspecified) and promises that the new one will be better, which suggests that much of his professional career was already behind him. None of his plays is known to have a later publication date, though a number of his plays cannot be dated.[33] The idea for the play, however, was evidently one that had occurred to him long before, for it is used in his previously mentioned vernacular story, the eleventh in his *Twelve Mansions*, entitled "The House Where I Was Born." The preface to *Twelve Mansions* is dated 1658, ten years earlier than the date of the preface to the play. The differences between the play and the story have a direct bearing on our consideration of the meaning inherent in the play and upon the larger question of the nature of Li Yü's dramaturgy.

Comparing the play to the story, one is impressed by the thoroughness with which the material is made to meet the requirements of the different forms. The story shows no signs of being a sketch for a *ch'uan-ch'i* play and the *ch'uan-ch'i* play shows no signs of being an adaptation of a story, yet the material in each is essentially the same. C. S. Lewis has remarked that in order to write a good love sonnet, it is as important to be in love with the sonnet as it is to be in love with a woman (or a man, as the case may be).[34] "The House Where I Was Born" and *The Amazing Reunion* are high instances of a craftsman's love for the vernacular short story and for the *ch'uan-ch'i* play respectively. The chief technical differences between the two treatments (aside from obvious differences, as that one is narrated and the other dramatically represented, etc.) may be summed up under the following three heads:

(1) The story is told with a maximum of suspense. The reader is never given any information the revelation of which can be put off until a later point. The play, on the other hand, entirely suppresses suspense and instead develops as much as possible the sort of irony that arises from the audience's knowing things that the characters do not. In the story, the reader's knowledge is as restricted as that of the characters themselves; he is down among them, as it were, looking at what passes through their eyes. He is being taken on an adventure. In the play however, his field of vision is as broad as if he were looking down at the action from heaven. His viewpoint is that of an omniscient spirit. He is forever responding with amusement or anxiety to the spectacle of characters racing toward exits that he knows to be cul-de-sacs and fleeing from evils that are really (from the standpoint of their own desires) goods. The reader of the story does not know that the old woman whom K'o-ch'eng purchases from the bandits is actually the wife of his adopted father; nor does he know (though he may well guess) that the young woman whom the old woman later advises him to buy is actually his fiancée Ts'ao-shih. The question that is uppermost in his mind is, therefore, "What will happen next? How will K'o-ch'eng deal with the disappointment of having purchased a grey-haired old woman? How will the purchase turn out to be related to what I have thus far learned of the story?" In the much broader area illuminated by the play, we know everyone's identity

and have a good idea in advance how the different parts of the story will fit together, so the question that is uppermost in our minds is, "How will these characters (with whose identities and individual peculiarities I am perfectly familiar) respond to the demands of this new and delightfully ironic situation?" We already know all that is determinate in their future history; what we do not know is the obbligato which their capacity for free choice will play upon the bass line of their destinies.

(2) The story's concentration upon suspense is accompanied by a marked devotion to continuity in the development of narrative, a devotion that affects not only the form, but the significance, of the material. The narrator never abandons the experiences of one character in order to relate the experiences of another unless the nature of the story absolutely requires him to do so; and in those cases, the break in continuity is always introduced by the phrase "the story now splits into two parts." In the play, on the other hand, breaks in continuity are embraced rather than avoided. In the play it is rare for any train of events to continue for more than two acts before the focus shifts elsewhere. The scope for elaboration of theme is consequently much greater. The story does not aim at complete representation; it does not try to be a paradigm of the totality of human experience. It aims only to be a complete story, to recount a single, shapely sequence of adventures. The story, if you will, is like a piece of sculpture, while the play is like the same piece of sculpture viewed in a hall of reflecting and distorting mirrors.

Thus in the story we begin (once the preamble is over) with an old man who loses his son, who is unable to have another, and who eventually wanders to a distant place in order to gain one. The story is all centered upon the old man; we learn of the other characters only at those points at which they begin to be involved in the old man's adventures. In the play, on the other hand, we focus first on a young man who wants to be a father, then upon a refugee official who wants to marry his adopted daughter to someone who will take his surname and act as his heir. Then we are shown this figure imposing a test of practicality upon the young man. Next we are shown the old man (the old man of the story) making his decision to go out and seek a son. Next the play focuses on the adopted daughter inscribing a love message on a handkerchief. Next we are shown Li Tzu-ch'eng giving bloodthirsty instructions to his generals. This systematic dis-

continuity of presentation affords opportunities to build up parallels
and contrasts that the storytelling approach does not afford.

In the story, for example,. K'o-ch'eng's neighbor Tung-shan is not
given characteristics that parallel those of Hsiao-lou, for the story is
not free to make discursive points about differences of philosophy between two such figures. He is not intended there to be taken as a person whose decisions are mistaken because they are prudent. He is not
an official posing as an herb doctor, as in the play, but simply a cloth
merchant, the person who taught K'o-ch'eng his trade (in the play it
is K'o-ch'eng's deceased foster father who is given these attributes).
He appears only briefly and is not mentioned again after his daughter
Ts'ao-shih (not his stepdaughter as in the play) is captured by bandits. In the play, Tung-shan plays an active role throughout and the
contrast between his behavior and that of Hsiao-lou is ever more
sharply defined. As a consequence of such contrasts, the play is more
centered upon ideas than in the story. It would be overly elaborate to
speak of the story as possessing a theme (apart from its narrative
theme); it is not overly elaborate to speak of the play as possessing a
theme.

In the story it is mentioned, but only as a bare fact, that Mme. Yin
becomes acquainted with Ts'ao-shih in the bandits' camp. In the play
we actually watch this event occur. One of the central acts (act 17,
"Exchanging Confidences," *P'ou ssu*) is devoted to it. The expansion
of this episode is not just a gratuitous padding of the narrative, but a
major reembodiment of the theme. Mme. Yin's attentions to Ts'ao-
shih are portrayed as acts of simple, original charity that we are
meant to compare with the kindness that K'o-ch'eng shows to Hsiao-
lou. Her treatment of Ts'ao-shih is an example of the chivalry which
the old can display to the young, as K'o-ch'eng's behavior shows the
opposite chivalry which the young can display to the old. Both Mme.
Yin and K'o-ch'eng display a willingness to take chances, a willingness to ignore prudential considerations, in making their respective
approaches to the young girl and to the old man. The people whom
they approach are both mistreated or ostracized by other people, the
old man for an eccentricity bordering on madness, the young woman
for her gloom and for the threat of the contagious disease from which
she is believed to suffer. Mme. Yin is drawn to Ts'ao-shih (as K'o-
ch'eng is to Hsiao-lou) by an admiration and a compassion that
ignore risks:

I would like to seek out a fellow sufferer so we could both tell each other our troubles, but how I am to do this, I don't know. My companions in distress are many, but those who feel as I do are few. Those purposeless, spiritless women wept a few times when they first entered the camp as captives, but after the third day all you could hear was the sound of their laughing. If you look for one who frowns and sighs, you can't find as many as one or two in ten. In fact the only one, really, is a young woman whose face carries the traces of disease; she weeps all day long. It pains me to hear her, and I would go and try to cheer her up, but I hear the others say she is afflicted with a strange disease that often infects those who go near her. Not only are the men afraid to meddle with her; even her own companions, the other captive women, are like that—there is not one who doesn't run away from her whenever they see her coming towards them. But then I am several times her age; even if I should die from it, what is there to be afraid of? I must go and find her, so we can tell each other what weighs on our minds.[35]

In retrospect, this totally impractical act, this chance friendship formed with no other end in view than the assuagement of immediate sorrow, turns out to be the crucial link in the chain of circumstances that leads to the reunion of the family. Looking back upon their experience (in act 31, "The Amazing Reunion," *Ch'iao chü*), the reunited characters use otherworldly imagery in linking their present happiness to their former steadfast adherence to a courtesy that disdained material limitations. Ts'ao-shih observes that "our meeting today as if we were immortals is all due to our meeting in hell and forming a ghostly friendship."[36] In chorus, they sing:

Two devoted couples sit with fragrant shoulders paired.
It is just as if the world were at peace and calamity had never been.
When we entered the fire we all imitated the fresh lotus
And never lost a petal, never lost a petal.[37]

This idea is echoed by the stage manager-cum-author at the conclusion of the play, when he says:

I'm pleased that the blossoms of my pen are not yet entirely
  withered.
One more time, a lovely flame-surrounded lotus blooms,
  upholding chastity.[38]

Here, the idea of a lotus surviving the flame applies not only to the
heroine preserving her chastity in a bandit's camp, but to the artist
saving something whole and pure from the corrupt currents of the
world. The sap that nourishes the lotus, we are to imagine, is a certain resilient gaiety of spirit. As the stage manager retrospectively
remarks in his last two lines:

You don't have to say that everything was happy,
But still, an amply gallant spirit was maintained throughout.[39]

By abandoning suspense and narrative continuity, then, the drama
gains a great freedom to compare the behavior of different characters,
to develop both aspects of a proposition, and, in short, to offer for the
reader's contemplation a complete, interpreted world: a world in
which being and meaning, suffering and the understanding of suffering, are one.

(3) A further technical difference having far-reaching artistic consequences is that the story tends to be one-sidedly expository, argumentative, and rational, whereas the play is heavily overlaid with medita-
tive and lyric elements due to the ubiquitousness of aria lyrics. These
lyrics impart psychological and atmospheric depth to the play and,
like the fragmented act structure itself, serve to create patterns of
parallels and double significances in the reader's mind. Often these
functions of the aria poetry are so closely associated that they cannot
in practice be isolated. A perfect example is the poetry with which
K'o-ch'eng describes his feelings for Ts'ao-shih in act 8 ("A Mute
Betrothal," Mo-ting). K'o-ch'eng is on the verge of embarking on the
cloth-peddling expedition with which he is to prove his resourcefulness to Yao Tung-shan (alias Mr. Ts'ao). He cannot understand why
he feels a vague reluctance or uneasiness about leaving, as if he "held
something in his hand that he cannot let go of." He paces up and
down by the bamboo fence that runs between his own thatched
dwelling and that of his neighbors, the Ts'aos. In a mixture of prose
and aria language, he complains that whenever he reaches a certain
point by the bamboo fence, he can go no further, as if its broken and

tattered bamboo segments formed "a snare of fencework." He notes the odd disparity between the objects of his attention and the feelings to which they give rise:

> This dwelling is a humble, circumscribed thing; why should it
>   be hard to leave behind?
> Why do I linger when I wish to go, as if my foot were
>   tethered?[40]

A little later, after he has read the quotation from the *Book of Songs* that Ts'ao-shih has left for him on a handkerchief, expressions of rapture merge with further images of captivity. He is caught in a "stubborn knot" of feeling. His heart is so bound, that he wishes the bamboo fence might stealthily encircle and imprison him. He recalls that this "illness of longing" had "injured" him before he even understood its nature. His captivity is now so deep that he fears he no longer has a will apart from hers. If she should order him to die, he would automatically obey.[41]

In return for the gift of the handkerchief, he leaves his jade cloth-measuring ruler for her to find, with another (slightly altered) poem from the *Book of Songs* inscribed upon it:

> She threw a girdle gem to me;
> In requital I gave a quince.
> No, not only as requital;
> But meaning I would love her ever.[42]

Poetic conceits involving the ruler emphasize the mysteriousness of their feelings and the disparity between the sentiment and the occasion. Leaving the ruler behind, K'o-ch'eng chants the lines

> If you want to know how long love lasts
> Wait for another year and measure it.[43]

Ts'ao-shih, having found the ruler and read the poem, says:

> Master Yao, Master Yao, I need no jade ruler to measure your
>   love.
> The earth's longevity and heaven's breadth are in that word
>   "forever."[44]

Finally, at the conclusion of the act, K'o-ch'eng observes of himself that

> From now on, an illness is added to my illness;
> The first onset merely introduced the theme.
> I fear that from this time on, a bamboo fence
> Will be added to the house that haunts my dreams![45]

This entire courtship act is characterized by a very odd, but very appealing, simplicity and naivety, a naivety that is all the more startling when one thinks of the intricately sensuous and erotic way in which courtship scenes are developed elsewhere in *ch'uan-ch'i* drama. Even considered in isolation, this act is startlingly original. But this originality, though it possesses all the unexpected force of an accidental event, is not accidental in its relation to the drama of which it forms a part. When K'o-ch'eng connects the bamboo fence (which stands for his romantic yearning) to the house that he repeatedly dreams of (which stands for his longing to belong to a set of parents), we suddenly realize that the way his feelings evolve for Ts'ao-shih is entirely consistent with what we already know of his character. He is a person who rationalizes from intuitions. He feels what he wants before he knows what he wants. He is also a person dominated by a deep desire to live in obedience to others. This desire is reflected in the fact that he wants parents far more than he wants a wife (for in traditional Chinese culture the relationship of a son to a father is the very archetype and definition of obedience, of willing service), as well as in the fact that when he does fall in love with a woman, his love is of that peculiar type that makes one feel incapable of disobeying the loved one's slightest command. Li Yü's portrayal of this state does not derive from *ch'uan-ch'i* convention. Chinese dramatic heroes more often than not display the most intense and delicate appreciation of the physical charms and artistic gifts of the women they love and this appreciation can easily assume the form of a haunting infatuation, but such infatuation is not ordinarily expressed in terms of rapturously willing servitude. The way in which the relationship of man and wife is traditionally conceived imparts a faintly bizarre, or a faintly ludicrous, flavor to such expressions of devotion, natural as they may seem to the westerner, who is unconsciously steeped in the lore of courtly love. But in K'o-ch'eng's case, it is an eccentricity that is in line with the overall eccentricity of his character; it is of a piece with his extraordinary eagerness to trust and serve any decent-looking stranger.

The above use of the word character is not intended to suggest that Li Yü set out to portray character in the sense that modern western novelists and dramatists do. Rather, he set out to articulate a theme by means of a dramatized story. But he has such a vital conception of the consistency of his story that he sometimes creates what westerners term "roundness of character" as a purely incidental and unconscious result of his effort to link event with event and situation with situation. Many characters, of course, remain perfect stereotypes. The characteristics of Mme. Yao may be comprehensively summed up in the phrase "virtuous wife." The bandits are as true to type as if each wore a sign around his neck saying "bloodthirsty ruffian." About the same proportion of rounded to flat characters may be found in Molière who, like Li Yü, was a dramatist who wrote plays around propositions and was no more shy of theatrical stereotypes than is a tailor of his bolts of cloth. The simplicity of these stereotypes is not a defect, but a convention that allows the reader to keep his attention trained on characters whose actions carry thematic interest. There must be a background as well as a foreground.

The play's pervasive concern with the value of naivety is reinforced by a series of deliberate departures from convention in the courtship scene. The barrier that runs between the lovers, for example, is not the garden wall of romantic story (deriving from the great Yüan prototype of Chinese romantic comedy, *The Romance of the Western Chamber*), but a humble and somewhat dilapidated bamboo fence. Though they communicate through an exchange of poems (and thus far obey the romantic tradition), they do so on a level so simple as to suggest parody. The poems they leave for each other to find are famous love lyrics from the *Book of Songs* (the one that Ts'ao-shih uses is in fact the first one in the collection), poems that any child would know. The slight alterations they make are merely interchanges of terms within the poem; they do not involve poetic skill. Their message-making sophistication is not far above that of the schoolboy who thinks of a variation of the "roses are red, violets are blue" formula to give to a pretty playmate. Also remarkable is the complete absence of eroticism in the act. Nothing could be more different from the sexually taut atmosphere of refined, literary courtships, in which the young man and the young woman are both suffused with an intense, trembling awareness of their physicality and every image contains a delicate erotic innuendo. And what is finally unusual in this act is the muteness of the betrothal, the severe reticence and propriety of the behavior of both lovers. K'o-ch'eng refrains from speaking or meeting with Ts'ao-shih in order to avoid violating the trust of her father, and Ts'ao-shih refrains out of modesty from inviting such an approach. She is ashamed even to have left the inscribed handkerchief on the fence and reflects that she would never have done it if the bandit threat had not impelled her to act precipitously. They notice and admire each other's reserve, and feel more bound to their oaths of fidelity on that account.

What we have in this act, then, is a thoroughgoing transposition of the traditional courtship scene into a rustic or plebeian key, a transposition that the reader is intended to find partly amusing and partly touching. But these details, like others we have noted, are in fact specific instances of a motif that pervades the play. All of the principal characters are "transposed" from backgrounds of wealth and privilege to a world of mean striving and material necessity. When the play opens, Yao Tung-shan has already become Ts'ao Yü-yü, the travelling herb doctor. Yin Hsiao-lou becomes a nameless beggar. Yao K'o-ch'eng is so thoroughly transposed that he does not even suspect that his recurring dream is a remnant of former privilege; all he has ever known is the world of travelling cloth salesmen to which his foster parents belonged. Mme. Yin and Ts'ao-shih both fall to the condition of volitionless chattel, packaged and sold in a human market.

This downward transposition is in some respects parallel to, and in other respects opposite to, the outward or upward pastoral transposition of The Paired Soles. The pastoral transposition took its characters out of trouble and necessity and, by freeing them from the exigencies of role playing, allowed them to resume their original natures. The plebeian transposition takes its characters into increased trouble and necessity, but, like the pastoral transposition, it allows them a certain role-playing latitude; and it is this latitude that allows them to reveal what is genuine in their natures.

The expressed values of the chief characters in the play contain conspicuous elements of antielitism, of antipathy toward the rigid

limits circumscribing the behavior of the upper classes. Both Yao
Tung-shan and Yin Hsiao-lou want to find a son characterized by
"practical resourcefulness" rather than "useless book-learning." At
the close of act 5 ("Quarreling Over an Inheritance," *Cheng-chi*), Yin
Hsiao-lou sings that he wants an heir inured to cold and hunger
rather than a "wife-doting, father-forgetting dandy," for "a poor man
will know the hard side of obligation."[46]

When Ts'ao-shih hits upon the idea of using the first poem in *The
Book of Songs* as a love message, she observes:

> They always laugh at sheltered girls knowing nothing of poetry,
> Yet having to inscribe pink leaves to communicate their
>   feelings.
> But when depth of feeling combines with ready wit,
> One need not envy the superiority of the learned.[47]

When K'o-ch'eng is at length restored to the privileged position in
which he was born, the honors that descend upon him are not as
brilliant as those which usually adorn the hero at the close of a
ch'uan-ch'i play. When congratulatory messengers come to announce
his scholarly success, it is not a first in the metropolitan examinations
that they announce, but a fourth in a mere provincial examination.[48]
Moreover, K'o-ch'eng has not contributed to any military victories
nor done anything else to attract the admiration of the nation or the
favor of the emperor. What is celebrated in the play is clearly inconspicuous private virtue rather than public distinction.

The Amazing Reunion is filled with references to buying and selling,
and all of its major relationships are established by means of commercial exchanges. The vulgar marketplace is the setting to which the
gentlemanly values of sincerity, benevolence, and righteousness are
transposed and in which they attain real fulfillment. It is through
analogy with the practice of tradesmen that the idea of offering
himself for sale first occurs to Hsiao-lou:

> I have it, I have it! The thirty-six mercantile pursuits all have to
> make advertising placards so they will be known throughout the
> land. Only then will anyone come and seek them out. Since I
> wish to attract potential heirs, my situation is just like that of a
> merchant. Why shouldn't I make people know of me?[49]

Having finished making his sign, he exclaims, "Now that's what I call a stylish advertisement!"[50]

Throughout the various purchase scenes, the business aspect of the transactions is heavily emphasized. Hsiao-lou tells K'o-ch'eng that he is to consider the sign his contract of purchase; it is heavy and strong and cannot be consumed by termites like ordinary paper documents. When K'o-ch'eng puts the sign in his sleeve before he has made clear his intention to pay, Hsiao-lou protests that the sign is part of his "investment."[51] In the story (though not in the play), much banter is derived from the conceit that the ten taels K'o-ch'eng pays to purchase Hsiao-lou is "capital expended" and the fortune he gains in consequence is "profit."[52] Yet accompanying the emphasis upon the commercial manner in which the relationship is established is an emphasis upon the reality of the supracommercial sentiments that are involved. K'o-ch'eng reflects that he can use Hsiao-lou's person as a stand-in for his missing parents:

> I can serve him tea and water morning and evening and thus fulfill my filial instincts. Who knows whether my parents' spirits might not adhere to his body and come forward to receive my offerings?[53]

Later he assures Hsiao-lou that he is "not to think of this as an adoption":

> I'll make you my natural father in the end;
> We are like relations from two once-dead but newly revived families.
> This is not an instance of tumbleweed tracks meeting in the road;
> Clearly it is an instance of bearing another child, reexperiencing labor pains.[54]

The attitude towards commerce that is implied here and elsewhere is friendly, even affectionate. To exchange money and goods, to draw up contracts, to seek advantages, are not necessarily activities characteristic of petty, morally undeveloped people, as the elite culture is disposed to claim. Such activities may be among the physical forms of honesty itself; they may become incarnations of sincerity. The payment of cash may be an activity by means of which all human purposes including the sincere purposes, are manifested.

The conditions of commerce are also the conditions of peace. When a shortage of provisions temporarily compels the bandits to become merchants (even merchants engaged in an enterprise as repugnant as the sale of human beings), their customary bloodthirstiness is perforce modified:

> For the time being, we'll break with custom and act like rulers.
> Yama the king of hell will change to a Bodhisattva.
> We won't draw knives for a month; our inward virtue will be high and vast.
> The heart of heaven is perceptive; how will it repay us?
> Not only those who act as emperors of the people,
> But even God, is about to tire of killing.[55]

The Amazing Reunion can be viewed as Li Yü's apologia for engaging in commercial activities (chiefly book publishing and book dealing), just as *The Paired Soles* can be seen as his apologia for being a semiprofessional director of an acting troupe. *The Amazing Reunion* is full of references to the sufferings and disruptions caused by the invasion and rebellion that accompanied the fall of the Ming dynasty; these are precisely the conditions in which Li Yü himself turned to commerce earn a living.

In *The Amazing Reunion*, commercial investment is an image not only of the quality of an individual's relation to other people, but of the quality of his relation to heaven or destiny. When K'o-ch'eng is about to rush off to the bandit's market a second time to redeem his captured fiancée, this further significance of commerce becomes explicit:

> I empty the bag's remains, collect the "golden planets," scoop together the "silver jellyfish";
> I hang all my possessions from my shoulder and send them as swift as flight up to the scales of heaven.
> If it is still not enough, I shall pawn my person.[56]

There is a connection between the willingness to invest everything in a commercial venture, expressed above, and the "wisdom of recklessness" which Hsiao-lou (and K'o-ch'eng and Mme. Yin) exemplify.

It is an attitude that might be characterized as "creative fatalism." as an anonymous boat passenger tells Hsiao-lou (who is eating his heart out at having forgotten to tell K'o-ch'eng his true name and address), "When you resign yourself to destiny, you can seek an advantage in every situation."[57]

In the act in which Hsiao-lou hits upon the idea of selling himself, his admonitory address to the sign he has just created emphasizes the riskiness of the venture, the possibility of total defeat:

> Advertisement, advertisement, the comfort of my declining
>   years depends entirely upon you. You must come to
>   my assistance. (sings)
> I give directions to the sign before beginning,
> So it can go into the street and sell my old bones.
> If it reports that none will accept this stallion's corpse
> Whom can the dead horse of the season hire to bury it?[58]

In act 17 ("Exchanging Confidences," *P'ou ssu*), Mme Yin's kindness to Ts'ao-shih is occasioned by a similar feeling of recklessness. Alone in the bandits' camp with no prospect of rescue or ransom, she wonders "what dog's belly my old bones will end up in."[59] The sincerity-exemplifying actions of the play are all leaps in the dark, devoid both of the comfort and the constraint of certainty.

It should of course be kept in mind that the free and daring exercise of choice the play celebrates is a quality exercised within, and occasioned by, conditions of extraordinary suffering and disruption arising from war. The significance of this background forms the subject of the "lead-in" (*yin-tzu*) or storytelling introduction to "The House Where I Was Born." Passages in the story which, like this introduction, are devoted to philosophical commentary are made possible by the conventional assumption (common in vernacular stories of this length) of the tone of a professional urban storyteller. The presence of this moralizing narrator is the only major technical difference between the two genres that tends to give the story rather than the play a greater freedom to be discursively philosophical. "The House Where I Was Born" is introduced by a two-verse *tz'u* (a poem of fixed but unequal line length) supposed to have been written by a woman of high birth who was taken captive by rebels during the fall of the Ming:

A calamity such as occurs but once in a thousand years·
Has chosen to occur during my own lifetime.
The state is broken, my family destroyed, and my person
    disgraced.
Not a single thing has avoided destruction,
The lord of heaven is so cruel.

I am wrong to think of it;
My bitter regret is useless.
Souls by the green grave-mounds are so numerous that
    individuals cannot be found among them.
But the road to the Yellow Springs is narrow, so narrow that I
    would surely meet my forbears on it,
And then I could not prevent my cheeks from turning red.[60]

Using this poem as his starting point, the narrator begins his performance by urging the reader not to adopt a severely moralistic attitude in judging the deeds of people who misbehave in conditions of
extreme stress:

> The standards we use to judge people in times of disorder should
> be different from the standards we ordinarily apply. . . . If a per-
> son's actions appear loyal and honest but his heart is no differ-
> ent from that of a traitor or flatterer, he will of course be harshly
> criticized by historians. But if an individual's person lives in a
> strange region while his heart remains true to heaven, he should
> be given his due for this by later generations. This is truly what
> the ancients placed first. . . . Since this woman met with shame,
> you might think she would be classed with those who have
> betrayed obligations and forgotten favors. Those who are still
> able to sing feelingly and mournfully, giving form to their feel-
> ings through pen and ink, should be considered worthy of for-
> giveness. Such people cannot be mentioned in the same day
> with the usual sort of women who lose their chastity.[61]

This passage, which is so strikingly "western" in the sharp distinction it draws between an action and the intention which accompanies the action, and in its disposition to affirm the independent
reality of spiritual states, is in the literal sense no longer relevant to

the story as it is developed in the play, for in *The Amazing Reunion* the heroine does not lose her chastity when captured by the bandits; the intelligence and originality she displays in preserving it in fact dominates one of the central acts (act 15, "Preserving Chastity," *Ch'üan chieh*). And although there are other major actions in the play for which the explicit justification is similar to that used above to excuse unchastity under stress—for example, Ts'ao-shih's forwardness in leaving a love message for K'o-ch'eng, K'o-ch'eng's decision to attend to trade rather than scholarship, and Tung-shan's decision to choose an unlearned husband for his daughter—the real relevance to the play of the story's lead-in is of a deeper sort. The events of both play and story take place in conditions of extraordinary insecurity caused by war. But that insecurity is merely an intensification of an insecurity that is inherent in the human condition, that pertains even in times of the utmost order and safety. The extreme instance brings out a quality inherent in ordinary circumstances. The response to the extreme instance in the story's lead-in is an awareness of life as a process of living in two mutually contradictory worlds—a world of practical concerns and external necessities and a world of spiritual ideals and gratuitous choices—and that is precisely the kind of awareness that emerges from the events of the play.

The dualistic atmosphere is established at the outset with the presentation of K'o-ch'eng's recurrent dream in act 2 and is maintained through the otherworldly language with which the characters at times refer to their experiences. As is the case with everything that pertains to the otherworld, the dream is vague, suggestive, unmotivated, hard to track down. K'o-ch'eng's only reasons for trusting the truth of the dream are based upon its recurrent nature and its total independence from his waking experience. He cannot remember having been in any house that resembles the one he dreams about.[62] The characters of the play are portrayed as living in a "strange region," and the odd behavior of the principal characters is occasioned by the "loyalty of their hearts" to a different region.

The characters' loyalty to the impulses that belong to the other mode of existence always appears impractical or even fanatical; it appears to involve an obstinate blindness to the plain facts of the sensually evident world. While the characters do not understand the causes of their presence in this world, they tend to assume the existence of an ultimately comprehensible reason for their earthly suf-

ferings. K'o-ch'eng's opening aria is given over to metaphysical specula-
tion on the accidents of his existence.

> Dwarfish pedants are stuffed to bursting,
> While clever Tung-fang, sighing for want of food,
> Yearns for rice grains as if for pearls.
> This long poverty, I know, arises from design;
> Heaven wants to manifest its full neglect.
> Only when it has wiped the old me out and changed it for a new
>   one
> Will heaven permit me to effect my grand designs.
> Look at scholars; they rely entirely on calligraphy and poetry
> To transform their persons into incense-breathing lions.[63]

K'o-ch'eng's anticipation of design is of course borne out by his
subsequent experiences. The heavens mete out suffering so that true
joy may be known. As the reassembled characters put it in act 31,

> Only now do we know destiny is not a shallow thing;
> If we had never suffered separation in our lives,
> We would have thought that human bonds were uncommonly
>   vulgar,
> That human bonds were uncommonly vulgar.[64]

It is just at this point that the final resolution of dream and reality
begins to occur, as Hsiao-lou and his wife invite the young couple to
ascend the stairs to the little upper-story room where they had their
own child. The little room is described in terms that impart to it an
otherworldly freshness and lightness. K'o-ch'eng and Ts'ao-shih sing
that "climbing to an upper story is better than climbing to a region of
immortals." As the following act opens they begin their climb. Singing, they describe their sensations as they rise:

> Holding our robes and climbing the stairs,
> We rise to a spacious view.
> Our bodies are as light as floating feathers
> And dust doesn't fly in clouds.
> Extraordinary figures are accustomed
> To walking in the surfaces of painted screens.[65]

Having arrived in the room itself, they observe that it is a fine little upper-story bedroom; high, but not vertiginously high; gayly painted, but not vulgar. The table is clean and the window bright. It is free of dust and has plenty of light for reading and embroidery. Suddenly, K'o-ch'eng's feeling of refreshing novelty changes to one of total familiarity. Not only the room, but the roads extending all around it, appear to match some memory. Yet he knows that he has never been to Yün-yang. "Surely," he muses in song, "I could not have ridden here on the wind, coming down from heaven, and then confined myself to roaming about this room without ever going elsewhere?"[66] Then he realizes that the room he is in is the little room of his recurrent dream, and is at once convinced that he is in the midst of another dream episode. His faith in the reality of his surroundings is only gradually restored as the true explanation for his seizure of déjà vu emerges. The little room is actually the place where he lived as an infant and small child.

Unlike *The Paired Soles*, *The Amazing Reunion* is not a play in which the supernatural is represented in such an unequivocal form as a spirit who changes the course of human events. Everything that happens in *The Amazing Reunion* is complete on the natural level. The natural events of the play nevertheless have a recurrent tendency to image forth a deeper or wider conception of reality involving the supernatural. That the play has this tendency does not mean that it is (even in a loose sense) an allegory. The relationship of the events to their implied parallels remains intermittent and flexible. One can say neither that the events are an illustration of heaven and hell, nor that heaven and hell are an illustration of the events. Either condition might pertain. Li Yü does not commit himself on that score any more than the writer of *Chuang-tzu* commits the philosopher to a human, or a lepidopteran, existence.

IV. Life as Error:
The Kite's Mistake

Worthwhile things have always derived from error;
If Liu and Juan had not gone astray, how could they have
    entered on the road to T'ien-t'ai peak?
Don't start walking unless you are prepared to learn what
    truth is;
You will find that the securest situations are those that
    lead to headlong spills.
Marriage especially cannot be grasped securely;
If you try to gain a beauty, you will end up with a hard-
    faced woman.
The warp and woof of life is all controlled by immutable
    fate;
It is useless for us bemazed mortals to seek to grasp the
    whole.
        Li Yü, prologue to *The Kite's Mistake* (c. 1670)

The error of our eye directs our mind:
What error leads must err.
        Shakespeare, *Troilus and Cressida*, V, 2 (c. 1602)

There is no such source of error as the pursuit of absolute
    truth.
        Samuel Butler, "Truth and Convenience," *Notebooks*
        (1912)

If you shut your door to all errors, truth will be shut out.
        Rabindranath Tagore, *Stray Birds* (1916)

> If a man wishes to be sure of the road he travels on, he
> must close his eyes and walk in the dark.
>   St. John of the Cross (c. 1580)

The Kite's Mistake is the most perfect of Li Yü's plays. The idea upon which the play is built—the cross-matching of an ideal, and a grotesque, couple, occasioned by the vagaries of wind-blown messages —is a simple one that despite its simplicity engenders a long series of effortlessly unfolding variations, all of which are fraught with novelty and humor. It is an idea that perfectly matches the structure of *ch'uan-ch'i* romantic comedy.

In earlier chapters we have noticed the ingenuity with which Li Yü makes any given segment of a story embody some aspect of his theme, or occupy some place in a developing pattern of ideological oppositions. *The Kite's Mistake* exists at a still higher level of craftsmanship; in it, content is so perfectly suited to form that we are scarcely aware of the dichotomy. Each event is already so much a part of the theme that we are not in the least surprised when it turns out to fit into the design. In this play, and in this play alone, Li Yü transcends ingenuity. The unity that is achieved against greater or lesser odds in other plays appears effortless in this one. Only in this play is there nothing that appears to have been worked into shape; the idea was (or appears to have been; we can have no idea how the play was actually put together) whole and perfect at birth.[1]

At the same time, *The Kite's Mistake* is the most detached of Li Yü's plays, the least committed to a moral position or to a philosophical point of view. It holds the whole tradition of *ch'uan-ch'i* romantic drama within its balance, distanced and miniaturized by comedy. Reading *The Kite's Mistake* is like looking at many earlier *ch'uan-ch'i* plays at once through the wrong end of a telescope.

In Li Yü's other plays, his commitment to a position or an idea often reaches an intensity that threatens the repose of the dramatic structure. Thus in *The Paired Soles*, the alternation of scenes concerning the moneylender Ch'ien Wan-Kuan and those concerning the noble recluse Mu-jung Chieh, conducts the reader through extremes of angry humor and ecstatic lyricism. The anger and the lyricism are both in earnest; both, we sense, could get out of control. We can feel these emotions straining against the narrative channels in which they are contained.

In *The Kite's Mistake*, on the other hand, the prevailing emotional climate is light and buoyant throughout. The villains are more than usually harmless and ludicrous. The good people are not heroes or geniuses, but people of conventional views and ordinary abilities who share in the clowns' and villains' tendency to error. In this play, Li Yü enjoins nothing upon the reader, unless it be something like the following: "Calm down, stop agonizing; nothing is as bad or as good as you imagine it to be." The premises of this play allow Li Yü to indulge his fascination with patterns and his endless gift for comic fantasy free from the distorting clogs of passion or thwarted idealism. There could be no more apt symbol for the play than the kite that is its central image: a light, colorful, wind-borne thing of wood and paper that floats above the world. "In casting forth a kite," says Li Yü in the prologue, "we cast forth a brand-new wondrous tale."

The thematic content of the play arises from a series of confrontations between the "beautiful" and the "ugly" that serve both to amuse and to enable the reader to derive gradually an enriched sense of the significance of these opposed concepts. Their application is not limited to matters of physical appearance; if it were, and if critical treatment were accorded only to the "ugly" characters, the play would be something other than a true comedy, as it is scarcely possible to regard a passive condition like a lack of good looks as a vice or folly.[2] In *The Kite's Mistake*, any aspect of personality and behavior that deviates from the ideal or the proper belongs to the category of the ugly (*ch'ou*) and it is from these deviant aspects of personality and behavior, rather than from their corresponding physical representations, that the play's ludicrous situations principally derive. One consequence of the inclusiveness of this concept is that the treatment of vice and folly in *The Kite's Mistake* is more global than in western comedies, which deal with isolated defects of behavior and whose titles, such as *Dyskolos* ("The Grouch," Menander) or *L'Avare* (Molière), often reflect their particularity of focus. We have no comedy entitled "The People Who Don't Act the Way They Should" and, as the imaginary title suggests, we lack a convenient global designation, like the word *ch'ou*, for comic misbehavior.[3]

The "ugly" characters, Ch'i Yu-hsien and Chan Ai-chüan, exhibit an extremely wide range of comic faults endemic to human nature. Being of dim intelligence, they are prone to ludicrous errors of judgement and to absurdly automatic behavior. Their perceptions are limited to the grossly material. Neither of the two has any use for poetry or learning. Lust and greed are their dominant springs of behavior. They are ordinarily petty, irritable, and intolerant in their relations with servants and family members.

Chan Ai-chüan is the comic star of the play; it is she who plays the key role in acts 13 and 16, which parody the two essential situations of serious romantic drama in China—the meeting scene and the dream scene. Her vulgarity is so unfailingly outrageous that the reader is apt to greet each of her new appearances with anticipatory delight. In her clandestine interview with the male protagonist Han Shih-hsün, she confuses conventional terms of reference used in polite discourse with hilarious effect. When asked "Have you bestowed a reply upon my second clumsy poem?" she responds, "I have already bestowed a reply upon your clumsy poem," and when the astonished Han Shih-hsün rejoins, "May I ask you to recite your refined composition?" she replies, "I've forgotten my refined composition for the time being."[4] Later, in the dream act, the language she uses in accusing Han of rape before a magistrate rivals that of Fanny Squeers (*Nicholas Nickleby*) in comic ungainliness: "(sings) He tore my drawers open! He tore my drawers open! I was gravely wounded and couldn't bear the pain, so I yelled like thunder."[5]

The behavior of the ugly characters is a rich source of comic delight, but it is also important to the conceptual structure of the play. They represent everything that the Confucian tradition of self-cultivation attempts to deny, transcend, or transform, and their erroneousness is meant to be valuable and cherishable as well as amusing. In conventional romantic comedy, such roles are usually confined to peripheral characters drawn from the lower classes, such as soldiers, maids, or tradesmen, and their comic scenes are not integrally related to the plot. Thus, while they may parody the orthodox system, they never significantly interfere with it. In *The Kite's Mistake*, however, the buffoons not only belong to families of the gentry, but occupy slightly higher social positions than the ideal characters with whom they are paired;[6] the action of the play, moreover, would totally cease to exist without their participation. The result of their elevation to a position of dramatic parity with the serious characters is a continuous contest of values. The example of the refined characters throws into relief whatever is stupid or crass in the behavior of their doubles; but the spontaneousness of the ugly characters is equally efficacious in revealing whatever is strained, artificial, or inflated in the behavior of the refined characters. The reader's response to the first process is a mental guffaw or snicker; his response to the second is a perception of balloons being punctured or of facades crumbling away to realities.

It is the confrontation with the strident vulgarity of Chan Ai-chüan that most strikingly deflates the seriousness of Han Shih-hsün's romanticism. The great pains he takes in the composition of a poem hinting at marriage are rendered ludicrous by her illiteracy, and his noble resolution to submit to prosecution as a thief if caught lurking before her house (rather than damage her good name through confessing to an assignation) is similarly mocked by her rampant lust.[7] One has the feeling that the unfortunate Han has wandered by accident into the wrong play and is being detained there through the malevolent humor of his creator.

It is not simply Han's fortuitous involvement with Chan Ai-chüan that causes his correctness to become a source of amusement. The ugly characters have a great ally. In the dialectic of the play, they stand for *tzu-jan* or naturalness, a blind wisdom of being arising from all that is unaltered by human efforts at improvement; and, appropriately, heaven itself takes part in their unconscious mockery of cultivation. Alone in his examinee's lodgings in Peking, Han-Shih-hsün bewails the fact that he has never beheld a beautiful woman and sings that he would consider his yearning satisfied for the time being if God would only grant him the vision of a beautiful woman in a dream.[8] The heavens' answer to his prayer is the dream of persecution by the revolting Ai-chüan.

The bias of heaven is in fact fundamental to the play, and its plainest representative is the kite that makes a mockery of Han's romantic aspirations and ethical principles by wandering into the wrong half of a divided courtyard. Ideals and ethics are powerless to prevent Han from stumbling into each of the frivolous, graceless, or immoral actions of his ugly double and his would-be bride. His romantic yearning impels him, in spite of damage to his self-respect, to indulge in Ch'i Yu-hsien's idiotic sport of kite flying.[9] Like Chan Ai-chüan, he allows a motive of selfish caution to induce him to assume another person's identity in sending a love message.[10] When he can no longer escape what he imagines to be a bad marriage, he resigns himself to the same cynical consolation, that of taking concubines, with which Ch'i Yu-hsien is placated after discovering Chan

Ai-chüan's former adventure with Han.[11] The meeting into which he is led by the kite, moreover, exposes him to the same charge of immoral conduct as does Ch'i Yu-hsien's attack upon the "ideal" heroine Chan Shu-chüan.[12] The natural world's opposition to Han's principles eventually impinges even upon his consciousness; at the close of act 28, it occurs to him that heaven is punishing him for his perfectionistic standards of beauty by pairing him with an ugly woman.[13] This realization is the prelude to the act of ritual humility (the forced marriage of act 29 and its consequences) through which he is absolved of his comic faults and united with his hoped-for ideal mate.

The role of Han Shih-hsün is a rare phenomenon in comedy; he represents a union of the inflexible or obsessed character with the reasonable and self-aware hero (the two types to which Northrop Frye applies the Aristotelian terms *alazon* and *eiron* respectively), the contest between whom ordinarily forms the basis of a comic action.[14] The most well-known western example of a comic hero who takes on the function of the crusty older generation in obstinately opposing his own marriage to the heroine is probably Bertram in *All's Well that Ends Well*, but Bertram is so extremely inflexible that his role retains nothing but the structural attributes of the role of romantic hero; he is a "transplanted *alazon*." The character of Han Shih-hsün, however, is evenly balanced between the self-aware and the obsessed. His plain superiority in judgement, learning, and refinement to Ch'i Yu-hsien and Chan Ai-chüan prevents us from viewing him simply as an object of ridicule; and the misunderstanding to which he falls prey is one that could plausibly mislead a reasonable person. Our perception of him as an obsessed character arises in part from the responses he provokes from the ugly characters, who complain frequently and at length of his character as a pedant and a spoilsport. He is also placed in perspective through such touches as his terror of noises in the dark while lurking at the Chan family's gate.[15] His role as a young military genius, moreover, is not reverentially treated; the grand stratagem through which he routs the rebellious barbarians in Szechwan consists of using artificial tigers to scare away the enemy's elephants, an idea gleaned from his classical studies.[16] The comic rigidity of his character is fully revealed in act 28, in which he resists every attempt of his guardian to persuade him to marry the Chan family's second daughter with a pedantic reiteration of his conviction that "what the eye sees is true; what the ear hears is false." The audience is of course aware here that Han's situation perfectly illustrates a limitation of his maxim: that the truth of what the eye sees is contingent upon the observer's powers of interpretation. As it happens, Han's reliance on solid evidence fails to further even his immediate argumentative aims, since propriety will not allow him to intimate to his guardian that he has any visual knowledge of the proposed bride. This gives him such an appearance of obstinacy that the exasperated Ch'i Pu-ch'en at length exclaims, "Surely you are not going to claim that what I hear is false, while what you hear is true . . . maybe the ears of a top graduate [*chuang-yüan*] are a little different from other people's ears!"[17]

The following act finds him still so immured in his erroneous inter-pretation of events that he fails to follow his own precept of testing truth through observation. The beauty Chan Shu-chüan sits before him in the bridal chamber, modestly concealing her face behind a fan. Han notes her reserved and proper demeanor, but construes the evidence according to his *idée fixe*; imagining that the figure before him is the same creature he met a year ago, he attributes her reserve to shame over her earlier behavior. "It's a little too late," he sighs, "for her to start acting properly," and without looking at the face behind the fan, he retires alone to sleep.[18]

As with all inflexible characters of comedy, Han must expiate his transgressions before being readmitted to his normal status as a social person. He must submit gracefully to looking like a fool when the bride's identity is revealed to him; he must prostrate himself before Chan Shu-chüan before her displeasure is assuaged; and he must suf-fer a drastically abridged night of lovemaking—the cocks are crowing when he finally retires to the nuptial bed with his bride.[19] The severi-ty of his punishment is tempered by the nature of his faults, which are never such as would deprive him of the reader's sympathy. A character whose sole function is to exemplify an obsession or self-de-lusion is generally punished by the loss of the heroine; the self-aware hero, on the other hand, generally gains the heroine as a reward for his intelligence, tact, and perseverance. Han Shih-hsün figures in both capacities at once, and his ruined wedding night is the compro-mise worked out between the contradictory fates in store for him.

The chief themes of the play are echoed and reechoed in scenes of broad farce and exuberant fantasy. The celestial matchmaker who leads the kite astray has his earthly equivalent in the two scurrilously

quarrelsome matchmakers of the capital, Iron-foot Chang and
Swindle-heaven Li.[20] The high walls of the Chan family's house fade
metaphorically into the walls of the besieged city in Szechwan.[21] The
barbarians' retreat before the "gods" stationed along the wall by
General Chan is a metamorphosis of Han Shih-hsün's flight from the
"beauty" who frightens him on the other side of a domestic wall.[22]
The moment when the ultimate social honor, the rank of top
graduate or *chuang-yüan*, descends upon Han Shih-hsün coincides
with the moment in which, dreaming, he suffers the ultimate social
disgrace: a public beating.[23] As the commentator remarks in act 30,
"the marvelousness of the situations in this play cannot be expressed
in words; all one can do is slap the table and yell crazily."[24]

In the sung epilogue to the play, Li Yü does not, as he does in other
plays, claim to have written the play in order to uphold virtue and
rectify public mores, but instead emphasizes the comic character that
is in fact the play's great novelty. Then, with wonderful levity and ex-
uberance, he closes with a couplet that attributes to laughter itself the
power of salvation:

> Plays originally were things devised to banish sorrow;
> When your drinking funds are all spent, come on and sing a
> stanza.
> What's the use of spending cash to buy the sound of weeping?
> It will only change your happy mood to one of doleful sobs.
>
> Only I refrain from selling sadness when I measure out my
> verses;
> A single fellow not laughing—that fills me with concern.
> Only when all the world's folk have changed to laughing
> Buddhas,
> And my brush is bald from saving souls, will I consent to throw
> it down.[25]

The phrasing of the sixth line in the above octet echoes, with
ludicrous effect, a well-known passage from the Confucian *Analects*:
"The failure to cultivate virtue, the failure to perfect one's learning,
the failure to enact what one knows to be good, the failure to change
evil habits—that fills me with concern."[26] The Chinese are of course
unaccustomed to being instructed in tones of hallowed and ancient

authority to laugh away their cares, so the sudden intrusion of this Confucian echo enhances the shock value and the gaiety of the octet quoted above. I have never observed anyone to fail to smile in surprise and sympathetic amusement upon being shown it in the original.

Tradition dies hard, however. The preface to *The Kite's Mistake*, written by an anonymous later admirer of Li Yü, gives no clue whatsoever that the play to follow has anything to do with humor, let alone that it is a particularly high-spirited and preposterous comedy. Instead, it applies to the play what is probably the oldest cliché of Chinese literary criticism; it interprets *The Kite's Mistake* as an allegory of the author's frustrated political ambition. It must be read in full for its flavor to be appreciated:

> Ch'ü Yüan said, "The common run of men are jealous of my mothlike eyebrows and so spread slanderous rumors, saying that I am adept at scheming." Fear of slander, dread of censure; such was the motive that lay behind the composition of "Encountering Sorrow."[27] But the Three Clans and the Nine Manors [terms associated with Ch'ü Yüan] maintain their fragrant name to all posterity. An upright man cannot be mistaken for a wicked one, just as a beautiful woman cannot be mistaken for an ugly one. This has been true since ancient times.
>
> The generous conduct of our author Li-hung [Li Yü] is a matter of history and his literary brilliance is as lofty as the heavens. His person was fragrant, his imagination rich and refined. He was virtually unique in his generation. He paid the penalty, however, for offending the vulgar prejudices of the age, and in consequence wandered with haggard countenance by the edge of the marsh [implied comparison to Ch'ü Yüan]. Alas, black and white are never distinguished in the world and the beautiful and the ugly are in danger of losing their outward aspects.
>
> I recollect that in the past, there have been two instances of great ugliness impersonating beauty and great beauty being confused with ugliness: the village lady who tried to cheat the splendor of Yüeh by frowning [reference to the story of Hsi Shih][28] and the court painter who concealed the beauty of a lady of the Han court [reference to the story of Wang Chao-chün][29] But

when I think of those jadelike features by the Wan-sha stream [story of Hsi Shih] casting their solitary reflection in the clear ripples, when I think of those corallike footsteps in the hall of chiming stairs, each falling in perfect measure, I realize that the imitator may frown and frown again, but the imitation remains an imitation.

Furthermore, though pink-cheeked beauties may have unhappy destinies, flawless jade cannot escape all notice. On everyday occasions, the sovereign may depend on paintings to search for blemishes [story of Wang Chao-chün] and cast me aside like some leftover thing, but one day I will say farewell to the throne in person and my radiance will move all who are present. Suddenly I will cast an alluring glance with my luminous eyes, and then for the first time the sovereign will truly perceive my face that resembles the spring wind. With what deep emotion will he then think of the long journey to the frontier that I must undertake within the day. With what bitter sorrow will he ponder his loss in the cold autumn palace!

A peerless beauty was dragged in the dust. In what age have people not pondered Green Mound [name of the tomb of Wang Chao-chün] at twilight? Her fate is still invoked in poems today. We may therefore know that those who use bright colors to disguise a swarthy skin cannot be confused with Wang Ch'iang [Wang Chao-chün], but on the contrary contribute to the undying fame of Wang Ch'iang. All those who are like Ch'iang then, may walk boldly and with self-confidence between heaven and earth. This is the allegory that Li-weng's [Li Yü's] play *The Kite's Mistake* is written to convey, though it may not have been the author's fully conscious intention to do so.

When we read this work, we come to realize that when ugliness impersonates beauty, its carving and painting is in vain; and that when beauty is confused with ugliness, it must reveal its true nature in the end. The same person who in the beginning excites terror at the warts of the witch from Wu-yen, and is regarded as a demon or a goblin, turns out in the end to be as lovely as Yang Yü-huan [Yang Kuei-fei] and Chao Fei-yen.[30] When people turn and look at a moth-browed beauty under a barbarous emperor and a barbarous sky, can they then believe in her beauty or not? Only slanderous rumors would be capable of injuring her.

Li-weng's literary genius bewitches and enraptures; I, who have no talent, can indeed be likened to an envious woman; but for now, I beg to be allowed to compete with others in showing my admiration for his work.

> written by Yü Lou of the Kou-wu society in
> his capacity as a relation to the family
> of a descendant of the playwright.[31]

This preface is so eloquent and persuasive, and is at the same time such a large-spirited tribute to the character and abilities of the playwright, that it seems a shame to disagree with its central contention that the heroine Chan Shu-chüan is an emblem of the *hsien jen pu te chih* or rejected sage. To insist upon exactitude in a text that was perhaps not intended to be exact seems an indelicacy. Probably, it was simply a generous attempt to "rescue" the play by attributing seriousness to it. Nevertheless, since this preface is printed in most editions of the play and therefore confronts most readers of it at the outset, it seems worthwhile to point out in some detail why its critical point of view cannot be taken seriously.

First of all, the atmosphere of plaintiveness and narcissistic yearning that accompanies the whole *hsien jen pu te chih* tradition from Ch'ü Yüan onwards is wholly absent from *The Kite's Mistake*. In this work, the usurpation of the beautiful by the ugly is an occasion of delight, of robust guffaws, rather than of pain. Second, if the author were projecting his personal frustrations onto the heroine, we would expect her to be the central figure in the drama, or that we should be made to feel some special sympathy for her predicament. At the very least, there would be some scenes in which, alone on the stage, she would give vent to Ch'ü Yüanesque feelings of rejection, loneliness, and indignation. But in fact her appearances are brief, intermittent and devoid of lyrical soliloquizing. She appears always in her relation to others—as a dutiful daughter helping to make peace among the quarreling members of her family—rather than as a suffering or yearning individual. The character who occupies the foreground, and to whose feelings we are continuously exposed, is the young man who makes the wrong choice. In the allegorical scheme of the preface, he would correspond not to the rejected man of ability, but to the misinformed emperor who chooses the wrong man. The play is about the experience of making wrong choices, not about the experience of being passed over as the consequence of a wrong choice.

The work of Li Yü's younger contemporary and friend Yu T'ung (1618-1704) forms an instructive comparison in this regard, for here we have an example of a playwright whose work is for the most part solidly based upon the tradition of the rejected man of ability, and it is easy to see that the emphases all fall in different places in his plays.[32]

It is true that Li Yü never held an official position, and that for a person of his literary and practical ability this would ordinarily imply some degree of disappointed ambition. But Li Yü was far from being an ordinary case. We have a poem of his, written on the occasion of his thirtieth birthday, that does indeed lament his failure to distinguish himself during the first half of his life.[33] But after the fall of the Ming dynasty, which occurred only a few years later, he appears to have put aside all thoughts of worldly advancement. Though only a junior licentiate or *hsiu-ts'ai*, he never again sought to improve his eligibility for office by taking a government examination; moreover, he adopted the sobriquet *hu-shang li-weng*, "leaf-hatted old fisherman of the lakes," a name that implies a settled determination not to participate in public affairs.[34] As we have seen in chapter 2, he wrote a play that upholds anonymity and retirement as the ideal mode of human existence, and in chapter 5 we will see him in a different play cheerfully pouring scorn on the whole concept of the tragedy of rejection. His writings leave one with the impression that he paid little attention to current political developments, devoting himself instead to his mercantile, literary, and esthetic pursuits. Unlike a number of other *ch'uan-ch'i* playwrights of the early Ch'ing, Li Yü never wrote a play the purpose of which was to mourn the fall of the preceding Ming dynasty, even though that event had an immediate, and initially very unfortunate, effect on his life.[35]

This is not to say that Li Yü had no interest in politics or governments, but his interest was general and theoretical. He wrote a book entitled *Shih-lun*, devoted to weighing the achievements of historical figures and revising traditional estimates of their character and accomplishments. He also compiled a much-read anthology of essays on government administration, the *Tzu-chih hsin shu*. A preface to one of Li Yü's plays informs us that an acquaintance of Li Yü's (the preface writer) remarked to him after reading the anthology that it was a great pity he could not make use of his rare insights by serving as an official. To this Li Yü replied, "The fact that I can discuss government affairs does not necessarily mean that I would be capable of putting my ideas into practice."[36] This seems more like the comment of a person satisfied with the role of spectator than that of a person rankling beneath the insult of obscurity. More conclusive than these biographical considerations, however, is simply the pervasive buoyancy and gaiety of Li Yü's writing and of *The Kite's Mistake* in particular. This alone would make the attempt to cast him as a latter-day Ch'ü Yüan appear farfetched, even if we knew nothing whatever concerning his life.

The true concern of *The Kite's Mistake* does not lie in the realm of frustrated ambition, but in an area much closer to the plain significance of *ch'uan-ch'i* drama: the area of romantic love. Love, passionate and idealized, was at once the scandal and the principal attraction of Chinese romantic comedy. By Li Yü's time, two extremely popular and influential plays wholly devoted to this theme, *The Romance of the Western Chamber* and *The Peony Pavilion*, had already deeply influenced the climate of Chinese culture. Typical of this influence is the well-known scene in *Dream of the Red Chamber* in which Pao-yü and Black Jade are shown eagerly reading *The Romance of the Western Chamber* on the sly, as a forbidden delight.[37]

Though not insensible to the allure of this romantic tradition, Li Yü was at the same time unwilling to abandon himself to it. There was too much in it that provoked his critical sense and his sense of the ludicrous. True, his leading men and leading ladies fall in love as do those of other playwrights, but they typically temper their passion with prudential and moral consideration; moreover, they do not devote more than a portion of their minds to their romantic affairs. They resemble real people in that their pursuit of romantic happiness is a strictly leisure-time activity; it must take second place to matters affecting the stability of their rice bowls.

Another of Li Yü's plays, *The Careful Couple (Shen luan chiao)*, directly criticizes the romantic tradition and makes an intellectually ambitious attempt to show how the tradition might be brought into line with reality and human nature. Those of its scenes that illustrate the novel ideas Li Yü wished to promulgate have a diamondlike intensity of focus; other portions of the play appear to have been composed at a much lower level of engagement. The thinking embedded in this play, however, deserves a moment of our consideration at this point, for here we can see in explicit form the point of view that underlies the laughter of *The Kite's Mistake*.

In *The Careful Couple*, Li Yü develops his critique of romance by building up portraits of two contrasting relationships between a married man and a courtesan. The members of the first pair are influenced by the romantic clichés of plays and novels, and are ready to believe in the possibility of an enduring relationship almost as soon as they meet. The members of the second pair are initially slow and cautious, make no promises that might be difficult to fulfill later, and subordinate their feelings to long-range family and career concerns. The point of the comparison is that the second couple, who by conventional romantic standards appear outrageously cold and pragmatic, are in fact more truly romantic than the first. Their relationship survives and prospers, whereas that of the first is at the mercy of every accidental circumstance.

One exposition of the thesis grows from a conversation between the two courtesans, Teng Hui-chüan and Wang Yu-ch'iang. Like most young women in their situation, they both hope to meet a man who will be sufficiently attracted to them to buy them from their professional mistresses and take them into his family. Wang Yu-ch'iang complains that none of the men who come visiting every day are of the type she would hope to gain as a husband. Teng Hui-chüan accuses her of having unrealistic expectations; she herself would be willing to marry anyone, so long as he was a literary person and was ardent and sincere in his attitude towards her. This provides an opening for Wang to give vent to her antiromantic point of view:

> Wang: It appears then that you care only about the warmth of his affection and are unconcerned whether that affection will lead to any conclusions later on.
>
> Teng: Naturally. Conclusions and results all belong to the future. How can they be forseen in advance?
>
> Wang: That's not so. The future behavior of men is very easy to make out. Those who are generous and trustworthy will never be lacking in feeling. Those who are frivolous and fickle will inevitably break their promises. The generous and trustworthy are cold in the beginning and become gradually more ardent. Since their warmth comes last, their affection naturally leads to a conclusion. The love of the frivolous and fickle is deep at first and becomes gradually shallow. Since

their shallowness comes last, their affection inevitably leads to nothing. Therefore, when we courtesans choose a mate, we must be sure to study his behavior with a pair of cold, discerning eyes. If he is merely another one of those men who wants to swear by the sun and the moon to eternal constancy at the first lingering glance, you may be sure that he is the sort of young man who can make beginnings but not conclusions, that he is powerless to remember feelings or keep promises. If you agree to become his wife, you will simply guarantee an unhappy old age for yourself. If you perchance do not believe my words, you can wait and see for yourself whether they turn out to be true or not.[38]

Though *The Careful Couple* shares with *The Kite's Mistake* an antagonism toward romance as conventionally conceived, it has none of the latter play's sense of fun. Li Yü never wrote a play more serious in tone and content. His aim in writing *The Careful Couple*, he tells us in the verse epilogue, was to reconcile two areas of the mind that ordinarily function in isolation and at cross-purposes to each other:

> I have read all the sorts of books that people write, and they all belong to one of two kinds.
> What is called "romance" and what is called "morality" eternally go separate ways.
> If a person is "romantic," he probably fails to be a true gentleman,
> But if person is "moralistic," how can he avoid being an inflexible pedant?
> We must combine these traits if we wish to avoid their mutual absence,
> Work them into a linked and woven chain, like a necklace inlaid with pearls.
> If, upon examination, this play proves to have no other merit than this,
> It still should win a word of praise from audiences at the capital.[39]

The criticism of romance implied in *The Careful Couple* is that it is inherently shallow and cruel; if you want happiness and humanity, romance cannot compete for a moment with the cold logic of cost accounting. *The Kite's Mistake* mounts its attack upon romance from a different direction. It implies that the complex of attitudes subsumed under the word romance is a fragile thing dependent for its allure upon an elaborate set of special conditions. Deprive romance of those conditions and it at once becomes ridiculous. The serious and the comic play in their disparate ways both emphasize the unreality of the romantic emotion, its inferiority to prosaic, light-of-day modes of perception.

The Careful Couple never caught the imagination of its audience as did *The Kite's Mistake*; the former is in the main known only to specialists in Li Yü, whereas the latter remains one of the principal plays in the *ch'uan-ch'i* repertory and is still sometimes performed in a drastically simplified Peking opera version.[40] It is not hard to imagine reasons for this difference in reception. *The Careful Couple* cannot be appreciated unless the reader attends to its train of thought and grasps the significance of the unaccustomed distinctions that it makes between characters. Its characters are puzzling types who cannot readily be identified with any of the various sets of role characteristics that one expects to encounter in a Chinese play. *The Kite's Mistake*, on the other hand, achieves its novel effects through fresh juxtapositions of entirely conventional role-types; moreover, its thesis lies with such perfect comfort in the invisible core of the story that the reader need not attend to it at all. He can simply allow himself to be swept along by the play's unflagging comic ebullience.

Like *The Careful Couple*, *The Kite's Mistake* presents us with a contrast between two types of romance exemplified by two different couples. Unlike *The Careful Couple*, it contains no implication that either type of romance is philosophically preferable to the other; they are merely seen as different, so different that each variety appears absurd from the viewpoint of the other. The ugly characters Ch'i Yu-hsien and Chan Ai-chüan represent natural or vulgar romance, the sort of sexual behavior to which untutored instinct compels us. The ideal characters Han Shih-hsün and Chan Shu-chüan stand for "refined romance," romance as a purely spiritual and intellectual emotion. Refined romance of course enjoys all the advantages of cultural prestige, but as we shall shortly see, the quality of naturalness occupies so high a place in Li Yü's scale of values that it leads him to view with unorthodox respect any action, however vulgar or silly, that possesses this precious attribute. The dialectic of vulgarity versus refinement is therefore never resolved in favor of a single side.

Let us see how this dialectic is presented in act 2, where the action begins. The way in which the protagonist Han Shih-hsün presents himself there is typical of self-introductions by leading men in *ch'uan-ch'i* drama; if we are sensitive to shades of emphasis, however, we will notice that the towering self-confidence and lofty idealism typical of his role are portrayed here with the greatest possible degree of energy. This is a standard stop to pull, but it is pulled as far as it will go. Han is made to build up his hopes and pretensions to the fullest possible extent so that the ridiculousness of his subsequent adventures can appear in the greatest possible relief. Even more than the usual protagonist of *ch'uan-ch'i* drama, he sees himself as a man of destiny. His every act must be fraught with great and hidden meanings:

> (sings) The cosmos is desolate;
> Upon what can I fix my yearning ambition?
> I know myself to be an ardent and loyal lover,
> But have not as yet been granted the chance to meet with
>   the ideal beauty of my generation.
> I know that the creator surely has a reason for it.[41]

In an ordinary *ch'uan-ch'i* play, these lines would be dull and fatuous; in the peculiar atmosphere of *The Kite's Mistake*, they are electric with potential laughter. It is often unnecessary for the satirist to make any internal change in his material; all he has to do to make it funny is to place a frame around it.

In the entrance poem that follows his introductory aria, Shih-hsün goes on to invoke the names of some of the greatest poets and beauties of all antiquity. His aspirations could not be expressed in loftier terms:

> In crow-black cap, quail-feather shirt, and calf's nose pants,
> I still consider myself the most dashing young man alive.
> After writing the prose poem on the three capitals,
>   Tso's fame grew great;
> Standing on the summit of achievement, his look inspired awe.
> If her hand be not like T'ai-chen's, let her not hold my inkslab;

If her eyebrows be not like Princess Kuo's, how dare I receive
her favor?
Exquisite ladies exist in books indeed,
But when Liang Hung grew old, he didn't marry.[42]

There is no trace of the mundane in these sentiments, no question of
gratifying a mere physical need. The natural man has been entirely
consumed in the intensity of the ideal.

Shih-hsün's self-introduction is followed by a formal ceremony
such as frequently occurs at the openings of ch'uan-ch'i plays, in
which the members of the household express their relationships to
each other in terms of ritual. The occasion is the paying of filial
respects on the first day of the lunar new year, a time when one's
dress and gestures must be punctiliously exact and when it is particularly forbidden to utter, even inadvertently, an inauspicious or
indecorous phrase. Shih-hsün's and his foster father's exchanges are
all marked by profound courtesy and extreme elevation of sentiment.
All the niceties of polite behavior are on display. It is not a common
family. Even its amusements are free of any mundane taint. Ch'i Pu-
ch'en sings upon entering that "my greatest joy is that my house is
pure as unsullied water; we play a few idle games of chess here at
Tung-shan"[43] [an allusion to the place of retirement of Hsieh An, a
famous statesman of the Chin dynasty].

Ch'i Yu-hsien, the grotesque anti-hero whose actions are to
shadow and parody those of Han Shih-hsün in the scenes to come, is
silent throughout most of the New Year's ritual. He is held in abey-
ance by the formality and solemnity of the occasion. The one speech
he does make is obedient to the part he must play in the family
tableau and expresses nothing of his real nature. It does, however,
establish in our minds that Yu-hsien and Shih-hsün are to be regarded as an indissolubly bonded pair:

Yu-hsien: My old friend and brother, from ancient times it has
been said that all are brothers within the four seas. How
much more then are we brothers, we whose families have
been close for two generations? (sings) Why speak of blood
brothers having different surnames? We are just as much
brothers for all that.[44]

Shih-hsün stands for everything that is bright, public, praiseworthy and external in the society, everything that is put on prominent display; he is his culture's finest product. Yu-hsien stands for the dark, shameful, and private, for that which must be hidden and censured; he is the ludicrous failure whose nature is incapable of retaining any of the shapes impressed upon it by moral injunction and education.

When the lord of the house leaves to pay a New Year's call on a friend, allowing Ch'i Yu-hsien to lay aside his restraint, the "unsullied" water of his household changes at once to very turbid water indeed. The manner in which Yu-hsien's real character emerges and fills the stage at this moment, like an evil genie from a bottle, is much like the later scene in which he will emerge from a shadowed corner next to the privy pot in order to force his attentions upon his sister-in-law.[45] We learn at once what was actually on his mind throughout the New Year's ritual:

> My old friend and brother, we stay shut up in the library all day long. I haven't seen a woman for a whole year. I'm not sleeping well these days and I can't avoid having lustful thoughts. Now that we are released from our studies in the library for the vacations, it is a perfect opportunity to try and have some fun. Why don't we both take a stroll over to the pleasure houses?[46]

Almost immediately, and as if in sympathetic response to the mood created by Yu-hsien, a group of local prostitutes come to pay their New Year's respects to the young men of the house. Yu-hsien rapturously welcomes them, quoting (in quite a startling context) the great sentence of Confucius on the power of the human will to transform the world: "If ye will but desire the virtue of humanity, it will appear forthwith." *(wo yü jen, ssu jen chih i).*[47]

The vulgarity of the scene that follows holds the virtuous Shih-hsün in check, just as the base Yu-hsien was held in check by the elevation and formality of the New Year's ritual. He stands far off and faces away from the rouged and powdered guests as they note that he has "a fine bearing" and a "fresh romantic face," while his companion Yu-hsien has "furs and horses" that are "light and sleek."[48] Yu-hsien tries to detain the prostitutes, tugging at their clothing and making crude gestures, but they must finish making the rounds of the wealthy houses in the neighborhood.

When they have left he at once takes Shih-hsün to task for being so inhospitable. The fact that he is base does not mean that he is without values. He has his own standards of decorum and is deeply offended when others do not conform to them:

> Yu-hsien: My old friend and brother, why are you so stiff and moralistic? When lady guests arrive, you have to laugh and chat with them if you want to look like a dashing, romantic fellow. Why did you just stand there facing the other way without moving your hands or opening your mouth? You looked as if you were bashful and afraid. You are really terribly innocent and naive.
>
> Shih-hsün: Usually I am not altogether naive; it is just that when I saw all those ugly women, I simply couldn't imitate your burst of sophistication.[49]

Later, in act 13, the female clown Chan Ai-chüan will have the same perception of Han's character. She is complaining of his failure to behave like a lover during a midnight rendezvous from which he has just run away:

> He looks like a dashing character on the surface, but beneath it he's just a simpleton. He talked about poetry for a couple of hours and lectured about neo-Confucian ethics for a couple of hours, but he not only didn't know how to do anything romantic—he never said even a single thing having to do with love.[50]

Ch'i Yu-hsien and Chan Ai-chüan are both clowns; their actions are meant to be clumsy, and their speeches ludicrous; but like clowns in the courts of old kings and emperors, they may on occasion have a special licence to speak the truth. Their disappointment in Han Shih-hsün is rather like what a popular musician might be expected to feel toward a university-trained composition major who, though able to put together an ultra-sophisticated twelve-tone composition violating none of the standards of avant-garde taste, is not only unable to strum a simple waltz melody on the keyboard, but shivers in distaste or embarrassment upon contact with the profane music.

For all their awkwardness, there is a spectrum of experience in which the clowns are comfortable and assured; and in which the man of refined taste is stiff and helpless. In the process of educating himself, Han has lost the most precious of all assets: his naturalness.

Li Yü was unusually alive to this type of contrast, for it was his great distinction to be equally at home in learned and popular styles. He was one of those rare figures who, having absorbed all the learning that a traditional, classical education could bestow upon him, then went on to write with complete naturalness and success in an easy, popular style. It is in fact this popular style that has constituted the chief problem for critics of Li Yü's work. They as often as not complain of the rusticity and vulgarity of his diction.[51] But this rusticity of language in Li Yü's work is not an expedient of poverty but a deliberate literary choice. In his *Random Lodge for My Idle Feelings* he says that drama is an art form designed for the ear; therefore it should contain no expressions that are unintelligible without a script. Moreover, drama is an entertainment designed to be watched by all classes of people; therefore it should contain no allusions that would be unintelligible to the unlearned.[52] Li Yü would doubtless have agreed with the remark of C. S. Lewis that any blockhead can write in the learned style; the true test of literary ability is to translate one's thoughts into a living vernacular.[53]

In the preface to his collected works, *One Writer's Utterances (I Chia Yen)*, Li Yü provides us with something like an artistic credo. In it, he takes pains to explain why he invariably chooses to write in a direct and simple manner. It is typical of his rhetorical adroitness that he not only manages to avoid all taint of self-praise, but indulges in some highly amusing self-ridicule, in the course of developing his doctrine of spontaneity. He begins by explaining his choice of title for the collection:

What is *One Writer's Utterances*? It is all the poems, prose pieces, and random jottings that I have produced during the course of my life. Nowadays, when literary men gather their writings into a book, they all use the word *collection* [chi] in the title. Why is it that I am the only one who replces this term with a different one? It is because none of my poems, prose pieces, or jottings have ever conformed to any literary rules; nor have they ever come up to any standard of form or style. I have never borrowed any methods from the ancients; I have never sought to imitate any of my contemporaries; nor have I ever entertained any thought of posthumous transmission. All I am is a private individual who says what he wants to say and then stops. Like the

season-announcing insect or the dog who serves as a night
watchman, I cry out automatically whenever I bump into something; I have no thought whatsoever of imitating strange and
wonderful effects when I write. A writer who uses the method of
imitation must necessarily seek to become skilled in the elaboration of exotic effects, and the effort of his whole lifetime must be
directed toward striking an endless series of bewitching poses in
order to escape the censure of clumsiness. But personally, I am
afraid that by the time he has managed to do away with the
greater part of his clumsiness and to replace it with refinement,
all that is personal and distinctive in his writing will have been
lost.

When an insect is startled by a change of season, or when a
dog encounters something that startles it, what sort of occasion
is it that they can afford to select the tones with which they
sound their alarms? If they could take time to make such a selection, then surely they could just as usefully refrain from barking
or chirping at all.[54]

Lest the reader suspect him of taking any pride in his freedom from
affectation, Li Yü hastens to add that his prohibition of artifice is not
intended to be applied to all writers. It is a rule intended only for people of ordinary capacity and limited knowledge such as himself. Small
talents such as his are inevitably led into falsity when they try to
achieve distinction through imitation. A world-bestriding genius
may naturally imitate anything he likes with impunity. If a passage in
his writing happens to recall the manner of some older author, the
older author could just as well be said to be imitating him. The work
of such geniuses, unlike his own work, can scarcely be looked upon as
the work merely of one man.[55]

The allegiance to naturalness as a literary standard, insofar, at
least, as his own work is concerned, could scarcely be stated with
greater emphasis than this. Even the exception granted to writers of
genius is not really an exception. They are allowed to violate the prohibition against imitation only because the largeness of their gifts
allows them to do this without violating the higher prohibition
against affectedness. The principle of naturalness remains supreme.

This principle is one of the chief touchstones of Li Yü's thought;
and its application is not confined to literary matters alone, but is

seen as the condition to which all activities of life aspire. If we turn to Li Yü's work, we will scarcely find a page in which some trace of this ideal is not to be found. We have already encountered it in several forms in the course of this study. In *The Paired Soles*, the ideal took the form of purposeful anonymity, the release from falsity and the gain in substance that occurs whenever a person (or superhuman being) with an exalted role loses himself in the manners and identity of a humble role. In *The Amazing Reunion*, the ideal took the form of purposeful spontaneity, the willingness to abandon prudence and to entrust oneself to instinct.

In *The Kite's Mistake*, the ideal is not embodied in any single character or action, for all the characters are to some extent defective. This is in itself a great innovation in the *ch'uan-ch'i* tradition and is one of the things that make *The Kite's Mistake* a true comedy in the Meredithian sense. In most other *ch'uan-ch'i* plays, even for that matter in most of Li Yü's *ch'uan-ch'i* plays, the protagonist is an ideal figure, a hero of romance. In *The Kite's Mistake*, Li Yü hit upon the device of splitting the psyche of the two protagonists into opposite halves, embodying their instinctive faculties in the persons of clowns and their rational faculties in the persons of the original leading man and lady. Significantly neither the male nor the female protagonist is introduced in isolation. In both introductory acts they are shown in active involvement with their irrational doubles. In each case, it is not an individual but a quarreling duo which is introduced.

It might be argued that since the quality of naturalness resides in the clowns, their point of view must therefore, so far as this play is concerned, correspond with truth. Here, however, a distinction must be drawn. The naturalness that these clowns represent is not the same as the naturalness that stands as an ideal at the center of Li Yü's system of values. When an activity is brought to perfection it will end in a state of naturalness. But a person's first essay at an activity will often have a kind of naturalness as well, the kind referred to as "beginner's luck," or "the uncanny charm of the primitive." It is quickly destroyed by one's efforts at self-improvement.

Ch'i Yu-hsien and Chan Ai-chüan stand at the beginning, not the end, of human endeavor. Their integrity is that of the "barking dog and the chirping insect," not that of the godlike genius who can "imitate without imitating." Their instinctive being has never suffered the least intrusion of logic or compulsion, so their actions, how-

ever helpless and limited, retain a paradisaical freshness and wholeness. Their instinctive responses encompass enough of the truth to
provide a constant corrective to the striving, reasoning intellects of
Han Shih-hsün and Chan Shu-chüan. An ideal figure, however,
would be greater than either type; he would infuse the instinct of the
clowns with knowledge and transmute the knowledge of the protagonists to instinct.

Since neither type of character is complete, they unconsciously
adhere to each other, even though there is constant friction between
them and even though neither can see the other's point of view. It is
as if, on some level, they realize they will get into less trouble when
they do things in tandem than they will when on their own. Many of
their speeches bear casual witness to the closeness of their associa-
tion. Ch'i Yu-hsien may complain that Han Shih-hsün is "the
world's greatest duck egg" and that he always thinks of "the most inappropriate thing to do in every situation," but in almost the same
breath he also describes him as the person "who sleeps with me and
sits with me, who is half a friend and half a teacher to me."[56] The
words that Chan Ai-chüan sings in rage to her sister in act 3 inadvertently convey a profound sense of dependence:

> The grave and decorous countenance of yours has all the refine-
> ment of an exalted lady's face. Your reserve and moderation are
> well suited to the august utterance of an empress. As for me, I'll
> just have to be a farmer's or a pedlar's wife. I must rely entirely
> on your kind support if I am to become the favorite of a man of
> high position.[57]

Shu-chüan, calming her down, observes that they are "two sisters, as
close as an object and its shadow."[58]

Han Shih-hsün obviously keeps Ch'i Yu-hsien out of a good deal of
trouble by keeping him in the library chanting passages from the
classics. While he may not be learning anything, he is at least not losing money at the gaming tables or endangering his health in a bawdy
house. But there are also occasions when Ch'i Yu-hsien is able to correct the intellectual and imaginative extravagance of Han. When
Han turns his nose up at the courtesans who come calling on New
Year's Day, Ch'i peevishly demands to know what Han expects in a
woman anyway. Han replies that she must have both beauty and

charm: but even these qualities are only half of what he has in mind. The lady must have wit and delicacy of feeling as well, or he will not be interested. He goes on to say (and this is where his hubris comes in) that he will not consent to any marriage unless he first has an opportunity to test the talent and judge the appearance of the bride. He will gladly consent to a delay, but he absolutely refuses to entrust the selection of a bride to chance. Ch'i has nature, experience, and tradition on his side when he rejoins:

> What you say is utterly absurd! Sick horses raised by Yangchow dealers are the only things people are ever permitted to examine! Surely you can't expect it to be easy for people to be allowed to study the faces of ministers' daughters! (sings) I've surely never noticed that the lovely daughters of noble houses are willing to allow people to compare thinness and measure fatness! (speaks) And even if you get to look at their outward aspect, how can you learn anything of their inward abilities? Surely you don't suppose you can set them a topic and have them take a test? (sings) Even the imperial court wouldn't hold examinations for women; how many times have penniless scholars been observed examining moth eyebrows? (speaks) My old friend and brother, I must urge you to think it over and reconsider; you must realize that (sings) you can't wait for the floods of spring to make the river clear; I fear that by the time you find a beauty, your days will have sunk to the west. Don't be stubborn; as long as the family is a proper one, fly directly to it.[59]

The clowns are forever expressing enthusiasm for things that are practical and concrete and that make a direct appeal to the senses. When Ai-chüan learns that her sister has written an answering poem on a kite that fell into her side of the courtyard, she thinks it is a pity that she responded only with a poem instead of "something a person could eat or use." If a kite had fallen on her side, she would have given at least a jade clasp or a gold pin in return for the sender's affection.[60] When Ch'i Yu-hsien instructs his houseboy to go and paste a kite together, he enthuses about the interest and novelty of inventions in general:

> I think the great mechanics and inventors of the past are the

most entertaining people there are. Whenever the time for it arrives, they make a device that people can amuse themselves with. They're not like those moralistic old philosophers Wenwang, Chou-kung, Confucius, and Mencius, who made those sets of classics that weary people to death. (sings) Intelligent folk needn't yield an inch to that bunch from Lu; at any time, at any season, they put their skill to some new and untried use, not something dull and stale like those vapid essays rotten with allusions, flat as dried meat, straight as a hairclasp, with no sudden twists, no surprises, anywhere. In my opinion, nine parts in ten of all that stuff should be expunged.[61]

The modern reader is aware of delicious ironies here, ironies that would never have presented themselves to the play's first readers, or even, for that matter, to Li Yü himself. This is one instance in which the passage of a few centuries has contributed greatly to the richness of the original joke. Here we have a forthright expression of preference for the physical experimenter as opposed to the abstract philosopher, a paean of praise directed to that realm of concrete manipulation now regarded as being proto-scientific as opposed to the realm of moral philosophy, now usually regarded as being merely unscientific or ascientific. But who is the person who gives vent to this exciting, revolutionary, and prophetic opinion? A champion in the world of scholarship? A reclusive genius steeped in unorthodox researches? No, guess again. He is a totally ineducable fool, a near idiot, whose enthusiasm for devices and contraptions arises from utter inability to respond to anything more elevated, whose tastes must for natural reasons suffer confinement to the realm of mere sense impression.

But a further irony, one which the reader will have anticipated, awaits us here. It arises from the fact that Li Yü is typically in sympathy with his buffoons and is inclined to put his most cherished preferences into their mouths. And the passage quoted above is one of the signal instances of this. Li Yü's aproach to writing, and to all things, was typically that of a maker or inventor rather than that of a literary man per se. This was apparent even in the material details of his daily life. He was forever devising contraptions to increase the convenience of his living quarters. In his *Random Lodge for My Idle Feelings* he describes a water-cooled stool and a heated and insulated desk-with-chair of his own devising that allowed him to stay cool in the summer and warm in the winter during hours of literary composition.[62] A biographical notice in a local gazateer of Lan-ch'i District says of Li Yü that

> He was extremely clever by nature and had all kinds of new ideas with regard to windows, furniture, clothing, household utensils, and eating regimens. People were invariably delighted when they saw these things, so he became popular and well known.[63]

His experience as a war refugee and his work as a book publisher and garden designer brought him into close contact with problems of a physical, mechanical nature. His plays are often concerned with the lives and problems of small tradesmen and craftsmen. They abound in references to mechanical objects and to ingenious, practical solutions to pressing dilemmas, as for example Ts'ao-shih's use of oil from the croton bean to simulate leprosy in *The Amazing Reunion*. [64] His attitude toward the making of plays was concrete and functional. He was the only drama theorist of traditional times to pay attention to the structure of the entire play as opposed to the technique of writing individual lyrics.[65] Moreover, he typically supports his dramaturgical theories by appealing to the *function* of drama, to its effect on a group of viewers. Even his view of the created universe is colored by the mechanical bent of his mind. When he refers to the supreme power it is usually the inventive aspect that is stressed. He sees God or heaven as a busy artificer whose activities are analogous to those of a cabinet maker or a playwright. Thus when Li Yü has his fool praise mechanics at the expense of philosophers, I believe we may be confident that this preference corresponds with a predilection of his own.

Li Yü is an author who combines an unusual fluency and facility of verbal expression with an unusually strong perception of the secondary and dependent relationship of words to things. He can make his characters describe, question, exclaim, and apostrophize with endless variety and brilliance, yet some of his finest effects are created nonverbally, by causing the essence of a dramatic or moral situation to reside in a concrete object resting on the stage, as when the "stubborn stone" comes to stand for the moral obtuseness of Ch'ien Wankuan in the culminating scene of *The Paired Soles*.[66]

Li Yü loves the stubbornness, the uniqueness, and the impervious-
ness to logic of solid things. In his plays it is one of the functions of
nature and the concrete objects which stand for nature to contradict
the predictions and upset the pretensions of theory mongers. But as
plays are in greater part structures of words, it is neither possible nor
desirable to represent regularly the concrete with the concrete. Some
verbal equivalent must be used. In Li Yü the equivalent is to be found
in ribaldry and in aggressively irrational babbling. One has the sense,
in reading Li Yü, of two entities in incessant competition with each
other. On the one hand, there is a brilliant debater clamoring to be
heard; on the other, there is a stammering idiot yearning to be born.
The behavior of the idiot is inherently eruptive and irrational. In
most of Li Yü's plays no definite place is assigned to him in the
philosophical scheme of the play, so his appearances are fearsomely
unpredictable. At any moment, including the most serious or romantic, his loud donkey bray may suddenly break into the texture of a
scene, infusing it with a bizarre, even inappropriate, sense of comedy.
Thus in *The Careful Couple*, Li Yü is not afraid to put grotesque jokes
involving venereal disease in close juxtaposition to a portrayal of an
entirely noncomic, ideal courtesan.[67] In *The Paired Soles*, he portrays a
couple who attain the ultimate romantic dignity of suicide for love
and then, without surrendering the perspective of admiration and
sympathy from which they are viewed throughout, turns them into
subjects of ribald joking and horseplay.[68] Now there are two possible
reactions the reader can have to such lawless eruptions of the idiot.
The sympathetic reader will cherish such moments as being the
essential Li Yü, examples of a rare literary flavor that can scarcely be
encountered elsewhere; the antagonistic reader will view them simply
as unaccountable blemishes, an author's wanton destruction of his
own chief effects.

The great distinction of *The Kite's Mistake* is that it provides a place
and a function for this eruptive element in Li Yü's literary nature. It
rationalizes the irrational. In *The Kite's Mistake*, the appearances of
the idiot are not vulnerable to the criticism of irrelevance; he is firmly
ensconced in the intellectual structure of the play. If you subtract the
idiot from *The Careful Couple* or *The Paired Soles*, the result is a purer,
more rational play. If you subtract him from *The Kite's Mistake*, the
result is a destroyed play. Only in *The Kite's Mistake* does Li Yü hit
upon a formula that allows him to express the warring elements in his

nature in an unassailably integrated, harmonious way. Nearly all his plays are admirably startling and original, but *The Kite's Mistake* is the play he was born to write.

We have been concerned up to this point with the rational and the natural as exemplified by different sets of characters within the play. The same polar principles can be discerned in the area to which I now wish to direct attention: the relationship in this play between design and event. *The Kite's Mistake* possesses in abundance two artistic characteristics that are often found in isolation, but rarely in combination: extreme artificiality of structure, and elaborate naturalism of presentation. If we stand back from the play we see a thoroughly designed structure of straight lines, perfect curves, and balanced masses. But if we move closer and look at what transpires within any given scene, the smooth man-made shapes all give way to the irregularly undulating shapes of nature. The characters have distinguishing traits that are not required by the role they fulfill in the intellectual scheme of the play. The scheme requires only that the mothers of the Chan daughters be concubines and that they quarrel. Li Yü, however, individualizes them. He makes Mistress Plum the older and more quarrelsome of the two. It is only out of duty and a sense of prudence that Chan Wu-ch'eng spends time with her; with Mistress Willow he really enjoys himself. The older is jealous of the younger's beauty while the younger is jealous of the older's authority. This provides their quarreling with motivation and makes it all appear so extraordinarily lifelike that the commentator is moved at the climax of their quarreling in the third act to nudge the reader's elbow: "Reader, allow me to ask you, is this situation true to life or not?"[69] Similarly, the "ideal" characters are not identical in their ideality; Shu-chüan is free of the hubris that marks Han Shih-hsün's behavior and has more sense of what is socially appropriate. Ai-chüan is more purely comic than is Ch'i Yu-hsien, who is on occasion sinister as well as comic. Li Yü's mind is filled with schemes and blueprints, but at the same time he never forgets that he is dealing with unique, mysterious, impenetrable objects whose lineaments he paints with the delicate attention to detail of a painter-naturalist. The playwright is indeed an artificer, so much of one that he must leave not a nail or shaving behind for the audience to see. As Ch'i Yu-hsien remarks of the contraption that is the chief emblem of the play itself, "I challenge the painter to blend his hues so subtly/That the cast kite will seem a sun-stained cloud on high."[70]

It is another example, in a different continuum, of Li Yü's endless respect for the blindness of nature that he never (in this play, at any rate) allows his design to interfere with natural causation. In fact he delights in making it appear in the highest degree unlikely that nature will ever come up with the event required by his design, so that when the event is at length stumbled upon, as it were, we are speechless with outraged amazement or amusement. Consider the succession of events that leads to the launching of a kite bearing a love message from Han Shih-hsün. Han himself is much too grave and intelligent a young man to enjoy such a frivolity as kite flying. The motivation, the fruitful error, must come from somewhere else. The *Ch'ing-ming* or grave-sweeping festival arrives, and young men from wealthy families mill around the city outskirts flying kites. When the clown Ch'i Yu-hsien sees them, he is suddenly stirred by the desire to go kite flying as well. He instructs his houseboy to go paste a kite together. When the houseboy enters with the kite, Ch'i objects that it looks too plain. The houseboy suggests that he paint some colorful design on it. Yu-hsien has no patience for this; he tells the houseboy to bring the kite in to Master Han and tell him to paint something on it. He, Yu-hsien, will go to the city outskirts and wait for the houseboy to arrive with the completed kite.[71]

In the meantime, Han Shih-hsün is alone in the library trying to assuage his melancholy by writing a piece of eight-line, tone-regulated verse:

> Don't say romantic youths resemble banished angels;
> With laden heart I vainly sing my boundless sadness.
> The light of spring still lingers on my brow and yet,
> Already, sounds of autumn moan about my ears.
> I long to dream, but who is willing to invest my dream?
> I want to sleep, but all night long forget to sleep . . .[72]

Just as he finishes the sixth line, Yu-hsien's servant bursts into the room demanding that he decorate his master's kite. Shih-hsun is furious at the servant for killing his inspiration and objects that he has no pigments. He doesn't even have red ink for punctuating his texts; how can he have colors for a kite? Besides, it is beneath his dignity; if Yu-hsien wants to have the kite decorated, he should have it taken to some common tradesman who specializes in such matters. How can he use his "huge-as-a-housebeam brush for painting little finger rings?"[73]

The houseboy begs Shih-hsün to put up with the annoyance and paint something on it anyway. He points out that his master is already waiting for him at the city outskirts; if he is tardy in arriving with the kite, he will suffer for it. He admits that there are no pigments and supposes Han will just have to put a few strokes on it with black ink. He begs Han to hurry, promises to return for the kite after eating a bowl of rice, and exits.

Left by himself, Han continues to fume over the silly demands of his adopted brother. Then it occurs to him that he can simply add a couple of concluding lines to the poem he was composing a moment ago, write out the characters on the kite, and give it to the houseboy to take away. He writes:

> Because no place to hide my grief remains on earth,
> I'll write it on this kite and send it to the sky.[74]

You will observe that the above sequence of events is continuously ventilated by chance. There are no reasons other than chance convenience for the characters' choices; they could at any point decide to do something different from what they actually do. And they have no conception of the ends to which their nearly random choices are gradually tending. Han hasn't the remotest premonition that the poem he wrote on the kite will actually function as a love message. Insofar as he imagines anything, he imagines the poem inscribing to be a kind of prayer addressed to the old man in the sky:

> (sings) I beseech you to gaze down on my prostrate heart terrified of poverty and worried about possessions. I beg to ask you, creator, if your wealth-creating intentions are reliable or not. Even though it is said that great men are always late maturing, I can't believe you will delay my marriage till my temples are streaked with white![75]

The other actors suspect no more of the shape of the play they are in than does Han. When the houseboy sees the poem on the kite, he jokes that since each word of such a masterpiece is worth a thousand gold pieces, the kite will be far too heavy to cast up to the sky.[76] In the following act, the sight of the poem provokes Ch'i Yu-hsien to one of his characteristic outbursts against brother Han:

> Every single thing he does is so tiresome and disgusting! If you turn this way, he writes a poem; if you turn that way, he writes still another poem. Even if he happened to kill somebody, he would end up giving a poem to the victim's relatives as compensation. There's nothing to be done. I'll just have to put up with flying it as it is'.[77]

Unconsciously echoing Han's idea of the poem as a message addressed to heaven, Ch'i fears that "that stinking poem will offend the lord of heaven with its odor and make him send down hosts of heavenly soldiers to exterminate all poets on the earth." If that should happen, he will "honestly report the name" of the one who wrote in his behalf, beg the heavenly avenger to remember that he "never sinned that way in all his life," and humbly beseech his clemency.[78] At this point, the play's anonymous commentator appends a (playfully sympathetic?) note:

> Stinking poems have come to fill up the whole world, these days. In the future, Ch'in Shih-huang must inevitably be reborn in order to carry out the wrath of heaven and prevent poets from ever gazing on their kind again. Old Ch'i is a very prescient fellow. He cannot be lightly dismissed as a crank.[79]

The apparent aimlessness of nature does not end with this phase of the story but pervades the subsequent scene as well. When Shu-chüan writes a poem matching the rhymes of the one on the kite, she has no more idea than does young Han that the poem will in effect turn out to be a love message. She is simply obeying her mother's injunction to practise her versification, for which the kite that has just fallen into their courtyard has provided a handy theme and subject. "It is a stranger's poem," she says, "why should I write a poem that matches it?" To this her mother replies,

> People who have a gift for verse can make a theme from anything their eyes light upon and take a rhyme from any

ready-at-hand word. Haven't you noticed that people often write rhyme-matching answers to poems inscribed on walls and on fans? All they are doing is to borrow someone else's theme in order to express the feelings in their heart. Anyway, you won't be showing your answer to the poem writer, so what problem can there be?[80]

She then instructs her daughter to write her answer below the first, using the rhyme words of the first poem in reverse order. After an interval of pacing and concentration, Shu-chüan departs to visit her sister Ai-chüan, leaving behind the following lines for her mother to read:

> From what region in heaven have these golden strains been cast?
> They fell straight here as if to rouse me from my sheltered slumber.
> A paper kite is only good for soaring past the clouds;
> Why was the varicolored string broken beside the sun?
> I can't be sure its purpose lay in sending me some message;
> Maybe it simply lacked a verse to match its sable lines.
> When grief grows great, don't turn to the domed heavens to announce it;
> It is precisely grief that dooms an angel to be banished.[81]

Shortly afterwards Ch'i Yu-hsien's houseboy arrives to claim the kite and Mistress Willow, forgetting that her daughter's poem is now written there, returns it. Shu-chüan hurriedly returns to protest the indiscretion of allowing her poem to be seen by men outside the family. Mistress Willow's first impulse is to send someone to recall the kite, but upon reflection she decides that to recall it would attract even more attention to themselves than to allow it to be returned. The equivocal situation of the women, and of the gradually coalescing plot, is neatly summed up in the act-closing quatrain:

> We matched a verse, but not to advertise our female genius;
> We sent it out, but don't be led by that to wild surmises.
> An unmoored, drifting kite was found, then again cast away;
> The poem's script is gone, but its intent is still arriving.[82]

"The intent is still arriving." That simple but far-reaching formulation sums up what it would be like to be a character within *The Kite's Mistake*, experiencing life from hour to hour and from day to day. In Li Yü's world view, "intent" is not something exclusively possessed by sentient creatures, but something that informs all the changes, all the processes, within the observable universe. We are accustomed to thinking of these phenomena as events; Li Yü is accustomed to thinking of them as actions. A consequence of this mode of perception is that human action possesses an impersonal, as well as a personal, layer of intent. Thus, when I do something, I of course have a conscious intent that is known to me even before I do it. I may very likely have a subconscious intent, as well, that is concealed from me. But in Li Yü's view, my action possesses a third type of intent, deeper than either the conscious or the subconscious; and this intent does not inhere in my mind; it inheres in the action, the process, itself and can only be revealed to me through the passage of time.

One consequence of this state of affairs is that people can never be completely aware of what they are really doing. People are created to err, to veer unconsciously from the direct path. And the more a person strives to gain conscious control over the direction and meaning of his actions, the greater will be the resulting divergence from the actor's aim. What you ask for is never what you get. Thus when Han acts with total blindness, the consequences of his action lead directly to the object of his deepest desire: a woman who combines rare beauty with rare sensitivity and intellect. But when he perceives the intent inherent in his initial action and consciously strives to imitate it, his actions lead at once to the object he most desires to avoid: a woman who combines rare ugliness with rare crudity and stupidity. The initial action was not an imitation of anything; any imitation of it therefore fails by definition to be a replica of the original. We might express this situation by paraphrasing the words of the preface writer: "When the artificial impersonates the natural, its carving and painting is in vain, and when sincerity is confused with calculation, it must reveal its true nature in the end." Having come this far, we can see that the preface writer correctly described the process inherent in the play's system of thought; it was merely his terms that were awry. What was error in one dimension produced truth in another.

V. Life as Obedience: *What Can You Do?*

What the law demands, give of your own free will.
>   Terence, *Adelphi*, line 490 (act 3, scene 4) (160 B.C.)

He who takes his orders gladly escapes the bitterest part of slavery. . . . The man who does something under orders is not unhappy; he is unhappy who does something against his will.
>   Seneca, *Epistulae ad Lucilium*, no. 41, sec. 3 (64 A.D.)

Now these are the Laws of the Jungle, and many and
>   mighty are they;
But the head and the hoof of the Law and the haunch and
>   the hoof is—Obey!
>   Kipling, *The Second Jungle Book* (1895),
>   "The Law of the Jungle," stanza 19

>   Obedience,
Bane of all genius, virtue, freedom, truth,
Makes slaves of men, and, of the human frame
A mechanized automaton.
>   Shelley, *Queen Mab* (1813), canto 3, line 177

What Can You Do? shares with *The Kite's Mistake* the distinction of being one of the two most well known of Li Yü's plays. It is also the most obviously daring of Li Yü's many theatrical experiments. What more fundamental violation of the conventions of Chinese romantic comedy, what graver threat to the equilibrium of the form, could be devised than to put a clown into the role of romantic lead? In this play, Li Yü stakes everything on a single gigantic experiment.

No play by Li Yü sounds sillier or less realistic in summary. A husband is so ugly that his three wives all run away in succession to the seclusion of his library, where they take Buddhist vows and live as nuns. But finally, after the spirits transform the husband into a handsome man, the wives all come running back again and vie for the privilege of being his chief wife. Surely this must be a piece of fluff, a brainless piece of amusement with somewhat less substance than the libretto of *Così Fan Tutte*. How could such a vacuous idea be elaborated into a play as long and detailed as a novel, which took as many days to perform as a Shakespearean play takes hours?

And yet, as we make our way through the play's successive acts, we find ourselves persuaded at nearly every point of the logical necessity, the truth to life, and the underlying moral seriousness of what we are reading. One begins to suspect that Li Yü could write a play on the events of *Alice in Wonderland* that would seem an exercise in strict realism of presentation combined with orderly sobriety of thought.

But even as the reader's suspicions of unseriousness are laid to rest, he is apt to find other scruples raised, other sensitivities offended. It is bad enough, from the postromantic western reader's point of view, that the story should be intended as a celebration of so hard and uncongenial an attribute as obedience—which, after chastity (a Christian, not a Chinese, virtue) must seem to him the most dubious and inexplicable of the traditional virtues. But it will impress him as outrageous, if not criminal, that the chief vehicle of the theme should be the submission that a wife owes a husband, particularly when he recalls some of the more inhuman details of that relationship in traditional China.

It is disappointing to a modern reader who wants to admire Li Yü in all respects to discover that in this respect he is a man of his times rather than a prophet of liberalism. But the expression of this disappointment or condemnation will miss its mark unless we first take care to ascertain what the play actually is and says; and this appreciative effort is impossible unless it is accompanied by a suspension of condemnation. The moral concerns that must inevitably arise in our minds will be directly addressed in the concluding pages of this chapter. In the meantime, let us as far as possible abandon our own point of view and submerge ourselves in the world of the play.

One of the conveniences of Chinese *ch'uan-ch'i* drama is that it recognizes the inherent interest of literary interpretation and includes elements of commentary as part of the varied entertainment it spreads before the reader. You do not have to go outside the work in order to get it.

Thus, if you wish to grasp the fundamental idea of a given *ch'uan-ch'i* play, you can as often as not find an epigrammatic précis of the idea in the opening or closing lyrics of the play itself. At the very least, you will find there some broad hints as to what the play is about. The much shorter dramas known as *tsa-chü* are apt to consist exclusively of unexplicated fable, but in *ch'uan-ch'i* drama, you expect the author to admit that his narrative has philosophical implications and to give you some direction in tracing them.

When we turn to the opening and closing lyrics of *What Can You Do?* we immediately notice that antagonism toward popular romance that we have already observed in *The Kite's Mistake* and *The Careful Couple*, accompanied by a vehement (though at the same time humorous) denial that there should be such a thing as feminine free choice. Thus in the verse epilogue we read:

> What did I have in mind when I began to write this play?
> One fact alone: romantic plays are far too numerous.
> To rank with the undying classics and escape mere cheap applause,
> You first must heave a massive boulder so it blocks the stream of love.
> If the secluded sex did not indulge in dreams that flout their nature,
> Who in the world would then take up the weapons of domestic discord?
> From this time forth, fair-featured ones will know that there is fate above,
> And that Ying-ying is an entirely fitting match for brother Cheng.[1]

Ying-ying is of course the heroine of the great love drama *Romance of the Western Chamber* (*Hsi-hjsiang chin*) and "brother Cheng" refers to the lusterless and unpleasant character whom her mother wishes her to marry and whom she abandons for the dashing protagonist,

Chang Chün-jui. It is as if Imogen should be considered fit for Cloten, or Sophia for Blifil. Romantic drama, then, is all wrong. Young women are to be taught to renounce what they love and to embrace what they hate. The introductory lyrics in the first act are as follows:

> The creator has no taste for female beauty;
> Crushing and killing lovely ladies, he exerts all the force of his destructive, chilling blast.
> Numberless tears pay court to the sea until rivers and oceans overflow,
> But these are of no more concern to the Lord of Heaven than are the morning and evening tides.
> That pink-cheeked damsels have slender fortunes is an established rule;
> One needn't fear that the retiring sex will sprout four wings.
> Even if they should hatch a hundred schemes, how could they move the will of heaven?
> In the end they would find it can't be altered.
>
> How many playwrights could revise the foregoing lyrics!
> Snatching up a heroine and delivering her to the handsome hero, they would stage a play of young romance.
> And comely women therefore grow to hate what suits them,
> And in pell-mell profusion do disgraceful things, and hasten out to secret rendezvous.
> This time, though, I break completely with established stage convention;
> A clown and a beauty joined in marriage is truly not what you would expect.
> But surely you must realize this sort of thing is very common;
> It is no rare or monstrous wrong, so don't cry out against it.[2]

Hung-yen po ming, "pink-cheeked damsels have slender fortunes" (line 5 above), is one of the oftenest repeated proverbs in the language.[3] It is a melancholy, ubiquitous refrain accompanying romantic tales of interesting beauties. Li Yü gives this saying all its customary prominence and in fact makes it the mainspring of arguments against feminine free choice that occur in the last acts. In so doing, he gradually imparts an unusual significance to the saying. Usually it has the quality of metaphysical complaint; we trot out the proverb as we cluck our tongues and shake our heads over the heroine's misfortunes. In *What Can You Do?* it assumes the quality of metaphysical justification. We look through the proverb as usual, but we look through it from its opposite side, gazing down at people instead of up at heaven. The death-dealing prerogative of heaven is not merely stated; it is, with cheerful ferocity, supported. The introduction is not only antiromantic; it is antihuman. It appears designed to create pain as well as shock, to hit us where it hurts most.

From the brief introductory act, we proceed at once to the central experiment of the play. Just at the point where we expect to see the leading man come on to the stage and introduce himself, a clown walks on instead and usurps his function. Now one way in which this might have been handled would have been to make the clown parody everything that a leading man does. He would describe himself as a dashing, talented, but penniless young scholar and invoke the names of all the heroes and poets of the past, but in a manner so clumsy as to provoke laughter. This, however, is not what happens. The clown is not made to try to imitate the manner of a romantic hero. Instead, he is given self-knowledge. He knows that his qualities are the opposite of those of a romantic hero. He knows that instead of being handsome, talented, and poor, he is ugly, stupid, and rich. And he proceeds to describe these qualities, the qualities he actually possesses, with the same gusto, the same self-satisfaction, with which a romantic hero describes his qualities. As he talks to us of his ancestors, his circumstances, and his prospects, we discover to our surprise that there is plenty of serious substance in his buffoonery. The dignity with which he unconsciously clothes himself seems to us entirely plausible. His opening lyric appeals to the principle of realism in order to challenge the right of romantic young men to hold pride of place in romantic drama and in the esteem of mankind:

> A painted face [clown] plunging on to the stage while the true leading man flies from the banquet—
> We do this thing not because we wish to turn the customs of the stage upside down,
> But merely because positions of elegance and luxury are chiefly occupied by people such as me.

I always laugh at the pathetic pride of literary men—
They may have the talent of Sung Yü and the looks of P'an
    Yüeh, they are all poor wretches anyway—
No match for the crude stupidity of such as I—I, whose wealth
    comes from the bounty of heaven.[4]

Here again, as in his use of the "slender fortunes" proverb, Li Yü is
from a romantic point of view committing treason. Wealth and
coarseness laugh, with his approval, at poverty and sensitivity. He is
in effect illustrating the principle that "the race goes not to the fleet of
foot," but in an inside-out manner; instead of using the principle to
mourn for the fleet of foot and cast taunts at the world, he uses it to
justify the world and cast taunts at the fleet of foot. That which
romance and human yearning perceives as injustice is in fact justice.

The poem that follows is the part of Ch'üeh Li-hou's self-
introduction that is most nearly allied to parody; however, it is not
parody by imitation but parody by reversal. Ch'üeh presents himself
as a prince of ugliness in terms that recall the self-introductions of
princes of romance:

Tso Ssu and Wang Ts'an exhausted the possibilities of romantic
    charm,
But ugliness did not achieve its ultimate shape until expressed in
    me.
This vile form will take no lantern as its friend;
This wrathful image is forever at odds with mirrors.
When I pass by azure curtains, cross beneath jasper towers,
The beauties hide their faces and drop their window blinds.
In leisure moments, I dare not ride out in carriages
For fear of being pelted with tiles and pebbles.[5]

Then, passing from the intoned to the spoken portion of his self-
introduction, he informs us that though his ancestors have been
steadily amassing wealth for many generations, no one in his family
has ever had any intellectual ability. Not only has no one been able
to attain such high honors as the *chü-jen* or *chin-shih* degree, there has
never even been a person in the family to win the relatively humble
distinction of a junior licentiate's turban. They have had to be content with no more than the level heavens for a cap (this is of course

what Li Yü likes about stupidity: its approximation to his cherished
ideals of naturalness and obscurity). "I myself," says Ch'üeh, "have
studied for the examinations for more than ten years, but even so I
can't get a drop's worth of writing out of myself, even if I hang myself
upside down."[6] But this Ch'üeh could easily put up with if it were not
for a yet more grievous problem:

> The form that heaven has bestowed on me is not only thick and
> coarse; it is deformed. There is not a single one of my five senses
> or four limbs that does not carry some defect. Not long ago
> there was an impudent rascal of a scholar who gave me the
> nickname Ch'üeh Pu-ch'üan ["Crippled Not-complete"] and
> wrote an essay purporting to be a eulogy of my appearance. It
> was very mean and cutting, but nevertheless quite accurate.
> (pointing, miming, and speaking at the same time) It says:

> "His eyes should not be called completely blind; they just have
> small white flecks; his face should not be thought completely
> marked and scarred; it just has many black spots; his hands
> should not be called completely bare; here and there some scat-
> tered nails appear; his legs should not be called completely lame;
> heels poke out in various places. His nose is not completely red;
> deep and faint, some swollen veins show through; his hair is not
> completely yellow; it also has a brownish-incense sort of tinge;
> his throat does more than stammer; when hurried it emits two
> sounds at once; his back is not entirely humped; the flesh stands
> out behind the neck three inches only. He also has a not com-
> pletely crooked mouth; it suddenly twitches and lies still as if
> pulled by someone hidden. And left over he has two eyebrows
> that don't entirely protrude; they alternately break and con-
> tinue like two tracks of scattered firewood."

> (he laughs) What do you think? Isn't every sentence in that
> eulogy the truth? Isn't every word of it exact?[7]

Now Ch'üeh comes to the climax and point of his self-description:
he may be as stupid as can be and as ugly as can be, but who can
deny that he is also as rich as can be? The fellow who gave him the

nickname and wrote the eulogy of his appearance is of course extremely intelligent and extremely handsome, but Ch'üeh is "just afraid that when Mr. 'Completely Not-crippled' doesn't have any silver pieces left to spend, he will have to come to Mr. 'Crippled Not-complete' for money."[8]

Ch'üeh then turns to his handsome servant Ch'üeh Chung, who manages all his financial affairs for him, and asks for corroboration on the following point: "Is it or is it not true that among all the people who come here to borrow money, there is not a single one who is not intelligent and handsome in the extreme?" Ch'üeh Chung confirms his master on this point ("there's a lot in what you say, sir") and shortly afterwards observes that he himself is a case in point. His features are strikingly distinguished; he knows his characters; he reads books; but still there is nothing he can do to better his lot, which is to "hold the lantern for others and follow the crack of the whip."[9]

Ch'üeh Chung is in fact just the sort of person whom we would ordinarily expect to assume the central role in a *ch'uan-ch'i* drama. His role-type is *hsiao sheng* or "subsidiary romantic lead." As the play unfolds, he shows himself to be a man of endless sagacity, prudence, courage, and loyalty, but these qualities are directed exclusively to the attainment of his master's interests. He has no interests apart from his master's. The radically contingent nature of his existence is epitomized by his name: he has taken his master's surname, effacing whatever his own was, and his given name, Chung, means "loyal." It is as if the words "property of the Ch'üeh household" were engraved on his face.

His service is merely one aspect of the vast good fortune enjoyed by Mr. Crippled Not-complete. That Ch'üeh Li-hou is ennobled and magically transformed at the close of the play is due to the wit and industry of the paragon of humanity who is his servant. All Li-hou has to do is to be receptive, to accept Ch'üeh's labor and advice. It is in fact Ch'üeh Li-hou's unusually pronounced vocation for receptivity that is at the bottom of his worldly success. His physical and intellectual incompleteness leaves him open to the bounty of humans and spirits.

The same point is made, though not of course with Li Yü's humor and hyperbole, by Chinese historians when they compare the character and achievements of the two rival contenders for the mastery of

China after the fall of the Ch'in dynasty, Liu Pang and Hsiang Yü.[10] Hsiang Yü was a military aristocrat, a man of outstanding heredity and opportunity, extraordinarily endowed with courage, nobility, and strategic genius; Liu Pang was a man of the people with no obviously outstanding personal qualities or abilities. His military position, moreover, was initially weaker than that of his rival. Yet it was Liu Pang who eventually prevailed and founded the succeeding dynasty for, aware that he was not exceptionally gifted, he was willing to be guided by able advisors; whereas the egocentricity of Hsiang Yü could not accept the jarring presence of alien viewpoints and personalities. Perhaps something of the same perception lies behind the American distrust of intellectual presidents. Americans have always preferred leaders of ordinary tastes and abilities, but with the horse sense to make judicious use of brainy or specialized advice.

It is an instance of Li Yü's extraordinary genius for comedy that he could see the potential for amusement in this ordinary principle. The method has been enunciated by Bernard Shaw: "Find the right things to say; then say them with as much exaggeration and levity as possible."[11] Li Yü must have been aware, too, that the joke was as much at his own expense as at anyone else's, for he definitely exemplified in his own person the class of poor and brainy people who depend for their existence upon the service they give to the relatively rich and stupid. Perhaps it eased his cares to write a comic justification of his own penurious and dependent existence.

The modern reader may well wonder why Li Yü devotes so much attention to the physical appearance of his characters in this play. His reflections upon the consequences of ability and stupidity are easily understandable in contemporary terms; not so those concerning beauty and ugliness. The reason for this emphasis lies partly in the great importance that was placed upon physiognomy in traditional China. A person's features were thought to be directly related to his fortunes, and there existed a highly developed "science" of physiognomic fortune-telling. We get a taste of this in act 2:

> Ch'üeh Chung: The other day, my lord, there was a phrenologist who said that your features are those of one who is naturally destined to enjoy immense wealth and status. I asked him how he could tell this and he answered that your lordship's person carries ten defects. This is similar to a

domino's having eight incompletes [*pa pu-chiu*]. He knew that
you very seldom come across dominoes that have eight incompletes, and from this he deduced that a physiognomy
with ten defects must indicate great wealth and status.
Ch'üeh Li-hou (laughing): He spoke cleverly! Cleverly indeed!"[12]

Here the reference to phrenology is plainly a joke, but it is a joke
that rests upon a cultural background of perfectly serious belief. It
was normal for people in all walks of life to wish to determine if a
stranger's features were auspicious or not before entering into relations with him, and many a Chinese story turns upon a particularly
percipient character's detection of auspiciousness or inauspiciousness
in someone's features.

Given this cultural background, the preoccupation with beauty
and ugliness in this play appears perfectly natural. It also has secondary advantages; deformity is dramatically colorful, particularly
when it can be represented with stylized exaggeration, as on the
Chinese stage. The play would be an entirely different kind of experience without the physical loathing, the shock of contact followed
by disgusted recoil, that follows hard upon each of Ch'üeh's various
marriages. That irrepressible physical reaction is the perfect objective
correlative for everything that is hateful in the concept of obedience.

Li Yü does not rely solely on members of the Ch'üeh household to
illustrate the relationship of talent and features to worldly success.
The nature of *ch'uan-ch'i* drama is expansive and reduplicative. Every
major relationship of characters is bound to have reflections
elsewhere in the structure. Thus the chief wife of General Yüan Cho-
shui, whom we first meet in act 5, is in some respects the female
counterpart of Ch'üeh Li-hou. More venomous and scheming than
Ch'üeh, her role-type is that of *ching* or villain. Being ugly, she enjoys
high position, ease, and authority. She has no difficulty keeping her
handsome and talented husband in thrall. "My present life is a lucky
one," she sings; "how proud I feel when I think of those beauties with
wretched destinies. Unlike them, I use a handsome husband to
gratify my amorous desires." In her self-introductory speech, she
makes fun of her physical grotesqueness in much the same way as
Ch'üeh Li-hou:

I am only seven feet in stature [the old Chinese foot is slightly shorter than the English foot] and my waist is barely two arm-spans around. My tiny golden-lotus feet can't be said to be "three inches" [the ideal length of a bound foot]. My delicate jadelike fingers, if you weighed them, wouldn't come to half a pound. My face is always put to shame by the sight of flowers; it is truly what is called a "flower-shaming face" [the Chinese expression ordinarily means "flower-shaming" and is applied to the faces of beauties, but it is also grammatically capable of meaning "flower-shamed"]. I always want to hide my features when I see the moon; I actually have what people term "moon-eclipsing features" [also capable of meaning "moon-eclipsed"].[13]

On the other hand, her husband and his two lovely concubines suffer the ill fortune that attends those with unusual natural gifts. As Ch'üeh Chung is the opposite of Ch'üeh Li-hou in ability and social status, so Yüan Cho-shui, whose role-type is that of romantic lead, is his opposite in ability and romantic destiny. Ch'üeh Li-hou is destined to marry beauties; even when (in acts 18 and 19) he does his best to find a plain-looking wife, he gains a beauty instead. Yüan has two lovely concubines, but is prevented from enjoying them by his wife; nor is he able to prevent her from selling them away in his absence. Yüan does enjoy high position, but it is a position maintained only by hard and precarious work, and is dependent as well on the fickle whim of the court to which he gives service. Ch'üeh, on the other hand, enjoys his wealth and, at the close of the play, his ennoblement and physical transformation, without having to endure any danger or exertion at all.

This is not to say, however, that Ch'üeh's apotheosis at the end of the play is uncaused. There is a deed he must perform without which the apotheosis could not occur. That deed is one of the principal actions of the play and, like the rebellion and submission of Ch'üeh's wives, it is a theme-bearing action. It is introduced immediately after the self-introductions of Ch'üeh Li-hou and Ch'üeh Chung and before any other narrative elements are begun. Li-hou asks Chüeh Chung to tell him how his financial affairs are going and learns that he has recently taken in more than eighteen thousand taels in rent and loan payments, and that it has been turned over to the storehouse. This reminds him of a financial worry he has. The imperial court has almost come to the end of its monetary resources and, because it is a year of bad harvests, is unable to collect further taxes. The supply needs of the imperial forces stationed at the frontier are extremely pressing and the court really has no practicable plan whatsoever for meeting the need. Li-hou is fairly widely known to be a wealthy man. He wonders how he can handle the situation if the court should hear of his wealth and ask to borrow money from him. Ch'üeh Chung agrees with his master that the situation is worrisome. He has heard that the court is buzzing with proposals that they borrow money from among the commoners. And their own house will certainly not be overlooked. He has a plan to propose, however, though he fears Li-hou might not be willing to accept it. Li-hou urges him to unfold the plan and Ch'üeh Chung responds as follows:

> In the Han dynasty, there was a rich commoner named Pu Shih. When he saw that the court was out of funds, he contributed a hundred thousand taels to aid the court in purchasing supplies for the army. He afterwards became an illustrious minister and his name was preserved in the ever-living annals of history. Why don't you take advantage of the fact that they have not yet asked to borrow money from you and go yourself to the head minister's office, draw up a contract, and do what Pu Shih did? If you contribute a few ten thousands of taels to help the frontier forces, the court will surely be very pleased. Perhaps when peace is reestablished and your services are reported, you will be given a ministership as a reward, who knows? (sings) This is the early touch of the whip that will get you started on the cloudy path of glory; it will be far more efficacious than the ordinary office seeker's paltry gifts of millet.[14]

Li-hou balks a little at the great expense of such a contribution, but gives in and accepts the idea when Ch'üeh Chung assures him that a hundred thousand taels would consume only a quarter of one year's profits. "What you say makes sense," he says; "it is a good thing you were able to figure it out." He then sings some lines of thanks to his servant who, also singing, rejoins, "I want to make up for your defective inheritance of natural qualities."[15]

In ch'uan-ch'i drama it is typical for the focus of attention to shift back and forth between dynastic military concerns and the personal romantic concerns of the chief characters. In *What Can You Do?* seven out of thirty acts are concerned with the dynastic theme and most of the remainder with Ch'üeh Li-hou's troubled love life. This ratio is about average for the form. The love story occupies the foreground, but there is always a background of fighting and politics. The ultimate reasons for the nearly invariable presence of this background are probably much more related to theatrical spectacle than to any purely literary requirement; no *ch'uan-ch'i* performance would have pleased an audience if it lacked the colorful feats of swordsmanship and tumbling that occur in battle scenes. But of course skillful practitioners of the form, such as our playwright, made a virtue of this necessity (thus providing us with an inspiring instance of obedience) and related their battle scenes to their foreground scenes in such a way that their presence is justified by more than the necessity of spectacle.

In general, the dynastic theme is not introduced at once, but enters somewhere in the vicinity of the fourth act with the introduction of a military official or bandit directly concerned with the fighting. Then, some acts further on, the foreground characters are also drawn into, or affected by, the dynastic problem. *What Can You Do?* is somewhat unusual in that its chief foreground character is drawn into the dynastic background almost the moment he appears. His romantic problems are not even broached until his relationship to this background is defined, and this relationship is in one sense the paradigm to which all that follows either conforms or deviates. Ch'üeh Li-hou's only natural asset is wealth. The first action that is urged upon him is to place a great portion of this asset at the disposal of an entity alien to himself. The action defines obedience: the willing performance of a required act repugnant to the self. Some acts later, a nonplussed magistrate asks Ch'üeh Chung if he is sure that his master will not regret his contribution later on, to which the servant replies, "He did it of his own free will. He wasn't pressured into it by any official. How then could he suffer regret?"[16]

The thing that most dumbfounds the various magistrates concerned with Ch'üeh Li-hou's contribution is that the contributor is a mere commoner. Examination graduates and office holders are trained from childhood to regard the reigning dynasty with feelings of the utmost loyalty and devotion. They have visible status; they are treated with a certain respect, even deference, by the various arms of government; they have a stake in the survival and prosperity of the dynasty. It is understandable that some outstandingly patriotic scholar or official might be moved to put his cash at its disposal in the event of a crisis; but for a mere ant of a commoner, an almost invisible member of the alternately nourished and exploited masses, to harbor such highly developed feelings of loyalty and responsibility involves such a leap of imagination, both for him and the official contemplating him, as to pass ordinary comprehension. It is not only astonishment that these officials feel, but sudden shame—shame for the self-satisfaction of their own class. As the pacification chief who registers the contribution observes in an act-closing quatrain,

> The insignia'd servants of the state are powerless to solve the
>   border's problems;
> Who could have known that dauntless integrity would emerge
>   from the registered masses?
> It has always been true that when propriety declines it can be
>   found surviving in the wilds,
> But I never knew till now how worthless we officials have
>   become[17]

That Ch'üeh Li-hou, though wealthy, has no status to speak of is made extremely clear by the bearing of the messengers in act 28 who inform him of the news of his impending ennoblement. The arrival of messengers is a frequent occurence in *ch'uan-ch'i* drama. Their behavior toward scholars and officials is invariably prompt and deferential, and their speech with them is limited to the few brief sentences necessary to transact their mission. Not so their behavior towards Ch'üeh Li-hou. Li-hou goes out himself to see who has come crashing through his gate (a person of status would remain inside while his servant did the investigating) and asks if they are playing some kind of practical joke. When the messengers say they have come to deliver good news, Ch'üeh objects that no one in his household reads or takes examinations; how can they be recipients of good news? The messengers reply that that is just what strikes them as odd, too, and ask him to call Lord Ch'üeh at once. Li-hou answers that he himself is surnamed Ch'üeh, and when the messengers express incredulity says, "If you don't believe me, see if you can find any part of my face or body that is not *ch'üeh* ["incomplete"]." The messengers then ask him to get his brush and inkstone and write out a reward authorization for them before they tell him the good news. When Ch'üeh asks how much they want, the reply is flippant: "only a hundred thousand cash." Only after Ch'üeh writes out an authorization for a thousand cash do the messengers finally come across with their information.[18] A person of official rank would never be treated with such familiarity. While the messengers would definitely expect a gratuity, they would not dare to haggle over the amount; they would leave it up to the official's sense of *noblesse oblige.*

The point of all this emphasis upon Ch'üeh's commonness is to make as vivid as possible the immense distance that lies between Ch'üeh and his concerns on the one hand, and the dynastic government and its concerns on the other. It is an *alien* entity to which he hands over his cash.

Unlike the officials who register Ch'üeh's contribution, the reader is aware that it has come about not so much from feelings of devotion to the state on Ch'üeh's part (it is rather his servant who is so motivated), as from a certain intellectual fuzziness that renders Ch'üeh vulnerable to persuasion and that keeps him from pursuing self-interest to extremes. A person with all his faculties intact would have reacted against sacrificing so large a portion of his profits and could easily have thought of objections sufficient to refute Ch'üeh Chung's persuasions. The same sort of stupidity-conditioned latitude marks his behavior towards his rebellious wives. When they barricade themselves in his library, he blusters and rages and threatens, but in the end fails to carry out any of the retaliatory measures that occur to him. He does not send them away, he does not have them beaten, and he does not order his servants to cease bringing them food. As each wife deserts him, he passively accepts the expense (once his initial rage and disappointment are past) of supporting another religious contemplative (to whom sexual abstinence is a less painful mortification of the flesh than is indulgence under these circumstances), and with a certain unshakeable positiveness of outlook that might well be impossible to a person of intact intellect, sets himself once more to the Sisyphean task of solving his marital problem.

Ch'üeh's voluntary gift to the government is paralleled by another piece of philanthropy in act 12, also devised and executed for him by Ch'üeh Chung. The latter is preparing to depart for the frontier to carry out his master's business. Li-hou's financial affairs will be managed during his absence by Ch'üeh Chung's younger brother, Ch'üeh I. As Ch'üeh Chung prepares to turn his books and records over to his brother, he reflects that many of his master's accounts are virtually uncollectable, as the debtors have suffered overwhelming financial reverses since taking out the loans. To continue to press for the repayment of these loans will only lead to widespread resentment and hostility against the house of Ch'üeh. He therefore resolves to imitate the example of Feng Huan, a famous retainer of the Warring States period, and cause his master to gain the love and devotion of the local populace by burning up all records of long-outstanding debts owed to him. Like Feng Huan, he does all this on his own initiative, reporting it to his master only after it is a *fait accompli*.[19]

Like Li-hou's contribution to the government, this financial sacrifice is something that the force of circumstance would at length have required of him anyway. The great honor that accrues to his person in the wake of these actions arises purely from the fact that he performs them *voluntarily*, before they become an unavoidable necessity.

A second point of interest (and of decided emphasis) in Ch'üeh Lihou's philanthropy is its vicariousness. This is even more apparent in the second action than in the first. Li-hou has so little to do personally with the record burning that he does not even have to assent to it. To the spirits who reward him with transfiguration, however, it is just the same as if he did it personally. It appears that we are intended to understand that one person can gain supernatural merit for another by taking upon himself the responsibility of doing the other's good deeds. As the play's commentator remarks apropos of the record burning, "No one could enjoy the service of such a loyal and intelligent servant if his ancestors had not accumulated virtue for generations."[20]

But all these details concerning the virtue and apotheosis of Ch'üeh Li-hou are, as it were, side dishes. They are not the main source of entertainment in the play. The play's introductory and concluding lyrics make no reference to Ch'üeh's philanthropy; they are concerned with attacking the philosophy of disobedience encouraged by romantic plays and with discouraging young women from entertaining unrealistic dreams. The richness and strangeness of the play lie in the grotesque, tragicomic scenes that show Ch'üeh's brides struggling skillfully to assert their freedom while Ch'üeh struggles clumsily to assert his authority. That is the contest that occupies center stage.

There is fairly good evidence that these scenes were the ones that first occurred to Li Yü's imagination. The material of the first story in Li Yü's early collection of vernacular language tales, *Plays Without Sound (Wu-sheng hsi)*, is identical with the material of the play except that everything concerning Ch'üeh's philanthropy and apotheosis is missing. The story is entitled "An Ugly Fellow Fears Beauty but Ends up with a Dazzler Anyway" *(Ch'ou lang-chün p'a chiao p'ien te yen)*. Ch'üeh has no devoted servant in the story, and we hear nothing of the problems of the imperial court. Nor is Li Yü there concerned to make any general observations on the relation of looks and brains to good fortune. The story is concerned exclusively with the domestic experiences of Ch'üeh and his three brides.

Since Ch'üeh is not transformed or ennobled in the story, its resolution and moral differ from the play. The play inculcates the value of willing cooperation with the inevitable; the story makes only the more specific point that you don't necessarily have to have an enjoyable sex life in order to enjoy general happiness and contentment. In the story, the sexual problem of the four main characters is the same at the conclusion as it is at the beginning; it is their response to the problem that changes. The place where the story and the play first diverge is in the return of Mistress Tsou and Mistress Ho to secular life. In the play, it is the refugees themselves who wish to return; they cast aside their robes almost as soon as they learn of the change in Ch'üeh's circumstances and then energetically apply themselves to preempting Mistress Wu's claims upon him. In the story, it is Mistress Wu who wants them to return so they can share the odious task of being Ch'üeh's bedmate. As they have no reason for wishing to return themselves, she must cajole and trick them back into the household.

Once they have returned, however, she establishes new procedures, approved by Ch'üeh, to reduce to a minimum the sexual unpleasantness they all must endure. Each of the wives' bedrooms is furnished with two beds on opposite sides of the room, separated by a table in the middle bearing an incense burner. Ch'üeh visits each wife's bedroom not more often than one night in three. On those nights, he shares their beds only during the brief moments necessary to the sexual act itself, and spends the remainder of the night in the auxiliary bed. He buys plenty of incense and allows the wives to burn as much as they like. Soon, each of them gives birth to a healthy child. Since none of the wives have any taste for Ch'üeh's embraces, there is no jealousy or dissension in the household. Their distaste for sex with Ch'üeh also keeps them from tempting him to overspend his vital powers and he lives on in good health till the age of eighty. Is not this good evidence, asks the narrator, that beautiful women are intended by heaven to marry ugly men?

He then advises his female readers to keep his story by their bedsides and to read it through again should they begin to grow discontented with their lot in life. If their beauty and talent have been matched with ugliness and stupidity, they can reflect that they are no worse off than the beautiful and talented heroines in his story. If on the other hand their husbands show some glimmerings of good looks or brains, they can congratulate themselves on their exceptional good fortune.

Finally, the narrator turns to his male readers and cautions them against pushing their wives to the point of desperation and rebellion through insensitive behavior, and urges them to treat their wives with the same restraint and consideration as does his hero.[21]

We may well suspect that the business of Ch'üeh's philanthropy and transfiguration would never have been brought into the plot if the requirements of the genre to which it was transferred did not urgently require it. Without this added element, there could have been no military episodes, nor could the play have ended with a festive occasion. The end of a prose story can trail indefinitely into the future of its characters' lives; the end of a drama must coincide with some particular event in those lives. In *ch'uan-ch'i* drama, nothing serves this purpose so well as the arrival of a glory-conferring decree from the emperor. The combined devices of ennoblement and transfiguration may be seen as a sort of makeshift dramatic equivalent for the gradual mellowing and amelioration of daily existence that forms the conclusion and point of the story.

The self-introductory speech of the "image-transforming" spirit at the beginning of act 28 performs marvels in the way of assuaging our impatience and incredulity by bringing the miraculous device as far as possible into line with nature and experience. The spirit comes onstage carrying an axe, a file, a wood plane, and other such tools.

After announcing his mission to the Ch'üeh household, he describes the role he plays in the world's affairs:

> If you went and told a person what I am about to do to Ch'üeh, he would no doubt laugh at you for repeating a preposterous impossible story. But when my mission is completed, people won't think the change in Ch'üeh's appearance is so strange. Every place in the world has the class of people known as poor scholars. Both their appearance and their gestures are poor and beggarly in the extreme. But the moment they become successful and enter into official service, not only does their whole spirit and manner change; even their physiognomy and complexion becomes completely different from what it was before. And this is not the only instance of such changes. The appearance of rich commoners has nothing in common with their appearance before they become wealthy. Back then they all look mean and dispirited just like all the other poor folk. There is not a single good point in their features. But after their luck changes and money comes into their hands, not only does their manner become dignified and stately; even their flesh fills out and grows fat. Surely you are not going to say that these changes are fantastic. What you must understand is that these processes of transformation do not occur because of their indulgence in eating and drinking; it is all due to my secret work as an image transformer. You must also understand that I do not bring about these changes because I am bent on flattering and placating the wealthy, as the people of the world are. It is because the accumulated merit of these people has moved the spirits that their minds broaden and their figures expand in testimony of this. There are also instances in which I visit rich people who have done unworthy things and use my tools while they are asleep to change their handsome features to ugly ones.[22]

Later, near the end of the same act, Mistress Wu observes that Ch'üeh's change is surely due to the power of the ghosts and spirits, but she observes that they may simply have been acting in accordance with some preexisting reason for the change and that what makes the event really strange is its swiftness.[23]

In addition to assuaging our naturalistic scruples, Li Yü supplies us with a great deal of metaphysical justification for the miracle in the course of depicting, in the preceding act, the conference of the spirits who effect the change. These justifications become particularly ingenious toward the end of the act, where we get to overhear some reasons for the extreme rarity of such interventions. At the same time we are incidentally presented with an extraordinarily bleak and fatalistic bit of Buddhist moralizing on the role and destiny of women. The entire passage is one of those in which the usual distinctions between the roles of author, character within the drama, and commentator become translucent. Its justifications of the ways of heaven are also justifications of the ways of artists, or at least of this artist faced with this problem; and we can overhear in these deliberations the busy ponderings of a fastidious craftsman trying to justify to himself the use of a major miraculous intervention.

The "dilemma-resolving minister" has just proposed to the other spirit officials that they petition the Jade Emperor to send down an image-transforming spirit to change Ch'üeh Li-hou into a handsome young man. Upon hearing this, the "crime-absolving minister" objects that the scheme may fail to win the Jade Emperor's approval because it will "hinder" Ch'üeh's wives. The other two spirit ministers ask how the wives could possibly be hindered by an event that could only be regarded as fortunate for them. The crime-absolving minister answers by directing their attention to the proverb I have mentioned earlier: "lovely ladies have hard destinies" (hung-yen po-ming). The meaning of this proverb, he says, is not that women first have lovely faces and as a consequence have hard destinies; rather it is because their evil actions in former lives demand stern retribution that they are condemned to be born as lovely ladies. If Ch'üeh's appearance is improved, his wives will only gain what they desire and will no longer think of repentance or the accumulation of merit for the next life. Who knows, in fact, how cruel and pitiless they may become. Therefore, God may not necessarily approve of the transformation. The other two spirit ministers agree with this reasoning, but they are still reluctant to allow such a notably beneficent person as Ch'üeh to remain in such a monstrous predicament for the rest of his life. Finally, they decide to request the Jade Emperor to allow his love for the man to extend to his three wives as well and spare them one life span's worth of karmic consequences. They recommend in their petition that the remission be granted in this one instance only and that it not be used as a precedent on future occasions. It is thus a rare, quasi-unique event that, considered as an item in the plot of a *ch'uan-ch'i* play, is a good instance of the generic criterion of "strangeness" (the etymological meaning of the term *ch'uan-ch'i*, you will recall, is "transmit the strange"). As the act-closing quatrain puts it,

> The meshes of the net of heaven have always been fine as silk;
> Only a special favor now allows its rule to be relaxed.
> The world's lovely ladies should all cry out in astonishment;
> How is it that their kind is suddenly having a run of luck?[24]

But this "strangeness" is small game indeed compared with the central strangeness of the play: the gigantic, hideous, yet obscurely positive and beneficent figure of Ch'üeh Li-hou, a figure from which all intellect and refinement recoils in shock and loathing and yet to which intellect and refinement must at length give service and submission. As in Li Yü's other plays, buffoonery and grotesque humor abound; as in *The Kite's Mistake*, grotesquerie is basic to the very conception of the play; but in *What Can You Do?* this grotesquerie is pushed to the very limits (and to modern sensibilities beyond the limits) of what the psyche can regard as comic. There is more than a touch of the horrible in it. When Mistress Tsou gets up from the nuptial bed in the middle of the night to vomit, or when Ch'üeh Li-hou, in an agony of rage and humiliation, roars out at the sequestered Mistress Tsou that he will use his money to marry someone far more beautiful than she is, the reader may laugh, but something in him cringes at the same time. And when he arrives at the scene in which Mistress Chou, badgered and bullied beyond endurance by the matchmaker and her mistress, is found hanging dead from a rafter in her room, he can no longer laugh, though the hurried machinations to which her suicide gives rise are certainly intended to be comic in themselves. This is the only one of Li Yü's comedies that forces us to contemplate with ironic detachment—almost, in fact, with flippancy—the suicide of a character who is not evil and who is of more than incidental importance to the story. Both the prose story and the play pitilessly draw the moral that her suicide is the extreme consequence of feminine rebellion against circumstance. In this work the comic mask turns out, upon examination, to be a gaily bedaubed Medusa face and laughter trails off into horror.

It is in some measure reassuring to notice that the commentator's response to the situations of the play is not altogether easy and lighthearted. It is apparently not only *modern* sensibilities that are affronted by the play's brutalities; readers in traditional times were uncomfortable with them as well. This encourages one to believe that Li Yü was partially aiming at an effect of pain, that he wishes to write a type of comedy that would to some extent wound and shock and affront the spectator. Thus, in the "general criticism" at the end of the play, the commentator observes:

> People of the world . . . cast blame on old Mr. Li for crushing fragrance, trampling on jade, eating up the moon, and destroying flowers. They say that having performances of this depressing, killjoy sort of play sets a vicious example that encourages spoilsports to go around burning zithers for firewood and boiling cranes for meat. They do not realize that that which has set the vicious example is heaven; no human being could compare with it in viciousness. And heaven has been setting this vicious example for a long time already. It is not something that only began happening today.[25]

Among the more distressing scenes in the play is the moment in act 23 showing the final collapse of Mistress Wu's plan of escape and her realization that she must return to Ch'üeh's household and learn to live with what she hates. Humiliations fall heavily and thickly upon her. Her former husband laughs at her protestations of fidelity:

> I know what is actually on your mind; you want to return because you were unexpectedly purchased by such a coarse lout of a husband. If you had married scholar Han instead, I fear that even if I came with silver to buy you back, you wouldn't necessarily be willing to return. I should really be grateful to that rustic-looking oaf for giving me an opportunity to meet you once more.[26]

Then, with Ch'üeh Li-hou looking on, he lectures her on the wisdom of submission and contentment, saying that "even if ten of you died [in protest], there would be no one to take up your cause." As she returns to the shore with Ch'üeh, her former husband's servant lectures her on the importance of the advice she has just been given and advises her never to forget it. After the servant's departure, Ch'üeh coolly informs her that instead of returning to her retreat in the library, she will begin acting as his wife at once. Hemmed in on all sides, Mistress Wu gives up the thought of further resistance. Then, in a passage that will remind English-speaking readers of the conclusion to *The Taming of the Shrew*, she turns to the female members of the audience and lectures *them* on the folly of rebellion and the wisdom of contentment. She concludes with a set of lyrics summing up what she perceives to be the meaning of her experience:

> I exhausted all my strategies and plans:
> My schemes were laid with infinite care and forethought;
> But after carrying them out I found myself still in heaven's trap
> as I was before.
> I can't overcome the meagerness of my karmic fortunes or the
> depth of my karmic sins.
> If your lot is to be born into the pink-cheeked breed,
> You needn't bother having any further dreams of romance.[27]

The commentator, as might be expected, remarks of Mistress Wu's exhortations that "seeing this play could cause all the quarreling couples in the world to return to peace and harmony," and that "its educative value is not inferior to that of the *Chou-nan* and *Shao-nan* sections in the *Book of Songs*." But then, reacting to the concluding lyrics quoted above, he observes, "These words make one's nose feel sour [i.e., they produce a tingling sensation in the nose caused by incipient tears]. One cannot bear to read them over very much."[28] Whether or not one regards this touch of pity as the last, delicate refinement of sadism, it reflects a fundamental difference between the quality of this scene and that of the scene showing the submission of Kate in *The Taming of the Shrew*, in which pity is not among the responses intended to be elicited. In fact, if we are to look among Chinese *ch'uan-ch'i* plays for a work that resembles Shakespeare's *Shrew*, *Shih hou chi (Tale of the Lion's Roar)* by Wang T'ing-na would provide a closer comparison than *What Can You Do? Shih hou chi* is a comedy about a woman who makes life miserable for her husband through her extreme jealousy. It has an episode in which she literally attaches a leash to him to insure his fidelity. Various methods are attempted to reform her, but none have lasting success. Only after she falls seriously ill and her soul, leaving her body, travels to the underworld where she is taken on a tour of all the regions of hell, does she give up the vice of jealousy.[29] In this play, as in *The Taming of the Shrew*, there is nothing complicated about the attitude we are intended to have toward the reformation of the main character. Both the jealous heroine and the shrewish heroine are spectacular misbehavers. Their reformations are corrections of extreme, disabling abnormalities. The severity and smugness of the judgements pronounced upon their insubordinacy may make modern readers wince, but this is an effect of cultural change; contemporary viewers would not have felt the attitudes implied by the conclusions of these plays to be overly severe or overly smug. We greet (or are intended to greet) their final changes of heart with an almost mechanical satisfaction. The play is done, the fun is over, the time to return has arrived.

But whatever attitude we take toward the submission of Mistress Wu, it cannot simply be one of dull satisfaction; it could not have been so even for Li Yü's contemporaries. Neither Mistress Wu nor Ch'üeh's other two wives are spectacular misbehavers; none of them are victims of crippling obsessions. On the contrary, they are all more than usually endowed with intelligence and common sense. If anyone knows what decorum demands, they do. If anyone is possessed of enough tact and intuition to live in domestic harmony, they are. But then, unexpectedly and preposterously, they all have the misfortune to fall into a marital situation of excruciating, spectacular unpleasantness. Like sensible people, they all struggle to get out of it. We are made to watch their struggles with a degree of sympathy and involvement. In Mistress Wu's case, these struggles attain great brilliance in conception and boldness of execution. But in the end, she finds herself still entrapped and discovers, gradually and reluctlantly, that her only hope of contentment lies in resignation.

The Taming of the Shrew and *Shih-hou chi* could only be made to resemble *What Can You Do?* if their conclusions were altered in the following way: the husbands, after devising a series of brilliant strategies to alter their wives' obsessions would at last realize that nothing can alter such twisted natures; that in fact all their efforts at reform and awakening have only made their wives more than ever confirmed in their original vices; and that their only hope of contentment lies in learning to submit to their shrewishness and jealousy respectively. Gradually, they would discover that it is possible to breathe and even, in a modest way, to flourish in an atmosphere saturated with these pollutants. The commentators would express some regret over their hard lots in life and blame it, with a sigh, on heaven. The introductory and concluding lyrics would inform husbands that their dreams of domestic comfort are all vain nonsense and are unsuited to their natures.

Now one may well raise the question, "Why did Li Yü not make use of some such fable as the above if he wished to write a play illustrating the value of creative compliance?" The idea would definitely not have been too bizarre for his creative intellect. His plays contain inversions of relationships far more daring than the mere idea of a husband submitting to the control of a wife. The use of a fable that concentrates on the submission of women puts him in the awkward position of preaching obedience to a set of circumstances that he does not have to face himself. It is as if an army chaplain, himself living in a safe, rear area, should preach on the beauty of courage and detestability of cowardice to a group of men who must regularly face death.

It might be argued that the amended *Shrew* plot—which, for convenience, we may call "the taming of the shrew's husband"—does in fact appear in *What Can You Do?* in the persons of General Yüan and his jealous wife. "In General Yüan," the argument would run "we in fact have a man of indubitable intellect and virtue who, far from rebelling against the tyranny to which he is domestically subjected by his wife, finds it both tolerable and expedient to submit." This is true enough as far as it goes, and it is true that the inclusion of this suggestion of male submission does have some faint tendency to balance the argument of the play. The scene of Mistress Wu's final entrapment and humiliation is in some remote sense rendered less intolerable by the fact that the person who rejects her appeal and lectures her on the duty of submission is a person who has had to take some domestic lumps (however mild in comparison) himself. But this does not alter the main thrust of the play. There are no scenes that show General Yüan passing through crises of rebellion or resignation. We are never forced to watch him squirming in defeat, compelled at swordpoint and before spectators to confess error and to assent meekly to dictums that are hateful to every element of self-regard in his nature. We may see creative obedience exemplified in various modes by Ch'üeh Li-hou, Ch'üeh Chung, and General Yüan, but the introductory and concluding lyrics speak only of correcting the behavior of women; they say nothing of the virtue of obedience in general.

In short, the entire play may be said to advocate the oppression and persecution of women. We may say, in addition, that the oppression and persecution it advocates is much more savage and much more thorough than anything that may be found in plays on the order of *The Taming of the Shrew*. What possible defense or, failing defense, what possible palliation can be found for the advocacy of such an extremely inhumane position? An appeal to the conditions of the author's intellectual environment—to the rudimentary development of certain humanitarian and egalitarian ideas—is totally futile and useless in this case. Such an appeal may excuse unconscious acceptance of inhumanity; it cannot excuse conscious glorification of inhumanity. The argument that the play is, after all, only a comedy and that it is foolish to take at face value a proposition whose only reason for existence is to provide occasion for a series of amusing scenes—this argument is worse than useless because it reduces the play to a condition of utter frivolity and makes the author into a sort of liar. A good comedist means what he says, and means it most of all when it most appears to outrage common sense and experience.

I believe there is only one possible line of defense for the manifest inequity of the play. Whether or not it is a sufficient defense, and whether or not it is a defense that actually applies in this case, remains to be seen. But the defense would run as follows: when we examine the argument that Li Yü makes for the submission of women, we notice that it belongs to a type of argument that depends for its effect of conclusiveness upon the use of a "weakest case." We have already observed that he does not trouble to portray any unusual degree of unpleasantness or rebelliousness in his female characters; that a shrew would be happier if she learned obedience to a good husband is for Li Yü too obvious for demonstration, and would do nothing to establish the generality of his proposition. Instead, he sets out to demonstrate that mild, reasonable, unshrewish women will be happier if they learn obedience to odious husbands. If obedience turns out to be good even for these exceptionally unfortunate and oppressed women, the argument says, then it must be good for all women.

Suppose, now, that a playwright is writing a play designed to

uphold not simply the obedience of women, but the value of obedience in itself; and that, as in the former case, he proceeds by constructing a "weakest-case" argument. It would do no good to this type
of argument to make much of the fact that persons belonging to
privileged classes (such as emperors, generals, or heads of households)
are benefitted by learning obedience, because it would not establish
the universality of the main proposition. There would be nothing in
this approach to shock or challenge the reader. He would dully or
complacently agree that an unlimited habit of command is bound to
corrupt anyone sooner or later, and that it is easier for powerful
figures to stay on the straight and narrow if they allow certain people
and certain principles to possess authority over them. It has all been
said a hundred times before in the dynastic histories. It has nothing
to do with *his* life. Another disadvantage is that such a figure cannot
supply very many, or very strong, examples of obedience. The full
odiousness of the virtue as felt by the practiser cannot thus be portrayed. "Downward obedience" (as listening respectfully to harsh advice, etc.) does not have nearly so much of the sting and the stench of
obedience as does upward obedience. The playwright, therefore,
draws his chief examples from as powerless and as oppressed a portion of humanity as he can find. He strives to make their situation
even more disagreeable and unjust than it usually is, and to show
even less consideration for their sufferings than is usually shown. The
more unjust their position is, the better it is for his argument. If obedience can alleviate the lot even of victims such as these, then it must
be good for other classes of humanity as well. The result of this
reasoning is a play that exhorts women to submit to their destinies
and at the same time intentionally supplies them with a destiny to
which it is even more preposterously difficult to submit than usual.

If women are actually viewed in this way in *What Can You Do?* —as
types of humanity, a special instance that illustrates the general
human condition rather than as a class apart—and if the flippancy
and harshness of the author's exhortations to submission do in fact
result from the argumentative strategy outlined above, then the appearance of bias and inhumanity that we have noted tends to disappear. The question is: what evidence is there for, and what against,
the proposition that the play should be read in this manner?

This is not the place for an exhaustive consideration of every detail
that might concern the validity of this interpretation of the play's

meaning, but a few general remarks concerning the evidence can nevertheless be made. As positive evidence, in his self-introduction Ch'üeh Li-hou laughs at "the pathetic pride of literary men," observing that though they may have "the talent of Sung Yü and the looks of P'an Yüeh . . . they are all poor wretches anyway, no match for the crude stupidity of such as I." The attitude expressed toward the aspirations of women in the introductory and concluding lyrics ("they hate the things that suit them") harmonizes with this attitude of Ch'üeh's toward "the pathetic pride of literary men." It is the business of the work as a whole to play the advocate for wealth, power, and crudity and to cast abuse on poverty, powerlessness, and sensitivity. It is what might be called a daring or paradoxical position, as it has never been adopted in any other *ch'uan-ch'i* drama, but it is a position in which the author believes he detects a considerable degree of truth. Women, as being most poor, most powerless, and most sensitive, naturally come in for the heaviest abuse in this scheme. If we take the women in the play to be the central types of rebellion and obedience (rather than a species apart), the other, nonfeminine elements of the play array themselves around their adventures in an orderly and significant way. If on the other hand we take the play to mean only that women should (as a species) know their place, the other episodes in the play (as for example Ch'üeh Chung's service to his master) lose their significance and become so much waste paper.

On the negative side, it must be said that nothing in the play *explicitly* forbids the reader from responding to *What Can You Do?* in a spirit of complacent sadism. I believe a person attuned to implications of tone and structure could not read it that way, but as many people are not going to read the play with any degree of care, implication must be considered a pretty weak defense against misreading where grave moral issues are involved. And even an attuned reader may at times suspect that the real reason the adventures of Ch'üeh's wives occupy such prominence is that their sufferings may, in a depraved sense, be pleasurably amusing to the spectator, whereas the sufferings of male counterparts would not. Read in this simpleminded way, *What Can You Do?* becomes a very cold, frivolous, and above all boring play. But it does partly lend itself to being so read.

After all factors have been considered, it must be admitted that *What Can You Do?* remains vulnerable to the charge of what is now called sexism (in Li Yü's time, this concept, to the extent that it existed, would have been included under the rubric "inhumanity": *pu jen*). But to observe that the play is sexist and, in so doing, to imagine that this term adequately expresses everything that the play is and says, is to betray a state of intellectual coarseness as grave in its own domain as the incalculably greater (because spiritual or moral) coarseness of sexism. The play is as susceptible of salvation as it is of condemnation; and the way of salvation provides, on the whole, a richer and more accurate perception of its content than does that of condemnation.

VI. Li Yü and His Critics

Comedy aims at representing men as worse and tragedy as better than in real life.
>Aristotle, *Poetics* pt. 2 (c. 322 B.C.)

The debauching of virgins and the amours of strumpets are the subjects of comedy.
>Lactantius, *Divine Institutions*, sec. 6 (c. 310 A.D.)

Comedy is the fountain of good sense.
>George Meredith, *The Idea of Comedy* (1877)

The aim of this brief chapter is taxonomic. It aims to arrive at a general characterization of Li Yü as a literary artist in terms that take account both of Chinese and of western critical categories.

When a member of one culture looks at the art of another culture, what he sees is apt to be quite different from what a member of the observed culture would see. The French valuation of Poe was different from the American and English valuation of Poe. The European valuation of Japanese wood-block prints was different from the Japanese valuation. The first Chinese novels to be translated into European languages in the late eighteenth and early nineteenth centuries were not those acknowledged masterpieces of psychological and satirical observation that we are now familiar with, but relatively humble and obscure popular romances that Chinese critical opinion has always disdained.[1]

The proper way to deal with such discontinuities of perception is not to try to eliminate contradiction by dismissing one viewpoint or the other as uninformed (for in matters of artistic judgement to be uninformed, or inappropriately informed, may at times be an advantage as well as a liability), but to attempt to arrive at a larger synthesis based on an understanding of the cultural factors conditioning the two reactions.

For readers of western background, Li Yü is among the most immediately appealing and accessible of Chinese authors. His principal qualities are all ones that are highly prized in the western literary tradition. He abounds in humor. He excels in naturalistic portrayal. He is gifted with a bizarre imagination and a knack for storytelling. Above all he was an original thinker, a man with a boldly questioning, joyously argumentative mind. Although never translated on a large scale, he was among the first Chinese authors to receive attention from western translators. In 1822, for example, John Francis Davis, an English colonial official and one of the early translators of the "obscure romances" mentioned above, published translations of the first three stories in Li Yü's short story collection *Twelve Mansions*.[2] There were other instances of early western attention as well.[3]

The Chinese attitude toward Li Yü during this period was not particularly favorable, however. Such references to his work as can be found are mostly either brief and contemptuous, or brief and harshly condemnatory. Typical of these brief notices is that of Huang Wenyang, compiler of a famous book of play summaries:

> Li Yü came from an official family and had a good education. He exhibited great intelligence from an early age and was able to compose songs and stories. He led a wandering, vagrant existence and people looked upon him as a strolling actor.[4]

When Li Yü is mentioned in passing, it is nearly always pejoratively; thus works of other playwrights are from time to time praised as being far superior to the "evil" or "frivolous" writings of Li Yü, or condemned as belonging to the same base type. In the twentieth century, Chinese critical estimates of Li Yü tend to grow longer, more attentive, and more balanced; but this is because these critics are no longer writing from a purely traditional point of view. The most favorable opinions of his work come from the critics who are most heavily influenced by western ideology, whether in the form of Marxism as in the case of Professor Liu Ta-chieh, or of western liberalism as in the case of Professor Liu Wu-chi.[5] The more traditional modern critics still include a considerable amount of condemnation in their appraisals.[6]

There is, however, one important exception to the general condemnation of Li Yü in traditional times, and that is to be found in the warmly appreciative prefatory and marginal additions to Li Yü's work made by his literary friends. It is of course no matter for surprise that these writings should be filled with praise; a writer does not after all contribute a preface to the work of another writer, still less to the work of a friend, unless he is prepared to say many good things about it. What is interesting is that these preface- and commentary-contributing friends include some fairly prominent literary figures of the time, such as the memoirist Yü Huai and the editor Tu Chün.[7] Their loyalty to Li Yü, though no doubt personally motivated, considerably complicates the picture of universal traditional disapproval of Li Yü that would otherwise exist; and while the critical observations made in these materials cannot be considered unbiased, because they are longer and more attentive they are generally more interesting than the dismissive notices one encounters elsewhere. These materials are our best indication of how a traditional sensibility was apt to perceive Li Yü when the genre of commentary demanded that the writer think favorably about his topic.

It must by now be apparent that in Li Yü we are dealing with a writer of controversial and shifting reputation. It will help us to find our way among the conflicting judgements of his work to gain some general sense of the Chinese literary terrain, a sense of the categories to which Chinese writers are traditionally assigned, and a sense of some of the assumptions and attitudes of Chinese literary criticism.

If one were forced to discover some vast, oversimplifying dual classification scheme for all Chinese men of letters, one could probably not do much better than the two categories with which the Chinese themselves are accustomed to conceive the variety of their literature: the orthodox and the untrammeled, the bound and the free. The ultimate prototypes for these categories are the rival princes of T'ang poetry, Tu Fu and Li Po, and standing behind these human figures are the complementary Chinese philosophies that they unconsciously personify: Confucianism, the philosophy of purposeful action and moral striving; and Taoism, the philosophy of acquiescence, anonymity, and escape. The orthodox writer writes with a positive moral purpose, has a preference for strict forms, tends to work and rework his lines, and aims for an effect of weightiness and complexity. The untrammeled writer conceives of himself as a "banished angel" (*che-hsien*) and is unconcerned with the moral struggle or with the success of the dynasty; his poetry reflects his union with the great impersonal forces of nature. He has a predilection for the freer forms, and aims for an effect of magical lightness and spontaneity. The orthodox figure is either in fact or in intention devoted to a life of service to the state. The circle of his moral concern extends to embrace the whole of society. The untrammeled figure holds government service in contempt and leads a wandering, somewhat vagrant, existence, either supporting himself with his pen or depending on the hospitality of relatives, friends, and patrons.

These stereotypes of course do not describe any particular Chinese author (not even the originals of the stereotypes) with any striking degree of accuracy, but they do exert a considerable influence on literary thought and practice. What we are concerned with at this point is not literary reality, but the system of reference points with which that reality is customarily measured.

We should note in passing that these two categories are entirely different from, and cannot be aligned with, western intellectual dichotomies such as Platonism versus Aristotelianism, or classicism versus romanticism. One type of poet is not more synthetic or more analytic, more abstract or more empirical, than the other type. Still less can the difference be defined in terms of the objective and the subjective: the classic artist who coolly adorns and balances, and the romantic artist who warmly explores and expresses. Both the orthodox and the untrammeled writers are subjective in the sense that they deliberately and consciously put themselves into their poems; both are concerned with their internal states. It is the quality of the self that they put into the poem that marks them as inclining to one category or the other. The untrammeled writer has the romantic attribute of relative freedom and spontaneity, but he also has the classical attribute of relative clarity and simplicity. The orthodox writer has the romantic attribute of relative subtlety and complication, but he also has the classical attribute of relative strictness and allusiveness. In short, these western categories will not help us to find our way among Chinese authors, for any Chinese author could be put in any of the categories, depending upon which qualities one chose to emphasize.

The notion of the "orthodox" and the "untrammeled" may not be very real when applied to particular cases, but it works better as a referential system for Chinese literature than does any western system. In particular, it can be observed in the two plays that stand at the beginning of the development of *ch'uan-ch'i* drama: *The Tale of the Lute* and *Romance of the Western Chamber*. *The Tale of the Lute* is the prototype of the "good play that upholds Confucian virtue." Its famous, central scenes all concern a conflict between moral principle and circumstance. In some scenes the moral principle is triumphant, as in Chao Wu-niang's persistance in devotion to her parents-in-law amid every circumstance of difficulty, ingratitude, and discouragement; in others it suffers temporary defeat, as in Ts'ai Po-chieh's reluctant submission to the power and determination of prime minister Niu. But moral effort is the common element that binds these scenes together; the common desire of the two central figures, regardless of their degree of success, is to swim upstream, to move against the current of the world and against their own more superficial desires.

Romance of the Western Chamber, on the other hand, may be characterized as a vast poetic celebration of swimming downstream. It lyrically portrays the triumph of nature and passion over duty and principle. It is the prototype of the naughty, semiillicit kind of play that bright youngsters in wealthy families read on the sly and that the court periodically sought to suppress throughout the Ming and early Ch'ing dynasties.[8] Nevertheless, its purely literary prestige (allowing for the low prestige of plays in general) remained very high; higher probably than that of *The Tale of the Lute*.

The same contrast may be observed in more moderate form in the two famous plays of the early Ch'ing, written some twenty years after Li Yü's death, that stand not far from the end of the development of *ch'uan-ch'i* drama: *The Peach-blossom Fan* and *The Palace of Eternal Life*. The former broods upon moral and historical problems and is ultimately antiromantic in attitude, though it includes the element of romance; the latter idealizes a love affair that nearly destroyed a dynasty, and is fundamentally lyrical in inspiration though it is not unconcerned with the moral and practical consequences of the love which it celebrates.

Where, then, do we place Li Yü with respect to these categories? It must be admitted at once that he does not fit either category extremely well, though he makes a much better untrammeled writer than he does an orthodox writer. He never held and, after a certain age, was never interested in holding, government office. He did a lot of travelling and often relied on patronage for support. His literary virtues are of the untrammeled sort: dash, spontaneity, facility; the ability to make sudden leaps and rushes that delight and surprise with their novelty. He was known for quickness of invention. He avoids complexity and allusiveness. His philosophy of literature is untrammeled; he valued spontaneity and originality above all other literary attributes. One of his "studio names," che-fan, means essentially the same thing as che-hsien: "banished angel."

But in spite of all this, he fails to fit in with the whole spirit and direction of untrammeledness, just as he personally failed to fit the persona of the inspired, unearthly poet-apparition wandering the earth as a stranger from celestial realms. Part of this has to do with a certain positive delight in simplicity and rudeness of expression. This in itself would not have been fatal, for the same taste had been successfully affected by untrammeled or semiuntrammeled poets of the past such as T'ao Ch'ien or Po Chü-i.

A much greater obstacle to his untrammeledness was a basic inability to be sympathetic to the untrammeled point of view. He could never have written a Romance of the Western Chamber or a Palace of Eternal Life, much less a Peony Pavilion, because he was incapable of regarding pure sensibility with enough seriousness to think it worth glorifying or indulging. Only in The Careful Couple do we find a few lines of aria lyrics imbued with intense romantic feeling;[9] and even here the point of the whole play is that the lovers in this scene do not lose their heads for each other.

Instead of the amorality of the great traditional love dramas, what you find in Li Yü's plays and stories is a steady, keen, analytic interest in the moral dimension of his characters' actions. But his morality is not the high, strenuous Confucian morality of the great orthodox plays of suffering and self-sacrifice. It is rather a practical, prudential, highly original morality that often sets itself in opposition to traditional moral judgements.

Li Yü may have been untrammeled in his philosophy of literature, but in the deeper matter of his philosophy of life he was not untram-

meled, but practical. He is much more concerned with making a living, and with making the best of his living, than he is with losing
himself for the dynasty or with losing the world for love. He measures
life and literature by the standards of this practicality.

Both the orthodox and the untrammeled modes are serious,
aristocratic, and potentially tragic in nature. They are both marked
by a freedom from mundane concerns. In both modes, the author is
thinking of an ideal so high that it transfigures the accidents of his
personal existence. The orthodox or untrammeled writer may refer to
the petty events of his daily life—he may even dwell lovingly on
them—but he does not do so in a petty spirit; he is not concerned
with the practical consequences of these events. In part he mentions
them to show how willing he is to be casual about them. His sense of
identity with the state or with humanity or with the great
naturalness is so complete that he thinks of his own discomfort or
beggary only as signs that intensify that identity by contrast. It does
not, for example, occur to him to interpret his discomfort as a sign
that he should engage in some lucrative commercial activity.

The work of Li Yü, then, is neither orthodox nor untrammeled,
but belongs to a third category that could be characterized as popular, vulgar, middle-class, trifling, pragmatic, or comic, depending on
the observer's class and culture. Li Yü is not alone in this category; it
appears early in the history of Chinese drama with the plays of Kuan
Han-ch'ing and such early ch'uan-ch'i plays as Tale of a Dog Killing
(Sha kou chi) and Tale of the White Rabbit (Pai t'u chi).The plays of
those two obscure professionals of the early Ch'ing, Chu Tso-ch'ao
and Chu Su-ch'en (one of which, Ch'in lou yüeh, Li Yü admired
enough to adorn with a set of marginal commentaries and a pair of
interpolated acts), also belong to this category, and there are many
others.[10] These plays, however, do not attract the particular hostility
and disapproval that are reserved for the plays of Li Yü.

The reason for this is probably that these other plays are genuinely
and unconsciously popular, whereas the plays of Li Yü are artificially
and militantly popular. What most probably offended his early critics
was not so much that he was vulgar or had a vulgar morality, but
that he mixed classes.

We must remember that in traditional China, artistic amateurism
was associated with esthetic distinction, and artistic professionalism
with esthetic tawdriness.[11] A gentry-member who wrote a few plays

for amusement in periods of retirement like T'ang Hsien-tsu was assumed to be exercising high artistic judgement. A commoner who wrote many plays for profit like Chu Su-ch'en was assumed to be exercising a vulgar mechanical skill. In each case, the person concerned is behaving in a way appropriate to his station and education. If there must be masterpieces to delight the cognoscenti, there must also be rougher commercial fare to delight the masses. Live and let live. There is space and sustenance for all kinds within the four seas.

The trouble with Li Yü was that he was not a pure example of either class. If he had been simply a gentry-member preaching gentryism or simply a professional practicing professionalism, there would have been no problem of acceptance. His peculiar offense was to be a gentry-member who preached professionalism. That he wrote plays and directed performances for money was not offensive; what was offensive was that he should do these things while mingling on equal terms with people in the highest reaches of society. It was offensive that he should parade his commercialism in a milieu in which it was felt to be out of place. That he wrote vulgar comedies was not offensive; what was offensive was that he should implicitly claim the status of high culture for these productions by criticizing the work of the great play-writing literati of the past.[12] His critics could have forgiven him for turning his back on his social origins and behaving like a merchant; what they could not endure without irritation was the unabashed volubility with which he affirmed the orthodoxy of his social and intellectual position in preference to theirs.

The problem was that Li Yü was creating a type of drama for which no precedent (and therefore no theoretical justification) existed. Like most innovators, he defended his newness by claiming that it was really oldness. But the spirit and outlook of his work has no close resemblance to that of any older drama in China; it could not have had, for the viewpoint from which it was written—that of a fully educated, fully articulate man of business—was altogether too new to be mistaken for something old.

This is not to say that Li Yü was the first Chinese writer to live upon his literary activities alone—Li Po and Chiang K'uei come to mind as early practitioners of that type of life, and there were many others—but he may well have been the first such figure to expect patronage and book sales to supply the expenses of a forty-member household and a private garden. Most earlier literati who were not officials still have something of the official manqué about them; they may have relied to a great extent on patronage, but they certainly did not regard themselves as go-getters or entrepreneurs. With Li Yü, however, we enter definitely into a realm of printing blocks and carpentry, business agreements and ledger books. His conversion to the world of trade was positive and total, and was not accompanied by any lingering yearning for lost refinement.

One of the chief indices of Li Yü's newness is his naturalism. Read the work of almost any earlier dramatist of the learned class, and you will be struck by the extreme formalism that marks the behavior of all the characters (other than clowns, villains, etc.) in the intervals of action and prose dialogue between arias. Even in situations that to a western reader seem to call for special spontaneity or emotion, the characters behave with the reserve, the strict adherence to pattern, of figures in a decorative frieze. This is true even of writers celebrated for their romanticism such as T'ang Hsien-tsu. His romantic abandon is expressed in the words of the arias, not in the things that the characters do or say between arias.

Though Li Yü was by no means averse to the use of friezelike patterns—probably nothing that partakes of the nature of pattern was antipathetic to his taste—he also delighted in capturing moments of unguarded spontaneity. The figures in the frieze may at any moment wink meaningfully at us, or smile sarcastically, or melt into some other familiar attitude that startles us with its resemblance to things we see in the ordinary course of domestic life.

This love of naturalistic observation was one of the things that most struck his contemporaries. In his "general criticism" (tsung lun) at the close of The Kite's Mistake, the commentator P'u-chai chu-jen (a pseudonym) praises the play for being "marvelous" (ch'i) and "new" (hsin). He then goes on to say,

> but this marvelousness resides in the most ordinary of natural principles and this newness consists exclusively of things that happen regularly. These days, plays of ox-devils and snake spirits fill the world so that at festivities and banquets, the spectators see ghosts and monstrosities all day long. It is said that this is the only way to startle people's senses. Who could have known that everyday family occurrences could furnish material for fine dramatic writing? It has never been done before. Once

this play appears, ghosts and monsters will vanish.[13]

Li Yü's famous acquaintance, the memoirist Yü Huai (1616–96), makes the same observation from a different, stylistic, angle:

> Li-weng [Li Yü] has great natural ability and many clever ideas, yet his great ability is not ponderously displayed and his cleverness does not consist of precious effects. What he so straightforwardly speaks of is nothing more remarkable than ordinary dressing and eating, yet one feels that imperial robes and embroidered vestments, dragon liver and phoenix marrow, could not surpass it. . . .[14]

Both of the above commentators point to the use of a natural style and the portrayal of everyday stituations as being distinctive features of Li Yü's writing. His work, we might say, displays a heightened concern for mimesis. Such a concern is one of the ways by which we distinguish "high comedy," that is, a comedy that inclines toward humor and satire, from a comedy that inclines toward romance. In *A Natural Perspective*, Northrop Frye points to a corresponding contrast between the comedies of Jonson and those of Shakespeare, accompanied by a corresponding contemporary response:

> He [Jonson] is never tired of insisting that serious comedy observes men and manners, in contrast to Shakespearean comedy with its "monsters," its desire to "run away from nature," and the like. In *The Return from Parnassus*, a play which makes some comments on contemporary drama from a pro-Shakespeare and anti-Jonson bias, it is said of Jonson that he is "a mere empiric, one that gets what he hath by observation, and makes only nature privy to what he indites."[15]

In short, we have seen something like this shift from romantic comedy to high or satiric comedy in the history of our own literature; it is not peculiar to China. If Jonson's imitation of "deeds and language such as men do use" does not seem as thorough to us as it apparently did to the playwright who called him "a mere empiric,"[16] we may recall that comedy, like other genres, has since tended to become steadily more tenacious in the maintenance of a realistic illusion.

Restoration comedy had already moved so far in this direction that by 1722 the critic John Dennis could see fit to defend the reputation of Etheredge by appealing to a passage from the seventeenth–century drama theorist René Rapin to the effect that "comedy is as it ought to be when an audience is apt to imagine that instead of being in the pit and boxes, they are in some assembly of the neighborhood or in some family meeting and that we see nothing in it, but what is done in the world."[17] The Italian comic dramatist and reformer of the commedia dell'arte Carlo Goldoni (1707–93) was famous for his ability to get the nuances just right in portraying the manners of his native Venice, and was fond of making such statements as "the secret of the art of a writer of comedies is to cling to nature and never to leave her."[18]

It is not surprising that in the eighteenth century the novel began to displace drama as the primary medium of comedy; its formal realism was as if designed to be applied to those detailed observations of contemporary manners that had more and more become the principal concern of comic artists.[19] An analogous process can be shown to have occurred in China. The figure who truly succeeded Li Yü, in the sense of having achieved the next logical step in the development of a comic mimesis, was not another playwright but the novelist Wu Ching-tzu (1701–54), whose *The Scholars* (*Ju lin wai shih*) is acknowledged (or should be acknowledged) to be the classic embodiment of the comic spirit in Chinese literature.[20]

Both in Europe and in China the emergence of high comedy was contemporaneous with the emergence of a new intellectual climate marked by rationalism, empiricism, and scepticism; and it is at least arguable that in both cultures the two developments may have been connected by something more than mere contemporaneity. Comedy first flowered in Europe with the revival of classical learning[21] and attained to ever-increasing dominance and variety as the outlook and methods associated with such figures as Bacon, Hobbes, Descartes, and Galileo began to hold sway over people's minds. It is surely interesting and suggestive, therefore, that Li Yü, the first sceptical Chinese playwright and the inventor of a new and very "high" kind of comedy, should have belonged to the same generation as the group of scholars associated with Ku Yen-wu (1613–82) who were the forerunners of the famous school of Han learning (*Han-hsüeh*; also called the "school of unadorned learning" or *p'u-hsüeh* and the "school of inductive research" or *k'ao cheng*). Ku Yen-wu and his group are generally credited with ushering in a new period in Chinese intellectual history by repudiating the vagueness and intuitionalism of the philosophies of Wang Yang-ming and the Sung neo-Confucianists, and insisting on such practises as the use of inductive reasoning and the testing of hypotheses in the light of all available evidence in the prosecution of historical research. These new principles led to many brilliant achievements in the fields of phonetics, etymology, historical criticism, and, especially, textual criticism during the seventeenth and eighteenth centuries. The eighteenth century, which saw the greatest development of this school, also saw the greatest development of the Chinese novel of manners.[22]

The development of comedy in China during this period, however, has one point of difference with its European development, the importance of which can scarcely be overemphasized. This was that the Chinese had no classical model of comedy to look back to; they were creating it for the first time. The Chinese development is therefore less conscious and definite (considered as comedy) than the European development. Unlike the first European comic dramatists, who modeled their work on the plays of Plautus and Terence, Li Yü had no ancient examples of comedy to refer to; nor could he defend his new version of *ch'uan-chi* drama through appeal to such classical definitions of comedy as appear in Aristotle's *Poetics* and Horace's *Ars Poetica*.

When we read *The Kite's Mistake*, we recognize it at once as high comedy and feel that we are on familiar ground. Li Yü and his contemporaries, however, were not on familiar ground. They did not look upon *The Kite's Mistake* as high comedy; they looked upon it as a *ch'uan-ch'i* play—that is, as a member of a genre characterized among other things by serious, idealistic romanticism. One begins to understand why the work might have struck contemporary readers as frivolous and why the preface writer was driven to the desperate expedient of discussing the play as an allegory of personal rejection.[23]

In the absence of an anciently recognized concept of comedy to appeal to, Li Yü's only polemical recourse was to invent his own arguments and definitions, justifying them, where possible, by appeal to the practise of earlier *ch'uan-ch'i* writers. This he does with his customary fluency and persuasiveness in the opening chapters of his essay-book *A Random Lodge for My Idle Feelings*. There is actually nothing "random" or "idle" about these chapters on drama. No western comic dramatist of any fame ever felt called upon to discuss drama so systematically or at such length; nor is there much to compare with them in China. The drama historian Aoki Masaru observes that these chapters are the most comprehensive exposition of a set of views on drama that had appeared in China up to Li Yü's time, and that the opening chapter on the structure of drama opens up an area that had previously never been discussed at all.[24] It is delightfully typical of Li Yü's optimistic, innovating spirit that in the absence of an Aristotle, he should himself become (as far as Chinese drama is concerned) an Aristotle.

As we have seen in chapter 1, these *Random Lodge* chapters contain some strongly promimetic passages that can with perfect propriety be placed beside the similar pronouncements of western comedists such as Jonson or Goldoni;[25] there are also many passages given over to emphatic condemnation of faults, such as the use of hackneyed themes and ornate language, that can be antimimetic in their tendency.[26]

Interestingly, however, this is not the aspect of drama that most concerns Li Yü. For him, the fundamental rule of play making is not so much to "cling to nature" as it is to avoid repeating the past. Plays must above all be new: new in language, new in matter, and new in concept. In defending this position, Li Yü appeals to the etymological meaning of the term *ch'uan-ch'i*:

> The reason men of old called play scripts *ch'uan-ch'i* ["to transmit the marvelous"] is that their subject matter was very unusual [*ch'i*] and particular; it was recorded and passed on [*ch'uan*] because no one had ever observed it before. This was the origin of the term. We can see, then, that nothing is transmitted [*ch'uan*] that is not marvelous [*ch'i*]. Now "marvelous" is just another way of saying "new." If a given sequence of adventures has already appeared on the stage in times past, then there can be nothing whatsoever of the marvelous in it even if a thousand or ten thousand spectators gather to view it. This is why playwrights must make sure that they grasp the significance of the expression *ch'uan-ch'i*. If you wish to write a certain play, you must first ask yourself whether the types of situations to be used in the proposed play occur in any other play scripts, ancient or modern. If they do not occur, then lose no time in transmitting it. If the opposite is true, you will just as surely be wasting your

effort as did the woman who tried to look beautiful by imitating Hsi-shih's frown.[27]

It is natural that Li Yü should have wished to establish this point, for the most striking (and potentially annoying) quality of his own work is its insistent note of originality. The refusal to use traditional, famous stories is but one aspect, and that the most trivial, of this originality. It is true that only one of his ten surviving plays depends to any significant extent upon previous materials and that even that play, *The Mirage Tower* (*Shen chung lou*), is made from a new synthesis of two hitherto unconnected tales.[28] But, as his prescriptive statements indicate, what Li Yü demanded of himself in nearly every instance was not simply to think of a new plot, but to think of a new *type* of plot: a story involving some unprecedented situation or relationship having conceptual and structural consequences affecting the whole composition. We have studied various instances of this at length in the preceding chapters. *The Fragrance-adoring Companion* (*Lien-hsiang pan*), which has not thus far been mentioned, is also a good example of the strangeness Li Yü reverenced. It concerns a triangular marriage-affinity group, the chief love bond of which is not that of the male protagonist for either of the two women, but of the two women for each other. They vow to become husband and wife in a future existence and to achieve a lesser union in their current one through marriage to the same husband.

The stories in Li Yü's two collections of vernacular language novelettes *Twelve Mansions* and *Plays Without Sound* (two of which were the prototypes for *The Amazing Reunion* and *What Can You Do?*) also make use of freshly invented plots centered upon novel situations. Their thematic elements are emphasized through such devices as arrangement in antithetical pairs, as in *Plays Without Sound*, and the organization of their plots around significantly named buildings, as in *Twelve Mansions*.

Li Yü's insistence on the importance of novelty in drama is highly idiosyncratic; he is almost the only Chinese playwright up to the early Ch'ing period who habitually devised rather than derived his subject matter. His most prominent precursor in this area, Juan Ta-ch'eng (c. 1587–1646), also liked to invent his own stories, but he never took the step of declaring novelty to be a fundamental quality of all true drama. In the preface to his *Riddle of the Spring Lantern*

(Ch'un teng mi), also titled *Ten Mistaken Identities* (Shih ts'o jen), Juan advances a half-humorous excuse for his originality:

> [the play's] subject matter is invented rather than borrowed from some popular story; such stories are also invented, so I preferred to rely on my own invention rather than that of others.[29]

The works of Juan Ta-ch'eng and Li Yü are often thought to betray similar attitudes and methods; one critic observes, for example, that the culminating offense of Juan's play *The Swallow's Letter* (Yen-tzu chien) is that it gave rise to the "vile scribblings" (e cha) of Li Yü.[30] Even more than Li Yü, Juan has a predilection for plot complications and mistaken identities. *The Swallow's Letter*, like *The Kite's Mistake*, is built around the idea of an unreasoning, airborne message bearer. The protagonist of *The Swallow's Letter* has a grotesque "shadow" figure who contrasts with him in somewhat the same way that Ch'i Yu-hsien contrasts with Han Shih-hsün in *The Kite's Mistake*. In the final acts of both plays, the leading romantic trio/couple give whimsical thanks to the airborne go-between for accomplishing its mission.[31]

The differences between Juan and Li Yü, however, are just as striking as their similarities. Juan's narrative structures tease, intrigue, or dazzle the reader through sheer mechanical complexity, while those of Li Yü bring successive aspects of a given theme or situation before the reader's attention until the subject is exhausted. *The Swallow's Letter* has three sets of complications of more or less equal importance: one concerns the swallow-borne letter of the title; another concerns a pair of paintings mistakenly exchanged and sent to the wrong people; and the third involves the fraudulent use of an examination paper. The situations to which these devices give rise are diffuse; the play cannot be summed up in a single image or idea. The complications in *The Kite's Mistake*, on the other hand, all derive from a single device, the misdirected flight to which the title refers. Moreover, each phase of the misunderstanding thus generated serves to illuminate a different aspect of a single subject: an opposition of the ideal and the grotesque as represented by the appearance, the attitudes, and the behavior of two sets of characters. The situations generated by this single opposition reflect upon each other in countless ways; one imagines flashes of insight and sighs of intellectual pleasure mingling with the ideal audience's amused smiles and startled laughter. *The Kite's Mistake*, in short, has both a theme and a fable; *The Swallow's Letter* has only a fable.

Li Yü does not explicitly discuss theme as a discrete aspect of drama, but he places great emphasis on a closely allied structural concept, *chu nao*, that appears to mean something like "primary component." In a section of *Random Lodge* entitled "Establish the *chu nao*," he states that however many characters there are in a play, all must exist for the sake of a single character, and that however many events involve this character, all must exist for the sake of a single event. This single character and single event constitute the *chu nao*.[32]

This is not quite what we usually mean, in literary contexts at least, by the word *theme*, but the practice of "establishing a primary component" nevertheless tends to result in a clarification and polarization of those moral and intellectual concerns that in western-style criticism are perceived as the thematic content of a play. In *The Kite's Mistake*, for example, the *chu-nao* is the character Han Shih-hsün as revealed through his encounter with Chan Ai-chüan;[33] everything else in the play in some way contributes to the meaning of that scene. But this encounter is itself the chief example of a confrontation of "ugliness" and "beauty" (the terms must be taken in broader than usual senses), the contest between which is the central philosophic concern of the play and which everything else in the play similarly serves in some sense to develop.

Li Yü's preoccupation with theme is another of the principal symptoms of his originality. Many of his other oddities—such as his use of invented material, his predilection for bizarre and low subject matter, his interest in naturalistic language and behavior, and his tendency to indulge in polyphonically involved plot complications—can be traced to his fascination with ideas. Of all the early Ch'ing reformulations of the *ch'uan-ch'i* concept, his was the most cerebral, even while it was among the most "vulgar." Like Aristophanes and Bernard Shaw, he is appropriately characterized as a problem dramatist, a dramatist for whom thought takes precedence over feeling; and high comedy turned out to be one of the consequences of his preoccupation with thought.

Both the subject matter and the approach of high comedy can be discerned throughout Li Yü's work in fictional and dramatic genres. Again and again, he turns to parodic and analytic portrayals of the ways his characters behave in social situations. Typical of his approach is a comic process that in the west has been a constant feature of the art ever since the appearance of Menanderean "new comedy": the portrayal of the defeat, exposure, or awakening of an inflexible or obsessed character—the type to which Jonson and later comedists applied the term "humour"—whose unreasonable or fantastic behavior conflicts with the peace of the normal human community.

One of the literary prose stories in Li Yü's collection, "The Strongman of Ch'in-huai" (Ch'in-huai chien erh chuan)[34] portrays the comic rise and fall of such a character with classic clarity and concentration. The protagonist, a local rowdy who believes himself supreme in all the martial arts, is a type comparable to one of the most ancient comic types in the western tradition: the miles gloriosus or braggart soldier of Greek and Roman comedy. His successive transformations from an obstreperous youth to a bullying tyrant to a cowering menial stripped of all martial pretensions occupy the foreground throughout, and are depicted with energy, gusto, and truth.

Another ancient western humor, that of acquisitiveness, is depicted with sharp but genial satire in the third of the Twelve Mansions stories, "The Abode of Three Dedications" (San yü lou). The story is worked out in a peculiarly Chinese fasion: the "anastrophic" reversal leading to the reestablishment of the normal society's ascendency over the aberrant society takes place only after a shift of generations has occurred in each group; the narrator, moreover, playfully ascribes this reversal of fortune to the workings of karmic retribution. Nevertheless, the fundamental oppositions of character and the burst of goodwill with which, at the close, the aberrant society is forgiven and invited to rejoin the mainstream, are the same as in any western miser or grouch comedy.

Sometimes, as in The Amazing Reunion, The Careful Couple, "The Abode of the Crane's Homecoming" (Ho kuei lou), or "A Maid Stays Faithful when the Wives Remarry" (Ch'i-ch'ieh pao p'i-p'a mei hsiang shou chieh), Li Yü's stories are designed to contrast "average insight" with "rare insight" as exemplified by the contrasting behavior of two characters or sets of characters. It is in keeping with the nature of comedy that these comparisons are as concerned with efficiency as they are with morality. [35] Sometimes the contrasted characters pursue goals that are equally egocentric; what sets the heroes and heroines apart from their doubles is the superior skill, foresight, or wisdom with which they conduct the pursuit. But even when a part of the ideal character's insight is to be unconcerned with personal advantage, it is demonstrated that his unworldliness "works"; he gains an earthly kingdom as a fringe benefit of the heavenly one. In short there is a tendency in his work—a tendency shared by all comedy—to prize success to the detriment of principle.

It is a general characteristic of human philosophy and culture to place a higher value upon virtue than upon cleverness. This is an attitude easily transposed to conceptions of class behavior; the gentleman (or as he is called in Chinese, the *chün-tzu*) is expected, in theory at least, to prize rectitude and to despise personal advantage. Any marked degree of ingenuity must therefore carry with it a flavor of ill-breeding and low character. This is perhaps one reason why, in Roman comedy and in the T'ang classical prose story, cleverness is an attribute found only in the tricky slave or wily maidservant, even though the raison d'être of the story is apt to involve the celebration of that very quality.

Li Yü does not hesitate to exploit the convention of the clever servant if the structure of a play calls for it, but the convention does not mark a periphery of his imagination; he is equally willing to endow an ideal, upper-class figure with conspicuous ingenuity if that will advance the idea of a story. Here again, we arrive at that cause of antagonism mentioned earlier in connection with Li Yü's social behavior: he mixes classes; he confuses categories.

Both in literature and in life, Li Yü epitomized the plebeian virtues of expedience, flexibility, and tenacity in the pursuit of gain. To his critics, he was doubtless the quintessential "petty man" *(hsiao jen)* held up to scorn in the Confucian *Analects*. He shows the partiality to the viewpoints of merchants and artisans that one would expect of a person who himself worked as a printer, shopkeeper, garden designer, and theatrical entrepreneur. His "Abode of Shaded Refinement" *(Ts'ui ya lou)*, for example, tells of the suffering and revenge of a bookseller gelded and sodomized by the infamous mid-Ming official Yen Shih-fan, and, as we have seen, *The Amazing Reunion* is concerned throughout with the pathetic and joyous adventures of various sympathetically conceived cloth merchants. That Li Yü demonstrates a greater regard for the prudential values associated with people of "small" spiritual character and social standing than for the traditional, grandly selfless, upper-class values of sincerity, righteousness, propriety, benevolence, and so forth can be taken as an indication of frivolity or vulgarity or decadence; but it would seem equally justifiable, as well as more productive for critical purposes, to take this attitude as one among many indications that he had found his way to a mode of thought new in traditional China—the mode of high comedy.

It is perhaps not surprising that high comedy should have appeared in China at this time; social and intellectual conditions had arrived at a state of ripeness for this development. What is remarkable is the assurance with which Li Yü treads the new territory, and the directness with which he addresses even the most alien classes of readers. There is nothing tentative or half-formed about his work and very little that is narrow or local in his outlook. It is remarkable how little it is necessary to make allowances for the distance of his culture from ours. Worlds have passed away and new ones succeeded them since he lived, but the voice with which he addresses us remains as fresh and natural as that of a near neighbor; the moral problems he considers continue to be the ones we encounter in the ordinary course of our daily lives. While he belongs in a deep and special sense to all members of the great and ingenious civilization that nurtured him, he belongs as well to all members of the worldwide civilized community. Just as surely as Aristophanes, Chaucer, and Molière are ours, he is ours.

Appendix: Act Summaries of Discussed Plays

The Paired Soles

1. Starting Off (*Fa tuan*)
The stage manager enters and sings (1) an aria on the novelty of using actors to portray actors, (2) an aria summarizing the plot, and (3)
an octosyllabic quatrain on the tenacious persistence in virtue of four
characters: the male protagonist, the female protagonist, a good
spirit, and a good official in hiding.

2. Exciting News (*Erh jeh*)
The male protagonist, T'an Ch'u-yü, enters and introduces
himself. He is from Hsiang-yang district in Hupei. He is without
parents, connections, or marriage prospects, and wanders from place
to place writing lyrics for actors to support himself. He has recently
come to San-ch'ü, Chekiang. He had planned earlier to go with
friends to see a *ch'uan-ch'i* performance now in progress, but his
writing work prevented him. He goes to the performing area and arrives just as the audience is breaking up. A group of spectators pass
by engaging in bawdy horseplay. Ch'u-yü then sees two of his friends
approaching and waits to ask them about the performance. His
friends rhapsodize on the beauty of Liu Chiang-hsien, and one of
them invites Ch'u-yü to go with him to the next performance to see
for himself. Ch'u-yü agrees.

3. Forming a Troupe (*Lien pan*)
Liu Chiang-hsien enters and introduces herself. She and her hus-

band Liu Wen-ch'ing belong to the Dancing Rainbow Troupe. She
has made a fortune as an actress through her skill in exploiting rich
admirers. Her daughter Liu Miao-ku is just old enough to begin
learning the trade herself. Chiang-hsien calls her in and tells her that
she is to join a new juvenile acting troupe being formed by her father.
She then gives her detailed instructions on how to make money as an
actress. Miao-ku is horrified at her mother's cynically acquisitive
principles and attempts to refute them. Miao-ku's father Liu Wen-
ch'ing enters, and reports that he has found young recruits to fill all
the role-types in his new troupe except for the role of "big painted
face" or military villain. He makes a sign announcing the vacancy to
paste to their entrance gate. At her father's request, Miao-ku thinks
of a name for the new troupe: the Jade Sprouts. She consents to join
it on the condition that she will not be asked to study immoral plays.

4. An Unusual Taste (Pieh shang)

Ch'u-yü and his friend arrive at the performance area early and
wait for the actors to arrive. They see Chiang-hsien and Miao-ku pass
by without stage makeup. Ch'u-yü is unimpressed by the mother but
is deeply struck by the daughter. They discuss the relative beauty of
the two but fail to see each other's point of view. Ch'u-yü secretly
resolves to follow Miao-ku after the performance and seek a way to
enter her family.

5. Dealing with Bandits (Pan tsei)

Mu-jung Chieh enters. He is a general opposing an army of bandits
in the vicinity of T'ing-chou prefecture, Fukien. He yearns for a simple pastoral life, but his many requests for permission to retire from
service have all been refused. Passing by his home on military
maneuvers, he stops to talk with his wife. They discuss the military
situation (it is deceptively calm just then) and the pros and cons of
retirement. As they are conversing, a despatch arrives from the front
announcing that the bandits are about to attack. Mu-jung Chieh
assures his wife that he has two cunning strategies in reserve, one for
dispelling the attack and one for destroying the remaining bandits in
their hiding places in the mountains. His wife urges him on
humanitarian grounds not to enact the second plan.

6. Deciding on a Scheme (Chüeh chi)

Ch'u-yü wrestles with his repugnance at the thought of becoming an actor and at length steels himself to apply for the vacant position in Miao-ku's troupe.

7. Entering the Troupe (*Ju pan*)

Liu Wen-ch'ing (Miao-ku's father) admits Ch'u-yü to the troupe and introduces him to the other players and to the new drama instructor. The drama instructor establishes the disciplinary rules by which the troupe is to be governed. Miao-ku lingers on stage at the close of the act and reflects admiringly on Ch'u-yü, whose marital intentions she has perceived. She resolves to accept him as a husband.

8. Bandits Issue Forth (*K'ou fa*)

Shan Ta-wang, the bandit chief, enters leading his forces. He is half-man, half-beast, and has the face of a tiger. He orders his assault troops (consisting of wild animals) to attack. Mu-jung Chieh (see act 5) routs the attacking animals by frightening them with land mines. Remembering his wife's admonitions, he refrains from pursuing the bandits into the hills.

9. A Grass-script Letter (*Ts'ao cha*)

T'an Ch'u-yü enters. He has been in the acting troupe for a month, but has not had a single opportunity to speak to Miao-ku. He writes her a love letter, using hard-to-read cursive script and recherché expressions to protect its contents from accidental discovery. He plans to roll the letter into a pellet and slip it into Miao-ku's rehearsal script when an opportunity occurs. Included in the letter is a request that Miao-ku urge her father to change his role to that of leading man.

10. Promoted to Leading Man (*Kai sheng*)

The drama instructor has the various actor trainees sing arias from plays they are supposed to have memorized. The leading man fails this test and in consequence suffers a beating. He is further humiliated when, at the instructor's request, Ch'u-yü gives a perfect rendition of the aria he failed to remember. After the instructor leaves, the leading man attempts to get even with Ch'u-yü by assaulting him physically and inciting the other actors to join in. Miao-ku tries to part the combatants and Ch'u-yü, taking advantage of her proximity, slips the rolled-up love letter into her hand. After order is restored, Miao-ku answers the letter by composing and sing-ing a couple of sets of aria lyrics. The other actors have no idea that she is not simply rehearsing a part in some play. In her response, she advises Ch'u-yü to pressure her father into changing his role by threatening to leave the troupe. After the rehearsal, Ch'u-yü gains an interview with her father and the drama instructor in which he suc-cessfully follows her advice.

11. Empty Intimidation (Hu wei)

Ch'ien Wan-kuan, a wealthy rural landlord, prepares to greet a group of visiting district officials. He is a former lover of Liu Chiang-hsien. Hoping to renew the relationship, he decides to hire her troupe to perform for the officials on a festival day honoring the water spirit P'ing-lang hou. He then learns from his houseboy that Chiang-hsien has a beautiful daughter who is also an actress. He decides to get a look at this daughter at the earliest opportunity.

12. Luxurious Hiding (Fei tun)

Mu-jung Chieh (see acts 5 and 8) has just received his long hoped-for permission to retire. With his wife and two servants, he hastens to a mountainous wilderness in Chekiang where he hopes to pass the rest of his life incognito as one of the common people.

13. Throwing Money Around (Hui chin)

Ch'ien Wan-kuan (see act 11) has now seen Miao-ku perform and is inflamed with a determination to enjoy her charms. He persuades her mother Chiang-hsien to sell her to him for a thousand silver taels.

14. Coerced by Profit (Li pi)

Chiang-hsien tells Miao-ku of her purchase by Ch'ien Wan-kuan. She is to be turned over to him immediately after the performance on the water spirit's festival day. Miao-ku protests that she is in a sense already married to Ch'u-yü, but her mother dismisses her objections with incredulous contempt. Left alone, Maio-ku's first impulse is to kill herself without delay, but then it occurs to her that she can incor-porate her suicide into the festival performance and thus give public expression to her grievances before dying.

15. Accompanied in Death (Chieh wang)

Ch'ien Wan-kuan comes to watch the festival performance and to take custody of Miao-ku. She has chosen to portray Ch'ien Yü-lien, the heroine of *The Thorn Hairpin* (*Ching-ch'ai chi*), in her own adaptation of the act (number 26) in which that figure jumps into a river to avoid a forced marriage. The stage upon which she performs is an outdoor one overlooking a river. When the moment of the heroine's suicide arrives, she throws herself into the river beneath the stage. Ch'u-yü then runs onstage, announces that Miao-ku was his wife, denounces Wan-kuan for causing her suicide, then jumps into the river as well. Wan-kuan runs away in alarm. The spectators form a search party to seize him and bring him before a magistrate.

16. Protected by a Spirit (*Shen hu*)

The water spirit P'ing-lang-hou (see act 11) transforms the drowned couple into a pair of flatfish and orders his fishy underlings to swim with them to Mu-jung Chieh's wild retreat. There, after being drawn ashore in a net, they will regain their original forms.

17. Collecting a Profit (*Cheng li*)

Various factions scheme and struggle for possession of the thousand silver taels that Wan-kuan gave to Chiang-hsien as a betrothal price. It eventually ends in the hands of the district magistrate.

18. Return to Life (*Hui sheng*)

Mu-jung Chieh's servant spreads his net for fish and, with his wife's help, pulls the flatfish lovers ashore. They cover the fish with their rain cloaks and go offstage to summon Mu-jung Chieh and his wife. When they return, the lovers have resumed their human forms. They are revived and made to tell their history. They can't recall what happened after their suicide, but Mu-jung Chieh and Ch'u-Yü conclude that they must have been rescued by P'ing-lang-hou. Mu-jung Chieh extends shelter and hospitality to the lovers and promises to arrange a wedding for them.

19. A Village Wedding (*Ts'un chin*)

Ch'u-yü and Miao-ku are married and treated to a rustic wedding banquet.

20. Emerging by Stealth (*Ch'ieh fa*)

The bandit chief Shan Ta-wang announces that he has been rebuilding his forces since his defeat by Mu-jung Chieh and that he has hired a skilled strategist to plan his next attack. The strategist enters and advises him to attack at once.

21. A Farewell Gift (Tseng hsing)
Mu-jung Chieh advises Ch'u-yü to leave the mountains and compete in the forthcoming provincial examinations. He gives him money and wine for the journey. The old and young couples part.

22. A Wicked Scheme (Chüeh chi)
Shan Ta-wang announces that his bandit forces have won many victories and taken many cities but have yet to attain full security. He has recently heard with alarm that the court is trying to locate his old adversary Mu-jung Chieh in order to restore him to his former command. His new strategist suggests that they find someone who resembles Mu-jung Chieh sufficiently to impersonate him, and pay him a thousand gold pieces to follow their instructions. He will "hide" where he can easily be found when the searchers come to their area. After being "reinstated," he will surrender his forces to the bandits. Since Mu-jung-Chieh is well known for his skill, word of his surrender will bring all the other loyalist generals to their side and victory will be within their grasp. Shan Ta-wang objects that no man looks like another down to the last detail, but the strategist assures him that the local officials will be so harassed that they will be eager to suppress their doubts and accept anyone who promises to stand between them and the enemy.

23. Feigned Hiding (Wei yin)
The impersonator of Mu-jung Chieh enters disguised as a fisherman. He is discovered and brought back to prefectural headquarters, which is immediately surrounded and attacked by the bandits. The imposter assumes command, makes a show of resistance, then surrenders his forces.

24. A Glorious Honor (Jung fa)
Ch'u-yü returns from the capital to Hsiang-yang district (Hupei) where Miao-ku is waiting for him. He has just passed the highest (metropolitan) examination and has been assigned to T'ing-chou prefecture (Fukien), the bandit-ridden area formerly governed by Mu-jung Chieh where the recent imposture has taken place. He and

Miao-ku want to express their gratitude to the water spirit P'ing-lang-hou by arranging to have another play performed at his shrine on his next festival day. They fear they might not be able to accomplish this in time, as the date is only a month away. Ch'u-yü sends a servant ahead to the shrine to hire actors and entrusts him with a letter to "fisherman Mo" (Mu-jung Chieh).

25. Assuming a Spirit's Identity (*Chia shen*)
Mu-jung Chieh receives Ch'u-yü's letter, which informs him of his examination success and his appointment to T'ing-chou, and that he and Miao-ku will shortly stop by to visit him on their way to his new post. Mu-jung Chieh's wife urges him to help Ch'u-yü in the performance of his new duties by telling him about the characteristics of the people and officials of T'ing-chou. Mu-jung Chieh wants to do as his wife suggests, but is reluctant to reveal his identity as a former official. He at last hits on the idea of writing a little book of advice that he will slip into Ch'u-yü's luggage during his visit. He will affix the name of the water spirit P'ing-lang-hou to the book so that when Ch'u-yü discovers it, he will think the book is another instance of the spirit's protection.

26. Transferring a Pamphlet (*I ts'e*)
Ch'u-yü and Miao-ku visit Mu-jung Chieh and his wife. They try to persuade the old couple to live with them and share their prosperity, but Mu-jung Chieh insists on his firm attachment to the wilderness. Upon their guests' departure, Mu-jung Chieh and his wife ride out with them on the little boat that takes them to their awaiting ship, and find an opportunity to slip the little book into their luggage.

27. Engaging Actors (*Ting yu*)
The servant sent ahead by Ch'u-yü recites a poem on the mysterious efficacy of spirits. P'ing-lang-hou has postponed the date of his festival a month by causing heavy rains to fall (the festival celebrations occur outside, so it cannot be held in the rain). The servant fortuitously runs into a couple of actors belonging to the former troupe of Ch'u-yü and Miao-ku. From them he learns that Miao-ku's mother Chiang-hsien now plays the leading male roles. He engages the troupe for the spirit's postponed festival and prepares to hasten

back to his master with the news.

28. An Ingenious Reunion (Ch'iao-hui)

Ch'u-yü and Miao-ku, now a couple of lofty status, glide by boat toward the temple outside which the play is to be performed. Wanting to test Liu Chiang-hsien's feelings, Ch'u-yü instructs the actors to perform the act (number 35) in The Thorn Hairpin in which the hero Wang Shih-p'eng offers prayers and sacrifices to the soul of his (presumedly) dead wife. Liu Chiang-hsien, in the role of Wang Shih-p'eng, gets through the first four arias, then breaks down and calls out to her (presumedly) dead daughter by name. Ch'u-yü and Miao-ku soon afterwards announce their presence and a turbulently emotional reunion occurs. A servant of Ch'u-yü then enters and informs him that bandits from the mountains have just plundered T'ing-chou, where Ch'u-yü is to take up official residence. Ch'u-yü directs Miao-ku to live with "fisherman Mo" (Mu-jung Chieh) until peace returns. The servant also produces the little instruction book, which he has just found in the luggage. Ch'u-yü examines it, grasps its intent, and marvels at the attentive beneficence of the spirit.

29. Cautioning a Magistrate (P'an yüan)   An elder of T'ing-chou prefecture enters, from whom we learn that Ch'u-yü has been in office for three months and has won the allegiance of the local inhabitants through wise government. Ch'u-yü has also collected a fresh military force and is about to lead it in an expedition against the bandits. Three additional elders join the first in an attempt to persuade Ch'u-yü not to risk exposing himself in battle. Ch'u-yü is politely inflexible.

30. Informing the Throne of Victory (Tsou chieh)

The impersonator of Mu-jung Chieh appears, and announces that he intends to observe the forthcoming battle and quietly slip away if the bandits get the worst of it. He exits. With the aid of the little book's advice, Ch'u-yü routs the bandits, cuts off their retreat, burns their mountain refuges, and captures their chief Shan Ta-wang. He then asks for the traitor who surrendered his forces to the bandits. His men reply that he slipped away. One of his generals then volunteers to go in search of the traitor. He has heard a report from Chekiang of a man in the mountains who resembles the traitor.

31. A Mistaken Arrest (*Wu ch'in*)

Mu-jung Chieh is arrested as a traitor by Ch'u-yü's general. His wife and Miao-ku (who is living with them) try unsuccessfully to dissuade the general and are likewise taken into custody and conducted to prefectural headquarters. Mu-jung Chieh (who has no idea of the events which led to the arrest) fumes over Ch'u-yü's ingratitude.

32. A Frightening Reunion (*Hai chü*)

Ch'u-yü is shocked to hear that the traitor is none other than his former benefactor, but he is determined not to allow his personal sense of obligation to impede the performance of his duties to the state. His inquiries appear to confirm the guilt of Mu-jung Chieh, as all the functionaries and citizens of T'ing-chou identify him positively as their former military governor. Ch'u-yü has already sentenced him to execution and offered him a last cup of wine when Mu-jung Chieh startles Ch'u-yü by revealing his authorship of the strategy booklet. Ch'u-yü then recounts what he believes to be the facts of Mu-jung Chieh's past official career, whereupon it becomes clear to Mu-jung Chieh that someone has assumed his identity. Ch'u-yü then has the bandit chief Shan Ta-wang brought in and Mu-jung Chieh, acting on Ch'u-yü's instructions, tricks him into a confession of his dealings with the imposter. The friends are reconciled and the wives are called in. Mu-jung Chieh resists an appeal to come out of hiding and instead persuades Ch'u-yü and Miao-ku to join him in hiding at the end of Ch'u-yü's term of service.

The Amazing Reunion

1. The Source of the Lyrics (*Tz'u yüan*)

The stage manager enters and, assuming the author's identity, expresses shame over the defects of his last eight plays and apologizes for venturing to add a new one to the list, but implies that the new one will at least be an improvement over the others. He then outlines the plot and sings a closing quatrain on the personal qualities of the four chief characters: the goodness of Yao K'o-ch'eng, the intelligence of Ts'ao-shih, the wisdom that is really stupidity of Yao Tung-shan, and the astonishing good luck of Yin Hsiao-lou.

2. Questions Asked in a Dream (*Meng hsün*)

Yao K'o-ch'eng enters and introduces himself. He has no money, no wife, and no parents, but it is only the lack of parents that really afflicts him. It pains him that he cannot even offer sacrifices to a portrait of his parents because he has no memory of how they looked. He often dreams, however, of a little house with a second-floor bedroom that seems to be his childhood home, but the dream always comes to an end as he approaches the house. It is getting late so he goes to bed, hoping to dream and see the house again. The night watchman's drum sounds offstage. K'o-ch'eng's dreaming soul enters and approaches the house, which is open and unlocked, with water set out in cups and incense in a censer, as if the occupants might be back at any moment. K'o-ch'eng's soul questions a neighbor, an old man sitting in an adjoining apartment, who, taking him for a ghost, testily informs him that the house was his (K'o-ch'eng's) when alive. He directs K'o-ch'eng to look at his old toys in the chest by the bed, if he does not believe this. K'o-ch'eng goes to the chest and removes clay figurines and toy horses, sticks and cudgels, drums and cymbals, and little swords and flags. He realizes that all of these objects were once his childhood playthings. As he plays thoughtfully with the toys, he suddenly remembers (or believes he remembers) that his father was a cloth pedlar and that he left him a jade ruler as a keepsake. He wonders why the ruler is not in the chest. The old man tells him he is wrong; the ruler was not his father's gift, but something he got later. He must nevertheless preserve it carefully for it will later prove the key to his marriage. The old man refuses to say more, though K'o-ch'eng repeatedly asks him where his parents live. Soon afterwards he awakens and puzzles over the old man's remarks about the jade ruler. He has been attracted to the beauty of the daughter of his neighbor to the east, but has had to keep out of her way to avoid suspicion. He resolves to wait and see if the prophecy is fulfilled.

3. Discussing a Son-in-law's Adoption (*I chui*)

Yao Tung-shan (the next-door neighbor of Yao K'o-ch'eng) enters in casual attire. He is from Szechwan. He is a *chin-shih* and has served the reigning dynasty in many high official capacities, but retired several years earlier because of disorders and dangers at court. Now, in order to avoid dangers arising from the rebellion of Li Tzu-ch'eng (who has been eating, rather than hiring, former officials) he has fled to Hankow, where he is posing as an itinerant doctor. He has adopted the common-sounding name of Ts'ao Yü-yü. He lives with his wife and an adopted daughter. He has no heir, for his only son died in childhood. He hopes to acquire an heir by marrying his adopted daughter to someone who will be willing to take his surname and act as his son. He and his wife and daughter discuss the problem. Tung-shan suggests that they need to find a capable young fellow (as opposed to a timorous scholar) who might be of some use in helping them escape from bandits. He has a person in mind whose surname is already the same as theirs and who has no family. He is thinking, of course, of the young man who lives next door. His wife approves, but worries that the young man is said not be be a true descendant of the Yao stock, but to have been purchased by the Yaos at the age of three or four for a few pieces of silver. Tung-shan tells her not to worry: "Magic fungus is without roots and fine wine is without a source." He must test the young man first, however, to make sure he is not a mere bookworm and is good at dealing with worldly affairs.

4. The Test of Adversity (*Shih chien*)

In pursuance of his goal, Tung-shan pays a neighborly visit to K'o-ch'eng and advises him to give up the study of books. "In times like these, there are only three professions to follow: those of the magician, the craftsman, and the pedlar. A magician or a craftsman can earn enough to eat even if he loses all his property; a pedlar, on the other hand, grows to be familiar with the countryside, so he knows where to hide and by what route to escape. Though it is the lowest of the three trades, it is still something that anyone can do without losing face." K'o-ch'eng responds that he knows nothing of magic or crafts but is sure he can be a pedlar, for his (adoptive) father used to sell cloth in the Sung-chiang region. The problem is that he has no capital to start out with. Tung-shan offers to lend him some money to use as capital in order to see how he makes use of the opportunity.

5. Quarreling Over an Inheritance (*Cheng chi*)

Yin Hsiao-lou enters in casual attire. He is an old man who lives in Yün-yang prefecture, Hupei. Because of his services to the state, he has received the hereditary rank of battalion commander in the Imperial Guard. His family has had but one heir for several generations. When a young child, his only son went out to play with a group of other children and never returned. As their area was troubled by tigers at that time, Hsiao-lou and his wife have long believed that their son must have been caught and eaten by one. Many friends and relatives have advised Hsiao-lou to adopt an heir, but he hasn't come to a decision as yet. His wealth is well known in the area, so he is afraid that the local people will all have selfish motives for desiring to become his heir. He therefore suggests to his wife that he go on a journey to seek prospective heirs who know nothing of his financial circumstances.

Just then two visitors, a cousin and a neighbor, come to his house, each accompanied by a son and a servant. Each tries to persuade Hsiao-lou to adopt the son he has brought along. Soon the two visitors are quarreling with each other over their respective claims and Hsiao-lou has to pull them apart. Each parent orders his son to come forward and give Hsiao-lou a son's obeisance. Hsiao-lou dashes away so as not to receive the bows. When he returns, the two parents press gifts of wine and meat on him. Hsiao-lou protests that he has vowed to abstain from wine and meat to do penance for being childless. The two visitors take their leave, reciting regretful exit poems. This experience strengthens Hsiao-lou's resolve to go on an heir-seeking journey. He decides to leave the next morning and not worry about procedures until he is on his way.

6. Inscribing a Handkerchief (*Shu p'a*)

Ts'ao-shih enters. She is the adopted daughter of Yao Tung-shan (see acts 3 and 4). She is unhappy about the excessive caution which prompts her foster father to test the abilities of Yao K'o-ch'eng before accepting him as a member of the family, and worries about the dangers he will face as a travelling merchant. She feels that since her parents have already expressed a wish that they marry each other, and since the times are dangerous, it might be justifiable for her to arrange a secret meeting with K'o-ch'eng in order to exchange marriage vows. She at length decides to write him a message on a handkerchief to avoid the shame and suspicion of a meeting. She selects the first poem in the *Book of Songs* as her love message, but makes a slight alteration in it, so as to avoid the appearance of praising her own beauty. She puts the handkerchief in her sleeve, so she can throw it over the fence at the first good opportunity.

7. Fumes of Rebellion (*Ch'uang fen*)

Four rebel generals enter in succession and introduce themselves. The first most likes to kill fat men; he uses their thick hides for drumskins. The second most likes to kill young scholars; he uses them as "fresh meat for sour soup." The third most likes to kill women; he pickles their lower quarters "to add flavor to tasteless vegetables." The fourth most likes to kill beautiful young girls; he likes to listen to their pretty screams as he drives the knife home. They have come together to meet with their commander in chief, the late-Ming rebel Li Tzu-ch'eng. This figure, blind in one eye, enters with his entourage and introduces himself, singing of his imperial ambitions and of his sudden rise to prominence. He then puts his four generals in charge of various armies which are to be deployed in four of the major geographical divisions of China. He tells his generals to provision themselves along the way and instructs them in the four methods of getting supplies: strictly requisition all granary supplies; make a clean sweep of the people's belongings; harshly interrogate all high officials to gain their hidden wealth; and capture a lot of women in order to collect ransoms or, failing that, to sell them.

8. Mute Betrothal (*Mo ting*)

Yao K'o-ch'eng is about to leave on his cloth-selling expedition when he sees Ts'ao-shih lingering near the bamboo fence that runs between her house and his. She drops the inscribed handkerchief over the fence and retires. K'o-ch'eng picks it up, perceives that it is a proposal of marriage, and is overjoyed. By way of reply he inscribes another poem from the *Book of Odes* on his jade ruler and leaves it in a crack on the other side of the fence. Ts'ao-shih picks up the ruler and realizes that the poem inscribed on it implies a promise of marriage. From this time on the two consider themselves engaged, though they have not spoken a word to each other.

9. Hanging up a Placard (*Hsüan piao*)

Yin Hsiao-lou (see act 5) enters. He has travelled through countless cities without meeting a son to his taste. He has just arrived at an inn in Sung-chiang and has been trying hard all night to think of a good scheme for inducing someone without parents to consider becoming his son. He suddenly hits on the idea of making a sign offering to sell himself as a father for the price of ten taels. He makes the sign, stands back and admires it, and addresses a prayer entrusting the comfort of his declining years to it.

10. Breaking up a Disturbance (*Chieh fen*)

Yin Hsiao-lou erects his sign in a little-frequented street and sits on a mat to await purchasers. He soon attracts two young men who heap taunts and abuse on him and at length start hitting and kicking him. K'o-ch'eng, who is out on a sight-seeing stroll, is attracted to the scene by the sound of the young men's taunts and Hsiao-lou's appeals for help. K'o-ch'eng orders the attackers to desist, demands to know the reason for their behavior, and delivers a stiff lecture on the duties of the young toward the old and helpless. The young men slink away. Left alone with Hsiao-lou, K'o-ch'eng questions him further and, gaining a favorable impression of his character, decides to enter into the bargain and purchase him as a father. Instead of handing the money over to Hsiao-lou in the street, however, K'o-ch'eng proposes that they both retire to a nearby tavern where they can talk some more and acknowledge their new relationship to each other with fitting decorum.

11. Buying a Father (*Mai fu*)

The two young rowdies enter with a servant. They are still seething with contempt for the strange old man they wanted to beat up and the strange young man who insisted on stopping them. They repair to a tavern to have a few drinks. They are seated on a balcony, from which they see "the two crazy people," Hsiao-lou and K'o-ch'eng, enter and take a table on the ground floor. The rowdies wonder incredulously if they could actually be carrying out the old man's transaction. The first young man suggests that they watch the pair closely; if they don't complete the deal he will do nothing; but if they do complete it he will play a practical joke on them. He will have the servant dress in his own clothes and pretend to be a wealthy young man. The servant will act as if he also wants to buy Hsiao-lou as a father and will offer to raise the price. If the servant manages to buy him, they can accuse Hsiao-lou of swindling a member of their household, and send him before a magistrate who will have him beaten within an inch of his life. "Won't that be smashing good fun?"

In the meantime, K'o-ch'eng, instead of merely paying Hsiao-lou the ten taels, turns all his money (sixteen taels) over to him, so that Hsiao-lou, as head of the household, will have complete jurisdiction in managing their income and expenses. The servant then enters in flashy attire and tries to purchase Hsiao-lou at double the price, but is rebuffed. After making several attempts to interest the pair in becoming related, first to his mother, and then to his sister, he departs.

K'o-ch'eng then pays a son's obeisance to Hsiao-lou and asks his name and where he is from. Hsiao-lou doesn't want to tell K'o-ch'eng his true name and place of residence until he has tested his character, so he makes up answers, saying that his name is Yi Hsiao-lou and that he lives in the provincial seat of Hukuang province. K'o-ch'eng takes it as a good omen that (as he believes) they come from neighboring cities in Hukuang province. He proposes that he take Hsiao-lou's surname as his own. Hsiao-lou doesn't want to make K'o-ch'eng adopt a false surname, so he persuades K'o-ch'eng that in this case, since the son was the purchaser and the father the person purchased, it should be the father who takes the son's surname. Hsiao-lou pays the bill and they leave the tavern.

Meanwhile, the young rowdies are infuriated at having "expended a fisherman's care in vain," and are at a loss to understand the behavior of the eccentric couple. They conclude that they have witnessed a prodigy of nature that portends the fall of the dynasty, and resolve to cast their lot with the rebels. "Since a son can buy a father, officials should follow suit and sell their princes."

12. Capturing an Old Woman (*Lüeh yü*)

A rebel commander enters with his men. They have come to Yün-yang, where they are searching houses for captives and booty. They enter the house of Yin Hsiao-lou, seize and interrogate his wife, dig up the cellar for buried wealth, and carry her off as a captive. The men mention to their chief that there is a chest full of child's toys in a little upstairs room. This they leave behind as having no value.

13. Guarding against Disgrace (*Fang ju*)

Ts'ao-shih enters, trying to think of a way to protect herself against rape in the event of capture by rebels. She has an idea. Her foster father has been supporting the family by practicing medicine, and she has often watched him prepare compounds. She has noticed that he never dares to touch croton oil beans. When the oil of this bean is swallowed, it produces violent diarrhoea; smeared on the skin, it results in ulcerated sores which, though horrible in appearance, pass away after an interval. With the aid of the beans she can make the rebels think she is a leper. She decides to carry K'o-ch'eng's jade ruler with her as well, so that if the beans fail, she can commit suicide with it. She fetches the two items and addresses a prayer to the beans to act as her talisman against rape. A clash of drums and metal offstage announces the approach of the rebels. Her parents fly from the house, calling to Ts'ao-shih to disguise herself and follow them. She burns some beans, smears the oil on her face, and lies down to await her captors.

14. Discussing Return (*Yen kuei*)

Hsiao-lou awaits the return of K'o-ch'eng, who has just gone out to gather news of the rebels. K'o-ch'eng returns and reports that the rebels have burned the capital and are sweeping across the coun-tryside unopposed. Hsiao-lou suggests that they return home at once. K'o-ch'eng replies that he has just been looking at boats with a view to buying return passages for themselves and their supplies. Unfor-tunately there are so many people clamoring for passage that the boatmen will only carry people; they won't carry merchandise. If he leaves his stock of cloth goods behind, he will have nothing to repay his creditor (Yao Tung-shan; see act 4) and they will both suffer hunger. Hsiao-lou then explains that he is actually a wealthy man with a hereditary position and that he has hitherto concealed his identity and pretended poverty in order to test K'o-ch'eng's loyalty. He urges K'o-ch'eng to return with him at once and not waste another thought on his trunks of cloth. They are now of no more concern to him than "a single hair in a carpet." Hsiao-lou promises not only to set him up financially, but to find a wife for him as soon as they reach home. K'o-ch'eng hastily tells him that a match is already arranged for him in his native town of Hankow, though the betrothal gift has not yet been given. As they will have to pass through Hankow anyway, he can stop off there and complete arrangements for a wedding. Hsiao-lou assures him that he has enough travelling money to pay the betrothal gift and to take the bride back with them. He tells K'o-ch'eng to gather their baggage so they can leave the next day.

15. Preserving Chastity (*Ch'üan chieh*)

The rebel general in charge of Hukuang province examines the captured women that are brought in by his subordinates and is attracted to Ts'ao-shih in spite of her sores (see act 13), and in spite of her warnings that her disease is contagious. In his eager desire, he puts his hands in her sleeves and gets oil on his skin and, sniffing and licking the "fragrant perspiration" left on his palms, swallows some oil as well. His face and hands swell up, he is seized with abdominal cramps, and his advances are soon interrupted by frantic dashes to the privy. He at length gives up the attack: "Enough, enough, enough! I have no predestined affinity with that woman! Lead her away at once! Get ransom money for her or sell her! Don't take her in to see me again! My stomach aches like fury! I've got to sit on the privy again!"

16. Separated en Route (*T'u fen*)

Hsiao-lou and K'o-ch'eng have been sailing back from Sung-chiang for half a month and are drawing near home. They sing arias describing the wild and desolate scenery through which they have passed. Hsiao-lou advises K'o-ch'eng to stop alone at Hankow to complete the marriage arrangements; he himself wants to continue straight home, for he is worried about his wife. K'o-ch'eng can rejoin him later. Just then a boat hand announces that they are almost at Hankow. Hsiao-lou and K'o-ch'eng are startled ("why didn't you let us know before?"), and hurriedly request the boat master to lower the sails so a person can go ashore. The boat master protests that they can't put up with such a delay when the wind is so fine, but consents to stop on the condition that the party concerned debarks immediately. Hsiao-lou hurriedly gives K'o-ch'eng a hundred taels for a betrothal gift and some odd silver for travelling expenses. He still has some last-minute advice, but the boatmen push K'o-ch'eng ashore and the boat resumes its journey before he can say what is on his mind.

A short while later Hsiao-lou suddenly realizes that in the hurry and confusion of K'o-ch'eng's sudden debarkation, he forgot to tell K'o-ch'eng his real name and address. Fearing they may never meet again, he frantically tries to lower the sails himself, so he can run back and find K'o-ch'eng; but he is quickly overpowered and roundly scolded by a group of irate passengers. Finally a passenger who is kinder than the others takes him aside and asks what his problem is. He advises Hsiao-lou to post signs announcing his true name and address in all the intersections through which K'o-ch'eng might pass. This suggestion alleviates Hsiao-lou's distress and allows him to finish the journey calmly.

17. Exchanging Confidences (*P'ou ssu*)

Mme. Yin (see act 12), now one of a large group of women held captive by the bandits, is attracted by the demeanor of a young fellow captive who keeps much to herself and who appears to be suffering from some disease. This captive is of course none other than Ts'ao-shih, K'o-ch'eng's fiancée. Mme. Yin treats her kindly, establishes a friendship with her, and gradually elicits from her an account of her previous circumstances and experiences.

18. Converting Stock to Rations (*Pien hsiang*)

Two rebel commanders enter. They have been put in charge of selling the captured women to get money for rations. They decide to enclose the women in burlap bags and sell them strictly by weight so as to get rid of all their stock, the ugly as well as the beautiful. They also decide to ask their commander to announce a cessation of killing and robbery for one month, so as to create a favorable climate for commerce.

19. Devastation (*Ching hsien*)

K'o-ch'eng returns to the village where he and Ts'ao-shih used to live, and finds the whole area deserted and burned to the ground. A beggar happens by and kneels before him in supplication. K'o-ch'eng sees that the beggar is an old neighbor, Mr. Chang, who used to be a substantial householder worth two or three thousand cash. From Mr. Chang, K'o-ch'eng learns that Ts'ao-shih has been taken captive and that her parents have fled. Mr. Chang asks K'o-ch'eng why he weeps at this news and learns the history of their betrothal. He is unable to tell him where the bandits have taken Ts'ao-shih, but he has heard that they intend to sell their captured women at Hsien-t'ao market. Perhaps Ts'ao-shih would be among them. "If you really love her, you can risk your life and go there; but if you can take her or leave her, I advise you to calm down and marry someone else." K'o-ch'eng thanks him, gives him a silver tael, and sets out for Hsien-t'ao market.

20. Following Traces (*Chui tsung*)

A servant of Yao Tung-shan (see act 3) enters. His master has resigned his office and left home with his family to avoid the disorders, leaving him behind to look after the house alone. A special decree has come down from the court making Tung-shan assistant secretary of war and commander in chief of the bandit-extermination campaign. A high official with many men and horses arrives at Tung-shan's house and demands that Tung-shan be brought out to hear the decree announcing his appointment. The servant says he has no idea where his master is and suggests that they try putting signs up or burning charms. The official is enraged and threatens the servant with execution for obstructing an official decree. Terrified, the servant kneels and volunteers that he has heard that Tung-shan is in Hankow, where he is posing as a doctor. The official orders the local magistrates to post a report to the emperor, and prepares to travel to Hankow to find Tung-shan. The servant offers to lead the way.

21. Hearing a Decree (*Wen chao*)

Yao Tung-shan and his wife arrive at a resting point in their flight from the rebels, and consider where they ought to go. Deciding in favor of their native place in Szechwan, they purchase passage from a boatman who promises to take them as near to their destination as the water routes will carry them. Aboard the boat, they sing many

arias describing the war-devastated scenes through which they pass.
They at length meet a boat going in the opposite direction carrying
the official search party led by Tung-shan's servant. Tung-shan
kneels and hears the decree of appointment. He knows that the appointment will almost certainly end in his own defeat and death, but
he nevertheless takes command in a spirit of zealous determination.
Upon coming to a place where a direct overland route to the capital
intersects the water route, he has horses and palanquins prepared
and sets out for the capital at once.

22. Astonished at Age (Ch'a lao)

The bandits set up their market. They have decided to get rid of the
old and ugly women first, and prepare four women for sale by putting
them in bags. The first is fat; the second, thin and ailing; the third,
lame and humpbacked; and the fourth (Mme. Yin), old. Two customers enter. The first picks the bag containing the fat woman and is
charged a high price, as the women are being sold by weight. He at
first claims to be unable to pay in full, but hastily meets their
demands when the bandits threaten to cut some flesh from his purchase. The second customer chooses the thin and ailing woman, is
charged a low price, and overpays the bandits by a tael. The bandits
offer him "an extra item" in return, which proves to be the head of a
small child. The customers hurry away with their purchased women.

K'o-ch'eng enters with another customer. They had both wanted
to turn away when they found that the women were being sold in
bags, but they discovered that no one is allowed to leave the market
grounds without making a purchase. They have no choice, therefore,
but to try their luck. The third customer chooses the lame and humpbacked woman. She is borne off on his shoulders, cackling with
delight at not having to limp around anymore. K'o-ch'eng chooses
Mme. Yin. He gapes in astonishment when he removes the bag and
finds he has purchased an elderly woman who, in refined tones, begs
him to treat her considerately. A bandit, thinking that K'o-ch'eng is
having second thoughts, brandishes a knife menacingly and yells at
him to take his purchase away. K'o-ch'eng responds, "There is no
need to trouble yourselves, gentlemen; I'm used to taking old merchandise. I am not reluctant to accept her; I just want to think of a
way to settle her comfortably." He departs with Mme. Yin and the
bandits close up their market for the day.

23. Grief of Separation (*Shang li*)

Yin Hsiao-lou has returned to his deserted home in Yün-yang. He grieves over the loss of his wife and adopted son, and suffers pangs of vain remorse over having misled the latter.

24. Acknowledging a Mother (*Jen mu*)

Moved by tenderness and respect for the old woman he has purchased, K'o-ch'eng proposes to her that they address each other as mother and son. In the back of his mind, he also imagines that she will prove useful to his adopted father as a concubine. Mme. Yin's feelings of astonishment and suspicion at K'o-ch'eng's suggestion at length yield to gratitude. In order to repay his kindness, she tells him of a beautiful young woman among the captives whom he can purchase and marry if he returns to the market at once. The young woman carries a long sticklike object in her sleeve that he should be able to feel through the bag which encloses her. Realizing that this young woman may be Ts'ao-shih, K'o-ch'eng seizes his purse and hurries off to the marketplace again.

25. Quarreling over a Purchase (*Cheng kou*)

K'o-ch'eng arrives at the marketplace with two other customers and finds there is only one bag left to be sold. While the other two customers wrangle, K'o-ch'eng feels the bag and finds that it is indeed the one he wants. He makes an offer, but the bandits are inclined to sell the woman to one of the other customers, because he was the earliest to arrive and bid. In despair, K'o-ch'eng tries to dash his brains out. Annoyed at this show of emotion, one of the bandit draws a knife and prepares to behead K'o-ch'eng, but another bandit hits on the idea of having the woman in the bag select her purchaser. The woman chooses K'o-ch'eng. K'o-ch'eng thinks it unwise to untie the bag in the marketplace, lest the others become aware of the extent of his good fortune. He therefore hires a couple of rebel soldiers to help him carry the bag to his temporary lodging.

26. Gaining a Wife (*Te ch'i*)

Mme. Yin anxiously awaits K'o-ch'eng's return. K'o-ch'eng arrives with the bag and at once rewards and dismisses the rebel soldiers. He fumbles eagerly at the knot, but cannot get it undone. Unable to restrain his anxiety any longer, he asks the woman if she is Ts'ao-shih and is answered by a voice that asks if he is K'o-ch'eng. Thus assured, he tugs at the knot again and it comes undone immediately. When Ts'ao-shih emerges from the bag, Mme. Yin is amazed to see that the couple embrace and weep. K'o-ch'eng wonders why Ts'ao-shih looks ill and Ts'ao-shih is amazed to see the old woman who befriended her in the bandits' camp. Explanations are exchanged and Ts'ao-shih acknowledges Mme. Yin as her mother-in-law.

K'o-ch'eng informs Ts'ao-shih that there is now an assistant military secretary in charge of the bandit-extermination campaign who is said to resemble her stepfather. He cannot believe that the two are the same, however, since her stepfather was a commoner who sold herbs for a living. Ts'ao-shih explains that her stepfather was really a great official in hiding. Now that he has resumed his official career, they will have no further financial anxiety. K'o-ch'eng worries that Tung-shan may not be willing to accept a commoner for a son-in-law now that he has been elevated to a high position. Ts'ao-shih assures him that his fears are groundless. She explains that Tung-shan desires to make him his son and heir, and that he loaned him capital in order to test his resourcefulness. K'o-ch'eng explains that he can't become Tung-shan's son since he has already been adopted by another person.

Mme. Yin mournfully recalls her husband's journey to find a son. K'o-ch'eng comforts her and bids everyone to sleep well so they can set out for his father's house in the morning. Ts'ao-shih writes a letter to her stepfather telling him where she is.

27. Hearing Family News (Wen hao)

Yao Tung-shan and his wife receive Ts'ao-shih's letter and are overjoyed to learn that K'o-ch'eng has ransomed her from the bandits and that they are now married as they had planned at first. Tung-shan is distressed, however, to observe that K'o-ch'eng is referred to in the letter as their son-in-law rather than as their son. It is not only that this mode of address goes against his plan to adopt K'o-ch'eng; he and K'o-ch'eng have the same surname (Yao). "How can a marriage be contracted between families of the same surname? It is a matter of the gravest moral and ritual importance." Tung-shan instructs his servant to cut the words "son-in-law" out of the letter and return them to K'o-ch'eng, telling him that mode of address is extremely inappropriate and that he must strictly remember to change it in the future. He further instructs the servant to tell the couple that he will shortly be crossing through their area with his divisions, and will stop to meet them then.

28. All Avenues Exhausted (*T'u ch'iung*)

K'o-ch'eng has arrived at the provincial seat of Hukuang, which is where Yin Hsiao-lou told him he lived. He seeks directions to his house from passersby while Mme. Yin and Ts'ao-shih wait in the boat. The people he asks are all certain that no such person lives in their city. From the last person he questions, K'o-ch'eng learns that the provincial examinations are about to be held. He considers trying his hand at them.

29. A Series of Shocks (*Tieh hai*)

On the boat, where they are awaiting K'o-ch'eng's return, Mme. Yin advises Ts'ao-shih to get made up so as to look like a bride when K'o-ch'eng calls for them to meet his father. Ts'ao-shih retorts that she has already been a bride for several days. It is Mme. Yin who should adorn herself to be ready when the bridal palanquin arrives. She then explains to Mme. Yin that K'o-ch'eng intends to have her marry his father. Mme. Yin indignantly protests that she comes from a great family and that her husband is still alive.

K'o-ch'eng returns to the boat and notices Mme. Yin's displeasure, but fails to understand it until Ts'ao-shih explains the old woman's opposition to remarriage. K'o-ch'eng then tells how he failed to find anyone who knew the name or whereabouts of his father. Perhaps they have been misled after all. He wonders where they can stay. Ts'ao-shih is confident that they will soon be able to stay at her step-father's house, where they will enjoy great honor and luxury.

The messenger that K'o-ch'eng sent to Yao Tung-shan enters, boards their boat, and delivers Tung-shan's cryptic message of displeasure at the use of the term *son-in-law*. Ko-ch'eng takes this to mean that Tung-shan is unwilling to take a commoner like himself into the family. He worries about the future of their marriage. Morever, they now have no home to go to.

At this point, Mme. Yin offers to take them to her home in Yün-yang. Her husband is a gentry-member with no offspring who would like nothing better than to adopt a son. K'o-ch'eng eagerly accepts her proffered hospitality, but explains that he cannot become her husband's son because he already has a father. He decides to delay his departure long enough to take the Hukuang provincial examinations. Ts'ao-shih in the meantime writes another letter to be given to her father when he passes trough the provincial capital, telling him where they are travelling and asking him why he feels as he does.

30. Leading the Way (La yin)

The servant of Yao Tung-shan enters, moaning from a beating he has just endured. When he and his master arrived at the provincial seat of Hukuang, his master sent him out to find K'o-ch'eng and Ts'ao-shih. He could find no trace of them anywhere, and in consequence suffered twenty blows and was ordered to find them within three days on pain of death. As he stands bemoaning his lot, K'o-ch'eng's messenger enters with Ts'ao-shih's letter. The servant brings the letter to Tung-shan, who resolves to set out for Yün-yang at once. K'o-ch'eng's messenger wants to go on ahead and inform the couple of Tung-shan's approaching visit, but the servant entreats the messenger to wait and accompany them as a guide. He has already suffered one beating for failing to find the young couple, and would be unable to endure a second.

31. An Amazing Reunion (Ch'iao chü)

Yin Hsiao-lou is "wearing out his eyes" gazing into the distance, hoping for K'o-ch'eng's arrival. As K'o-ch'eng approaches Mme. Yin's house, he is stupefied to see his adopted father call out to him from the bank. "Why should he be here rather than in the provincial seat of Hukuang?" Hsiao-lou hurries aboard and embraces K'o-ch'eng, weeping; then, catching sight of his wife, he embraces her and weeps. K'o-ch'eng and Mme. Yin are astonished at each other's behavior. K'o-ch'eng draws Mme. Yin aside and asks her why she is willing to embrace his father the moment she lays eyes on him when, before, she was unwilling to marry him. Mme. Yin in turn asks K'o-ch'eng why he is willing to embrace her husband the moment he lays eyes on him when, before, he was unwilling to accept him as his father. Hsiao-lou breaks into the discussion, exclaiming, "My son, regaining you alone would in itself have been a joy as vast as heaven! How did you manage to bring my old wife with you as well? How can I not die of joy!" The nature of the coincidence that has occured then begins to dawn upon the other three, who can scarcely contain their excitement and pleasure as their comprehension grows. After Mme. Yin, Ts'ao-shih, and K'o-ch'eng tell Hsiao-lou all that has happened, everyone repairs to the house and performs the rites of mutual recognition. Hsiao-lou and Mme. Yin then lead the young couple to the stairway that goes up to the little second-floor room where they had their own child years ago. It has remained empty for fifteen years, but now it is to serve as a bedroom for the young married couple.

32. The Original Dream (*Yüan meng*)

K'o-ch'eng and Ts'ao-shih mount the stairs to their new bedroom, which is pleasant, fresh, and airy. K'o-ch'eng does a double take. The room is somehow utterly familiar to him. He then realizes that this is the room he dreams of visiting night after night. He tells Ts'ao-shih of this and worries that their present happiness may be only another of his dreams. In order to prove to her that he knows the room, he tells her that there is a chest of toys behind the bed and accurately predicts what she will find there upon opening it. Ts'ao-shih, thoroughly astonished by now, calls her parents-in-law to the room. The sight of the toys reawakens Mme. Yin's grief for her dead child. The old couple are at a loss to explain the phenomenon of the dream and suppose that their child's soul must have attached itself to K'o-ch'eng in fond remembrance of his old home. It is Ts'ao-shih who guesses that Hsiao-lou's boy was not eaten by a tiger after all, but was kidnapped by someone and sold to the Yaos in Hankow. She says that everyone in Hankow knows (though K'o-ch'eng does not) that the Yaos bought him for a few taels of silver from a stranger who was passing through the area. Hsiao-lou then excitedly asks K'o-ch'eng if his left foot has an extra toe. This is in fact the case, and it is thus ascertained that K'o-ch'eng is none other than the child that the Yins lost years before.

33. Squabbling over an Heir (*Hua ssu*)

Yao Tung-shan arrives at Yin Hsiao-lou's house in Yün-yang with his wife and his divisions, and tempestuously disputes Hsiao-lou's claim to be K'o-ch'eng's father. The men make no progress in reaching an understanding; but while they argue and bluster, Mme. Yin quietly takes Mme. Yao aside and explains what has happened. Mme. Yao then pacifies her husband and everyone assumes his proper role.

A messenger arrives, announcing that K'o-ch'eng has passed the provincial examination in the fourth place. This is the third honor conferred upon him in the same day, for his father and father-in-law have each procured a title for him as well. The play concludes amid rejoicing and valedictory musing.

The Kite's Mistake

1. The First and Last (*Tien mo*)
   A *mo* enters and declaims (1) a *tz'u* on the role of errors in human destiny, (2) a *tz'u* summarizing the plot, and (3) an exit quatrain consisting of paradoxical formulations of contrasts within the play.

2. New Year's Congratulations (*Ho sui*)
   Han Shih-hsün pays his New Year's respects to his foster parent Ch'i Pu-ch'en and his son Ch'i Yu-hsien. As soon as Ch'i Pu-ch'en leaves to return a New Year's call, his son Ch'i Yu-hsien complains that he hasn't seen a woman in more than a year and urges Han Shih-hsün to go with him to the local pleasure houses. A group of prostitutes arrive at the house and pay their New Year's respects to Ch'i Yu-hsien. Han Shih-hsün holds himself aloof.

3. Strife in the Ladies' Quarters (*Kuei hung*)
   General Chan Wu-ch'eng introduces himself. His wife is deceased, but he has two concubines, Mistress Plum and Mistress Willow, each of whom has a daughter. Mistress Plum and her daughter Ai-chüan eavesdrop as Chan Wu-ch'eng sits talking with Mistress Willow and her daughter Shu-chüan. Overhearing some uncomplimentary remarks about Ai-chüan (who is ugly and ill-bred), the eavesdropping pair burst in upon the group and a quarrel between the concubines ensues which General Chan is powerless, as usual, to resolve. General Chan is called away to quell a barbarian rebellion in Szechwan. Before his departure, he instructs a servant to have a partition built to separate his quarreling wives. Mistress Plum will live to the east, Mistress Willow to the west.

4. Farewell at the City Outskirts (*Chiao chien*)

Ch'i Pu-ch'en sees off his friend General Chan at the city outskirts. Chan entrusts Ch'i with marriage of his daughters in the event that he does not return.

5. Training for Warfare (Hsi chan)

A Man barbarian chief enters, followed by his multitudes. He plans to conquer China through elephant warfare. His troops perform maneuvers at his command. The cavorting elephants are played by actors.

6. Constructing a Kite (Hu yao)

Ch'i Yu-hsien enters and complains lengthily about the character of Han Shih-hsün, whom he considers a killjoy and a bookworm. He orders his servant to glue together a kite, take it to Han Shih-hsün to decorate, and bring it to him at the city outskirts.

7. Inscribing a Kite (T'i yao)

Han Shih-hsün enters and complains of the character of Ch'i Yu-hsien, whom he considers a spoiled young man who ignores both his own improvement and the care of his father's property. Ch'i Yu-hsien's servant interrupts Han Shih-hsün in the composition of a poem with the request that he decorate the kite. Han protests that he has no colors with which to make a design, but finally, at the servant's urging, he paints his poem in black upon the kite, adding a final couplet to suit the occasion: "There is no longer any place on earth where I can bury my sorrow, so I will write it on a kite and send it to heaven."

8. Composing a Response to the Kite (Ho yao)

The servant meets Ch'i Yu-hsien at the city outskirts. Ch'i flies the kite, singing that the "stinking poem" on it will make God send down a host of heavenly warriors to destroy all poets. They exit, flying the kite.

Mistress Willow enters, followed by her daughter Chan Shu-chüan. The kite falls into their courtyard. Mistress Willow has her daughter answer the poem on it with a harmonizing poem on the reverse side. A servant from the Ch'i family comes and reclaims the kite. When Chan Shu-chüan learns of the kite's return, she is upset that her poem will be seen by a strange young man and tries to recall the Ch'i family's servant, but he has already disappeared.

9. Giving Instructions to the Kite (*Chu yao*)

Ch'i Yu-hsien returns home and tells Han Shih-hsün of the mishap with the kite. Han Shih-hsün advises him to join him in working at his studies rather than to worry about the kite. Ch'i Yu-hsien falls asleep over his books and can't be shaken awake.

The servant returns with the kite. Han Shih-hsün inspects the harmonizing poem on the reverse side, marvels at its skill, and wonders who could have written it. His servant Pao-ch'in tells him that there is a "daughter number two" in the Chan family with great poetic gifts. To conceal his find from Ch'i Yu-hsien, Han Shih-hsün has Pao-ch'in replace the answering poem with fresh paper. Ch'i Yu-hsien then wakes up and, seeing that the kite is back, runs off to resume flying it.

Han Shih-hsün takes out the harmonizing poem again and wonders how he could convey a poem hinting at marriage to its author. Pao-ch'in is confident that he can make a second kite fall into her courtyard, which is very spacious. Pao-ch'in advises him to identify himself only as "a son of the Ch'i family," because people these days are only impressed by wealth and power and would pay no attention to a poor and isolated person. Also, if they took offense, they would not dare to complain because of the Ch'i family's status. Han Shih-hsün enthusiastically agrees to this and sets to work composing the poem, with which he takes great pains, as Pao-ch'in glues together another kite. Pao-ch'in returns with the kite and Han Shih-hsün reads the completed poem. He then addresses the kite, urging it to a successful completion of its intermediary role.

10. Requesting Troops (*Ch'ing ping*)

Chan Wu-ch'eng arrives in Szechwan with his military secretary. He finds the officers' positions filled with aged, weak, and cowardly incompetents who have bought their rank and now request demotion and replacement to escape danger. Enraged, Chan Wu-ch'eng orders them to perform their duties or suffer the consequences prescribed by military law. He further finds that the rank and file have been reduced to debility and sickness through the supply hoarding and grain peculation of their superiors. His spy reports that the rebelling barbarians are numerous, fierce, and skilled in elephant

warfare. Chan Wu-ch'eng strives to create an appearance of strength
to fool the enemy and sends his military secretary to the capital with
an urgent request for additional troops and officers.

11. The Kite Makes a Mistake (*Yao wu*)

Han Shih-hsün enters with Pao-ch'in carrying the kite, observing
that he has now become as foolish as Ch'i Yu-hsien. He is about to
have Pao-ch'in cast the kite, when he catches sight of Ch'i Yu-hsien
in the distance coming towards them. Pao-ch'in goes to head him off,
leaving Han Shih-hsün to cast the kite. When the kite is just over the
middle of the Chan residence he lets go of the cord. The wind blows
it into the eastern courtyard. Feeling sure that is where the Chans'
second daughter must live, he retires to await developments.

Chan Ai-chüan enters with her maid intoning a "languishing beauty just awakened from slumber" poem. The kite lands in their courtyard. The maid retrieves it and tells Chan Ai-chüan how just the
other day a kite, also with a poem on it, fell into her sister's side of the
house. She tells how Chan Shu-chüan wrote a harmonizing poem on
the reverse side and how a servant from young master Ch'i (Ch'i
kung-tzu) came to reclaim it the same day. Chan Ai-chüan exclaims,
"If that one of hers was the seventh son's [*ch'i kung-tzu*], then this one
of mine must be the eighth son's!" The maid replies, "No, it's not the
ch'i that means seven; he is the son of Lieutenant Governor Ch'i, our
father's old classmate." Chan Ai-chüan enthuses over the qualities of
the terrific young fellow who can write poetry and likes to fly kites as
well. She thinks it is a pity that when the kite fell on her sister's side
of the house, her sister responded only with a poem instead of
something a person could eat or use. If it had fallen on her side, she
would have given at least a jade clasp or a gold pin in return for the
sender's affection.

The maid observes to Chan Ai-chüan that her speech reveals she
has men on her mind. Ai-chüan answers that she is, after all, of mar-
riageable age and all her acquaintances (Chang on the east side and
Li on the west side) are married or having children. She gets shivery
all over at the thought of a handsome young man. The maid offers to
act as her intermediary when someone comes to reclaim the kite if
Ai-chüan will give her a matchmaker's fee. Ai-chüan promises to give
her two sets of clothing and a gold pin after the first meeting.

The maid then explains that the kite must have been sent by the same young man who sent the first kite in hopes of receiving another reply from Shu-chüan. She advises Ai-chüan to assume her sister's identity because Shu-chüan is known for her poetic ability and people would not believe that Ai-chüan was the author of the harmonizing poem, and because if gossip of the affair leaked out, people would blame Shu-chüan instead of her. Ai-chüan agrees to this and urges her maid to act quickly before Shu-chüan beats her to the goal.

12. Impersonating a Beauty (*Mao mei*)

The gatekeeper of the Chan house enters, reciting a poem on the injustice of hereditary determination of social position. Having nothing much to do, he falls asleep. Chan Ai-chüan's maid enters. In order to get rid of the gatekeeper she wakes him up and sends him to town to procure a (ludicrously) long list of toilet items for Ai-chüan. She takes his place at the gate. Pao-ch'in appears to ask for the kite. The maid expresses mock astonishment at the frequency of kite errands. "Our house must be a storage chest for kites." Pao-ch'in says that he doesn't know why, but those kites just seem to have legs; they always wind up going to her house. The maid arranges to have Han Shih-hsün come to the gate just after the first watch (8:00 P.M.) so that her mistress can give him her reply to his poem in person. Pao-ch'in protests that his master is not courageous, but the maid assures him that she will see that everything goes smoothly.

13. Startled by Ugliness (*Ching ch'ou*)

The gatekeeper returns so laden with purchases that he compares himself to a street vendor. Ai-chüan's maid takes his purchases inside. The gatekeeper wonders complacently if Ai-chüan will reward him with a goblet of wine when she sees what fine purchases he has made. The maid returns, finds fault with each of the items, and orders him to go exchange them if he wishes to avoid a beating. The gatekeeper exits, grumbling and sighing, and the maid again takes his place at the gate.

Han Shih-hsün comes up to the gate after the sounding of the first watch. It is pitch-dark and he is terrified of being mistaken for a thief. Trying to locate each other, he and the maid collide in the dark. After being led in by her, he has a private interview with Ai-chüan. He cannot see her face in the dark but is astounded and revolted at the vulgarity of her conversation. The maid brings in a lantern. After

one look at Ai-chüan's face, Shih-hsün realizes he has made a terrible
mistake and flounderingly attempts to withdraw from the situation as
Ai-chüan tries to force him to go to bed with her. Finally, catching
sight of the maid from a distance, he says, "Oh no! The mistress of
the house is coming!" Ai-chüan releases him and he collides with the
maid again. After escorting him out, the maid returns to Ai-chüan to
collect her go-between's fee, but she is instead roundly scolded for
spoiling the affair "just when things were starting to get interesting."
Ai-chüan retires for the night tormented by unfulfilled desire.

14. Sent to the Examinations (Ch'ien shih)
    Ch'i Pu-ch'en enters in everyday attire and announces his inten-
tion of seeing Han Shih-hsün off on his journey to the capital to take
the examinations. He exits.
    Han Shih-hsün enters. He is still reacting to the shock of his
meeting with Chan Ai-chüan. He resolves to laugh at the incident
rather than try to understand it, and reflects that Ai-chüan's maid
was actually his benefactor; if she hadn't brought about the rendezvous, he might have married Ai-chüan on hearsay only. He resolves
for the future never to listen to hearsay and to avoid insisting on marrying a girl from a powerful and distinguished family.
    Ch'i Pu-ch'en and Ch'i Yu-hsien see Han Shih-hsün off on his trip
to the capital.

15. Strengthening the Fortifications (Chien lei)
    The Szechwan barbarians attack the city in which Chan Wu-
ch'eng is stationed. Chan Wu-ch'eng "strengthens the fortifications"
by disguising three of his best men as Kuan Yü, the planet Jupiter,
and the planet Mars respectively and stationing them at strategic
points along the wall where, through a combination of boldness and
the use of their assumed personae, they turn back a ladder assault, a
tunnel assault, and an artillery assault. The barbarian chief orders his
horde to kowtow and placate the "gods." Feeling that he can make
no headway against a city with so much supernatural protection, he
abandons the attack and leads his men elsewhere.

16. Terrorized by a Dream (Meng hai)
    Han Shih-hsün enters in formal attire followed by a lodgings at-
tendant carrying brush and inkstone. He has just returned from tak-

ing the examinations. That day, the emperor personally questioned the candidates on whether a strategy of pacification or extermination should be used on the *Man* barbarians of Szechwan. Shih-hsün set forth the dangers of "nourishing tumors" and elaborated a plan for putting down the rebellion. He believes that his arguments are fit for practical application, and hopes that the emperor will employ him in their execution. He has the attendant show him to bed. Alone, he beseeches God to grant him a vision of a beautiful woman in a dream. Upon falling asleep, he dreams that the horrid Chan Ai-chüan and her maid come to pay him a visit. Shih-hsün's anguished protests as the two drag him toward a bed attract the attention of some night watchmen who take him before a local magistrate. Shih-shü tries to explain that he was being attacked by the women, but the magistrate, impressed by the material evidence of the kite bearing Shih-hsün's calligraphy, believes Ai-chüan's claim that Shih-hsün tried to seduce and rape her. The magistrate has his attendants drag Shih-hsün away for a beating. Just at this moment, Shih-hsün is awakened by the arrival of messengers carrying the news that he is now a *chuang-yüan*, the examinee with the highest score, and is to proceed immediately to an imperial reception.

17. The Go-betweens' Quarrel (*Mei cheng*)

Two professional matchmakers of the capital, Iron-foot Chang and Swindle-heaven Li, arrive at Shih-hsün's gate, anxious to procure a *chuang-yüan* for their clients. Catching sight of each other, they at once begin to quarrel, recalling each other's failures and swindles as they trade scurrilous insults. At the height of the quarrel, Shih-hsün's servant emerges from the house and tells the matchmakers that his master will not consent to any marriage without first seeing the bride. The go-betweens agree to appear in public with their clients the next day. Shih-hsün is to indicate his acceptance or rejection by a nod or shake of the head.

18. Arduous Selection (*Chien p'ei*)

Shih-hsün goes on a tour of the capital city to appraise its beautiful women. The matchmakers appear on balconies with four different women in turn but Shih-hsün finds fault with each of them and has his servant reject them with a shake of the head.

19. Discussing a Marriage (*I hun*)

Ch'i Pu-ch'en enters. He worries that the behavior of his son Ch'i Yu-hsien is growing ever more dissolute. He feels that the only solution is to get him married. Since he has been entrusted with the responsibility of the Chan daughters' marriages, he decides to match them with Ch'i Yu-hsien and Han Shih-hsün, pairing the elder and ordinary Ai-chüan with his son and the younger Shu-chüan, known for her talent and beauty, with Han Shih-hsün. He recalls, however, that if Han Shih-hsün should happen to pass the examinations, he might get married to someone in the capital. He therefore resolves to postpone negotiating Shih-hsün's marriage until his return, but to see about his son's at once. He sends a matchmaker to Mistress Plum, the mother of Ai-chüan.

A messenger arrives and announces Han Shih-hsün's having become a *chuang-yüan*. Ch'i Pu-ch'en orders him to take congratulatory flowers to Han Shih-hsün. He meditates upon his now fulfilled responsibility to his dead friend, Han Shih-shün's father, and upon divine retribution and reward.

The matchmaker enters and announces Mistress Plum's agreement to the marriage of her daughter Ai-chüan to Ch'i Pu-ch'en's son. Ai-chüan can't be sent to Ch'i Pu-ch'en's house until her husband returns to determine the makeup of her bridal trousseau, but Ch'i Yu-hsien can go to the Chans' house to give the engagement gifts and consummate the marriage.

20. Marching off against the Southern Tribes (*Man cheng*)

Han Shih-hsün enters, complaining about the terrible dearth of beauty in the capital. He scarcely saw two or three passable women out the the hundreds he looked at during his recent, imperially sanctioned tour of the city. He has heard that Yangchow has many beautiful women and would go there except that he has been recommended to lead a force against the rebellious tribes of Szechwan. He frets about his bad luck in finding a mate, singing that even if he is not yet withered and grizzled when his army returns, his "spring desires" will have faded.

A messenger enters and reads an imperial edict ordering Han Shih-hsün to take charge of a division and proceed to Szechwan. He orders his forces to form for immediate departure.

21. A Nuptial Uproar (*Hun nao*)

Ch'i Yu-hsien arrives at the Chan residence for the wedding, singing nostalgically about former adventures with prostitutes. Chan Ai-chüan, veiled, enters and the ceremony is performed. The two are ushered into the nuptial bedroom to consummate the union. Yu-hsien removes Ai-chüan's veil and is dumbfounded at her ugliness. Ai-chüan, who expected to see Han Shih-hsün's features, is amazed, for her part, at the "change" which has occurred in his appearance: "How could you have lost your youthful freshness? Is it because you have been suffering from love? We were talking together so nicely that night when we were interrupted by my maid—you thought it was my mother and ran away. Since then I have yearned continually for this day! I was so miserable!" Ch'i Yu-hsien is enraged by this revelation of Ai-chüan's amorous escapade: "Fah! You ugly, lecherous woman! Are you so blind you can't tell one person from another? I never came to your house! I never saw your face! I never ran into any maid! You have been the object of who knows what scoundrel's dirty lust!" Mistress Plum hears the uproar in the nuptial chamber and surmises that it must be due to her daughter's maiden modesty and her young husband's impetuosity. Ch'i Yu-hsien calls to the servants to prepare a palanquin so he can return home. Mistress Plum intervenes to see what the trouble is. Confronted with Ch'i Yu-hsien's accusations, Ai-chüan is forced to give her mother a toned-down version of her encounter with Han Shih-hsün: "Last year during the *Ch'ing-ming* festival, there was a kite of Master Ch'i's which fell into our dwelling. He came to get it in the middle of the night and I exchanged a few idle words with him; actually nothing of importance passed between us. That night, I couldn't see clearly by the lantern light, so just now I thought he was the same person and referred to last year's conversation. I had no idea that he wasn't the same Master Ch'i."

Mistress Plum is terrified of the scorn and derision to which she will be exposed if Mistress Willow on the other side of the wall finds out about this escapade of her daughter's, so she does her best to smooth over the matter. Ch'i Yu-hsien is persuaded to accept the marriage through assurances that he will be allowed to take as many concubines as he likes. The couple retires again to the nuptial chamber. Ai-chüan sings, "Master Ch'i, Master Ch'i, my original seal hasn't been touched; it's as good as new! If you don't believe it, try it out and see!" to which Ch'i Yu-hsien responds, "Then the endangered city is still protected. Your offense of having invited plunderers in can't be proved by the documents!"

22. Devising a Plan (Yün ch'ou)

Chan Wu-ch'eng enters singing. He continues the besieged city imagery which closed the previous act. The city is protected but the surrounding areas are alive with barbarian troops. He awaits *chuang-yüan* Han Shih-hsün's arrival. Having heard that Han is a newly capped youth, he expects him to know nothing of warfare, but resolves to test him nevertheless. Han Shih-shün arrives. After the formalities of greeting, General Chan explains the military situation. Han suggests using mock lions to scare away the elephants and disperse the enemy. General Chan entusiastically accepts the idea.

23. Defeating the Elephants (Pai hsiang)

The barbarian chief enters with his troops. He is preparing to resist the forces of Chan and Han. He despises the first for being old and decrepit and the second for being young and "stinking of milk." They exit.

Chan and Han enter with their troops. They inspect the terrain and instruct their troops. Han's men are to await the enemy's attack, feign defeat, turn and flee, and then show the false lions. Chan's men are to prepare an ambush.

The barbarians enter. A stage battle takes place with cavorting "elephants" and "lions." Han Shih-hsün sings that he scorns the barbarians' illiteracy which makes them incapable of recognizing an ancient military ruse. The barbarian chief sings that his troops are on the run, exhausted and scattered. They fall into the ambush and are chased offstage. Chan's men return with captured heads and elephants, reporting a great victory. The troops that have fought are feasted; those that have not yet fought are sent out immediately to mop up the enemy remnants.

24. Leading the Way to Lust (Tao yin)

Ai-chüan enters, singing regretfully of her earlier indiscretion. It has been less than half a month since she became Ch'i Yu-hsien's wife and he already wants to take a concubine. She calculates that if he stays with the concubine one night out of three, she will be left in an empty room two months out of every year, while if he sleeps with her every other night, she will be a widow for half of her married life. "The thought is enough to make your hair stand on end." She reasons that since she won't be able to keep Yu-hsien faithful anyway, it might be better to allow him to amuse himself with prostitutes than to take a concubine, or still better than prostitutes, to allow him to have clandestine affairs. A prostitute wouldn't cling to him the way a young wife would, but he would still be free to come and go to one as he wished. If the object of his sexual ambition were a girl of good family, however, there would be no one to transmit his letters and no opportunity to speak his desires. Perhaps he would borrow his ugly wife to ease his longing. She recalls that her husband recently ran into her younger sister Shu-chüan by accident, observed her beauty, and has since been thinking of her in his dreams. She resolves to arrange for them to have an illicit relationship; this, she hopes, will have the added advantage of putting an end to Mistress Willow's boasting about her superior child-rearing methods. She goes to see Ch'i Yu-hsien, who is peeping through a hole in the wall and calling out to Shu-chüan in whispers. Ch'i begs her to help him in seducing Shu-chüan. Ai-chüan feigns reluctance, but at length agrees to arrange for them to be alone together on the condition that Ch'i drop the idea of taking a concubine. She warns him that he will have to be slow and gentle. "You won't get anywhere acting the way you did on our wedding night." Yu-hsien replies, "You don't have to tell me that. If you're worried about it, just play her role this evening and you'll see how I'll manage it."

25. Victory Banquet (K'ai yen)

At a banquet in celebration of the victory over the barbarians, Chan Wu-ch'eng has his military inspector propose his second daughter Shu-chüan to Han Shih-hsün as a bride. Han evades the proposal by objecting that he can't accept a marriage proposal without the approval of his foster father Ch'i Pu-ch'en. Alone, he sings indignantly about the dishonesty of the military inspector, who praised Shu-chüan's beauty and talent. He resolves to be even more on his guard against fraud.

Upon hearing of Han's response, Chan Wu-ch'eng decides to send Ch'i Pu-ch'en a letter saying that Han has already agreed to the marriage, but is waiting for Pu-ch'en's consent before sending betrothal gifts.

26. Repelling a Lewd Attack (*Chü chien*)

Ai'chüan invites Shu-chüan to her room to look at a double lotus blossom. Ch'i Yu-hsien is concealed there in a dark area behind a clothes rack next to a privy pot. After Shu-chüan's arrival, Ai-chüan finds a pretext to leave the room and Ch'i Yu-hsien emerges from his hiding place. Shu-chüan jumps back, scolds him, and calls for Ai-chüan. Yu-hsien tells her that she needn't call; it was Ai-chüan's wish that they become intimate. He invites her to notice that the doors are all locked and asks for her compassion. Shu-chüan seizes a sword hanging by Ai-chüan's bed (as an antidevil talisman) and prepares to defend herself. Ch'i Yu-hsien invites Shu-chüan to kill him if she will not accept his love. Taking him at his word, she lunges at him and he darts away terrified. Shu-chüan chases after him and Ch'i calls frantically for his wife. When Ai-chüan returns, Shu-chüan is furious with her but is persuaded to drop the matter. Flinging the sword down, she says, "Here, you can have your three-foot devil-suppressing piece of copper back!" and storms out.

Ai-chüan coldly informs her husband that he lost his chance to have an affair, and that he is not to mention the subject of a concubine again. Ch'i Yu-hsien is furious with the sword for spoiling everything but he has a scheme to get even with it: "In the future I'm going to melt it down into a pisspot! Night after night I'll vent my anger on it!" Ai-chüan rejoins, "I'm afraid you'll shrink from the labor."

27. News of Victory (*Wen chieh*)

Ch'i Pu-ch'en enters in everyday attire, worrying about the fortunes of Han Shih-hsün in his distant military mission. A messenger arrives with a letter from Chan Wu-ch'eng. He reads first of the military victory and that Han is returning to report on the mission. He then reads that Han has agreed to marry Chan's second daughter, though deferring the bestowal of engagement gifts until his consent can be gained. He is overjoyed at this coincidence (that such empathy could exist!) and moved at Han's filial feeling toward himself. Ch'i Pu-ch'en asks the messenger to send a go-between to Mistress Willow, but he replies that Mistress Willow already has a letter from her husband explaining everything. All Ch'i needs to do is to send the betrothal gifts to Mistress Willow and send the messenger back to Chan Wu-ch'eng with a reply.

28. Forced Marriage (*Pi hun*)

Han Shih-hsün enters in official attire with his men. He has just come from the capital where he has received a special promotion. The emperor wanted to have him marry the prime minister's daughter, but Han, having never seen the girl, was afraid of the match, which he escaped by memorializing the emperor to the effect that his marriage had already been settled by his family. He has requested a leave of absence to visit home with the (private) intention of continuing on to Yangchow to choose a mate. Having arrived at Ch'i Pu-ch'en's gate, he has his retinue announce his arrival. Ch'i Pu-ch'en enters and the two greet each other warmly and ceremoniously. Soon, however, Han is mystified to hear Ch'i Pu-ch'en congratulating him on his marriage. With increasing horror he realizes that Ch'i Pu-ch'en is talking about the Chan family's second daughter whom he identifies as the coarse and hideous Ai-chüan. He makes strenuous efforts to argue his way out of the marriage, but the only result is that Ch'i Pu-ch'en at length loses his temper and threatens to bring the case before the emperor if Han refuses to go through with the ceremony the following day. Alone, Han experiences a paroxysm of regret that he didn't consent to marry any of the women at the capital, some of whom one "could even look at." It was his foolish insistence on a meticulous standard of beauty, he feels, which has led to his being paired with a monstrosity. He resolves to submit to the ceremony and to pass the night with the bride, but to sleep in a separate bed. The following day he will go to Yangchow to take some attractive concubines, and never return to look at his wife for the rest of his life.

29. Astonished by Beauty (*Ch'a mei*)

Mistress Willow enters exulting over her daughter's marriage to a *chuang-yüan*. She invites Mistress Plum, whose son-in-law Ch'i Yu-hsien is just a common citizen, to attend the ceremony, with the obvious intent of rubbing salt in the wound, but she declines the invitation. Han Shih-hsün arrives and glumly submits to the ceremony. In the nuptial chamber, Shu-chüan shyly hides her face with a fan. Han goes to bed without speaking to her. When Shu-chüan sees that she has been abandoned, she goes to her mother's room to sleep and tells her mother of Han's strange behavior. Her mother has the maid awaken Han so she can question him. He is at length induced to repeat the story of the poems on the kite and his secret encounter with her "daughter." Shu-chüan, of course, denies having committed any indiscretion beyond that of having written a poem on the kite. It is nearly dawn when the misunderstanding is cleared up by having Han examine Shu-chüan's face by lantern light. He apologizes profusely to all concerned and retires with his new bride for what little remains of the night.

30. Suspicions are Dispersed (Shih i)

Chan Wu-ch'eng enters in official attire with his men. He is returning to the capital, but plans to stop off at his home which is just one relay stage distant. They exit.

Mistress Plum and Mistress Willow enter with their daughters and sons-in-law, to greet Chan Wu-ch'eng on his return. While they are all paying their respects to each other, Han Shih-hsün and Ai-chüan notice each other and start in surprise. Han Shih-hsün whispers to Shu-chüan that Ai-chüan is the person he met at their house a year ago. Moments later Ai-chüan's maid comes in with tea, and Han recognizes her as well. Shu-chüan is furious and goes at once to whisper this new intelligence to her mother so the culprits can be accused to their faces. Han is terrified that when Ch'i Yu-hsien learns of the affair, he will accuse him of flirting with his wife. Ch'i Yu-hsien, for his part, sees Shu-chüan in conference with her mother and is terrified that they are about to denounce him for his attack on Shu-chüan and that Han will accuse him of flirting with his wife. Each frantically tries to think of a pretext for drawing the other away from the group before his guilt is revealed. An idea occurs to Han; he suggests to Ch'i Yu-hsien that they walk out to meet their returning father-in-law. The two hurriedly exit.

Mistress Willow then denounces Mistress Plum for the behavior of her daughter Ai-chüan and, in particular, for her daughter's assumption of Shu-chüan's identity. Mistress Plum tries to dissuade Mistress Willow from accusing her before their husband, arguing that she too may suffer ill consequences from his displeasure. Ai-chüan's maid is convinced that she will be tortured to death in the coming investigation, so she entreats Mistress Willow and her daughter to relent. When the maid threatens to commit suicide, the two soften their stance, a reconciliation occurs, and both sides agree to hush the matter up.

Chan Wu-ch'eng enters with his men, followed by his two sons-in-law, and then by Ch'i Pu-ch'en. Greetings are exchanged all around and the four pairs of characters (the two fathers, the two concubines, the virtuous couple, and the "ugly" couple) each sing valedictory *tz'u*. A chorus of rejoicing concludes the play.

What Can You Do?

1. The Outline (*Yai lüeh*)
The stage manager enters and sings (1) a *tz'u* blaming stage plays for
giving young women illusions of free choice and promising that this
play will defy convention and uphold reality by portraying the union
of a clown with a beauty; (2) a *tz'u* summarizing the events in the
play; and (3) an octosyllabic quatrain hinting at paradoxical contrasts
within the play.

2. Worried About a Bride (*Lü hun*)
Ch'üeh Li-hou enters and introduces himself. He is coarse and
deformed in appearance and, like all his family, is too slow of intellect
to be a scholar. In compensation for these defects, however, he enjoys
immense wealth, a blessing never bestowed on the handsome and
talented. The imperial court has run out of money in the course of
pursuing some expensive border wars and will soon be requisitioning
money from wealthy commoners such as himself. His loyal servant
Ch'üeh Chung suggests that since he will soon be required to give
money anyway, he may as well come forth at once with a voluntary
contribution of a hundred thousand silver pieces. That way he can
earn a good name for himself at court and will very likely be given an
official position in return. After some persuasion, Ch'üeh Li-hou
accepts his servant's proposal.
He then turns his attention to a different problem. In accordance
with an arrangement made long ago by his parents, he will soon be
marrying a Miss Tsou, who is renowned for her beauty and intelligence. Because of his various deformities, Ch'üeh Li-hou has had
no experience whatsoever with women. He therefore asks his maid,
I-ch'un, to sleep with him so he can practice for his marriage. I-ch'un
at length consents, but insists that they do it at night with all the

lights extinguished. This gives Ch'üeh Li-hou the idea of hiding his appearance from the bride until after their wedding night.

3. Worried About the Groom (*Yu chia*)

Tsou Wu-huai, a former *chang-shih* (chief administrative advisor to an imperial prince), enters worrying about the approaching marriage of his daughter. He arranged the marriage with the Ch'üeh family when she was still a babe in arms. He had assumed that a son born to people as wealthy as the Ch'üeh's would surely have good features. Besides, his daughter was born merely to one of his concubines, so he expected her to have no better than common features and abilities when grown. He had never dreamed that she would grow up to be an exceptional beauty, while the groom would turn out to be such a monstrosity as to be a village and household joke. He has barely been able to keep word of the groom's deformity from his daughter. He realizes that the marriage is extremely unsuitable, but cannot go back on his word as he has already accepted the betrothal gifts. He calls her in to say goodbye to her, laying stress on the womanly virtue of obedience in his parting advice. Miss Tsou for her part worries that her father will find life burdensome now that she can no longer be on hand to write his social verse for him. Her nurse, carelessly mumbling the derogatory nickname by which the groom is known (Ch'üeh Incomplete), almost reveals the secret of his appearance to her, but manages to cover up her inadvertency just in time.

4. Shocked at Ugliness (*Ching ch'ou*)

Miss Tsou comes to the house of Ch'üeh Li-hou and is married to him. Without giving the bride a chance to see his features, Ch'üeh quickly consummates the marriage and falls to snoring as the maid I-ch'un listens outside the bedroom. Mistress Tsou is shortly afterwards overcome by foul odors coming from Ch'üeh's mouth, feet, and armpits and leaves the bedroom in order to throw up. Ch'üeh then wakes up and comes out as well, calling for Mistress Tsou. When Mistress Tsou, seeing him, realizes that her husband not only smells bad but is deformed in appearance, she bursts into tears and only becomes more upset when Ch'üeh tries to console her with the thought that at least she has married someone with money. At I-ch'un's suggestion, Ch'üeh goes back to bed and leaves her to handle the situation. I-ch'un has Mistress Tsou go with her to the library in order to calm down. Mistress Tsou observes that the library, though cleaner and quieter than the rest of the house, is furnished and decorated throughout in a vulgar, showy manner, a fact that demonstrates to her that Ch'üeh's mind is as imperfect as his person. She resolves to cut off relations with Ch'üeh on the occasion of their "first-month party" (a traditional celebration of a new couple's completion of their first month of wedded life), to have an image of Mother Mercy (the goddess Kuan-yin) set up in the library, and to pass the rest of her days shut up with the image of the goddess, praying for a happier life in her next existence.

5. Concealed Jealousy (*Yin tu*)

Yüan Cho-shui introduces himself. He is a prominent and distinguished general, temporarily living at home on leave, but expecting to be given a border assignment at any time. At home, he suffers a good deal from the constraints placed upon him by his wife, who is ugly and given to jealousy. He is nevertheless thankful that she at least refrains from openly offensive and domineering methods of control. He also has two concubines, Mistress Chou and Mistress Wu. Mistress Chou is only moderately attractive, but is good at running the household. Mistress Wu, on the other hand, is a stunning beauty. Since his wife never allows him to spend any time alone with them, both concubines languish from neglect. Yüan has a wine party with his wife and concubines during which his wife is careful to keep from becoming tipsy, so as to keep her husband under vigilant observation. An imperial messenger arrives with an order for Yüan to go to the southern frontier. Shortly afterwards, Yüan's wife makes him retire with her for the night, hand in hand. Mistress Chou and Mistress Wu linger onstage and lament the unhappy lot of lovely women.

6. Flight to Religion (*T'ao ch'an*)

Mistress Tsou surrounds herself with Buddhist images in the library. She has been in the Ch'üeh household for a month. Ch'üeh Li-hou has no idea of her intentions and imagines that she is praying to conceive a child. Mistress Tsou then announces her intention to become a nun and bids farewell to him forever. Ch'üeh pleads and argues with her, and calls in I-ch'un to add her persuasive efforts to his. He is then momentarily called out of the room and Mistress Tsou and I-ch'un seize the opportunity to barricade themselves in the library. When Ch'üeh returns, he at first falls on his knees and pleads with Mistress Tsou to come out; then he threatens to stop supplying her with food, but she at once signifies that she would welcome death by starvation rather than return. Finally, Ch'üeh shouts at her that he will use his money to marry someone much more beautiful than she is.

7. A Fraudulent Matchmaker (*Mei ch'i*)

Mme. Ho and her daughter, Miss Ho, introduce themselves. Mme. Ho is a poor widow who has for years been seeking a suitable husband for her daughter, who is her only child. Though Miss Ho is a great beauty, her mother's poverty has thus far prevented her from making an acceptable match.

Chang I-ma, a matchmaker hired by Ch'üeh Li-hou, enters and announces to Mme. Ho that she has found an ideal son-in-law for her. She fraudulently claims that the prospect is handsome and talented as well as fabulously rich. Mme. Ho insists on getting a look at Ch'üeh before agreeing to the match. Chang, who has a scheme in mind, agrees to this and says she will take Ch'üeh to a Buddhist temple where the mother and daughter will be burning incense, so they can get a good look at him.

8. Hiring an Actor (*Ch'ing yu*)

Ch'üeh Li-hou enters and announces that Chang I-ma has informed him of her negotiations with Mme. Ho, and has advised him to hire a handsome man to go to the temple and pose as himself. Ch'üeh fears that it would be indiscreet to hire an outsider to engage in this deception and reflects that his own servant, Ch'üeh Chung, has an entirely acceptable set of features. He therefore calls Ch'üeh Chung into his presence and explains what he desires him to do. Ch'üeh Chung, however, objects vigorously. Not only would the plan tend to confuse the proper distinctions between the roles of master and servant, but it could give rise to future ill feeling and suspicion as well. Even if his features gave satisfaction, it would be highly awkward and inappropriate for the bride to live in the same household with the person whom she originally imagined would be her husband, and of whose appearance she had approved. He therefore suggests that Ch'üeh Li-hou have the leading man from an acting troupe he has recently engaged undertake the impersonation.

He then leaves and returns with the leading man.

When the leading man hears what his proposed mission is, he politely observes that Ch'üeh Li-hou's features are actually uncommonly fine; but since vulgar eyes are incapable of perceiving their distinction, he will be willing to offer his services in return for a suitable reward. The leading man is then loaned a set of Ch'üeh Li-hou's rich clothing to use for the occasion.

Finally, Ch'üeh Chung persuades his master that he should accompany the leading man and the matchmaker when they go to the temple. That way, they will be able to deal with the morning-after outrage of the bride by claiming that they had no intent to deceive. They can blame it all on the matchmaker for pointing out the wrong person.

9. A Misapplied Physiognomic Inspection (*Wu hsiang*)

A monk enters, prepares his temple for the reception of gift-bearing visitors, and exits. Ch'üeh Li-hou's party enters, walking toward the temple. The actor compares his current assignment to the work he does on the stage. They exit. Mme. Ho enters with her daughter and Chang I-ma. She burns incense in front of the temple. They then catch sight of Ch'üeh's party from a distance. Asked for her opinion of the substitute's features, Miss Ho replies that though they are handsome enough, the man has a somewhat flippant or dissolute air reminiscent of a professional actor. Mme. Ho decides to follow Ch'üeh's party into the temple and look at the young man more closely before coming to a decision.

Inside the temple, Ch'üeh Li-hou asks the actor to describe Miss Ho's appearance, as he has cloudy vision and cannot see well at a distance. The actor responds with an aria full of stage language praising Miss Ho's beauty. Ch'üeh Li-hou then starts to assume what he thinks are fetching poses, in the hope that if the actor fails to pass the ladies' inspection, they might still give approval to *him*.

Miss Ho notices Ch'üeh assuming grotesque attitudes and is greatly amused. Chang I-ma tells her that he is the servant of the handsome young man. Noticing the smiles on the ladies faces, Ch'üeh thinks that his posturing has met with their approval and is greatly encouraged. Mme. Ho decides that the young man (i.e., the actor) will do. She was doubtful before, but the sight of his servant's extreme ugliness has made her realize that his features are acceptable after all.

Mme. Ho. exits with her daughter and Chang I-ma reports her acceptance to Ch'üeh. The actor sings, aside, an aria in pity of the lovely bride as Ch'üeh laughs with satisfaction.

Ch'üeh's party exits and the Ho's reenter. Told by Chang I-ma that Ch'üeh will soon send a betrothal gift and choose a wedding day, they close the act hoping that the groom will be as fine in intellect as he was agreeable in appearance.

10. Aiding the Border (*Chu pien*)

Ch'üeh Li-hou's servant Ch'üeh Chung announces that a pacification chief has recently come to the area to collect money for the border wars. He goes to the pacification chief's headquarters to await an opportunity to present a petition he has drawn up for his master that offers a hundred thousand silver pieces to the war effort.

The pacification chief enters and orders his runners to submit their reports on requisitioned funds. The runners have been unable to collect anything, but have brought a local official back with them to present his excuses in person. The latter explains that the local people have been so impoverished by recent floods and droughts that they cannot even pay their usual taxes, let alone a special war requisition.

The pacification chief then calls for the petitions to be brought in. When he reads Ch'üeh Chung's petition, he is amazed to discover such loyalty as Ch'üeh Li-hou's in a mere commoner. He promises to submit a memorial to the emperor at once announcing the great contribution. Ch'üeh Chung is anxious to prevent the money from being diverted to private use by dishonest officials and so secures permission to deliver the funds to the border region in person. The chief is as impressed at Ch'üeh Chung's presence of mind and powers of persuasion as he is at his master's patriotism, and predicts that in the future both will occupy high stations.

11. Getting Drunk on Nuptial Wine (*Tsui chin*)

Ch'üeh Chung reports back to his master on his visit to the pacification official. The day of Ch'üeh Li-hou's marriage to Miss Ho has arrived. He has no idea how he should deal with her inevitable disappointment, so he asks his servant for advice. Ch'üeh Chung replies that Li-hou was mistaken in the strategy of self-concealment he used with Mistress Tsou. Instead, he should establish his authority at once, if necessary having the bride's maids or servants beaten in her presence, so she will not dare to oppose him in anything. Ch'üeh Li-hou is delighted with this suggestion and practices the role by ordering some servants about roughly.

The bride arrives and the marriage takes place offstage. The two are then conducted onstage and seated opposite each other. When Mistress Ho's veil is removed, she realizes that she has been deceived, but she continues to sit silently. Ch'üeh Li-hou has the wine cups filled and urges Mistress Ho to drink. Instead of drinking, she lowers her head and bursts into tears. Pretending outrage, Ch'üeh orders a maid to persuade her to drink. If so much as one drop remains in the cup, the maid is to receive thirty strokes. Mistress Ho declines to drink and the maid is taken away and beaten. Ch'üeh then gives the same order to a second maid. The second maid kneels as she offers Mistress Ho the cup and beseeches her to drink it, saying she is ailing and unable to withstand a beating. Mistress Ho reflects that since she will not in any case be able to escape Ch'üeh's embraces, she may as well try to render herself insensible to their nastiness by drinking herself unconscious. Perhaps, she reflects, she can even drink herself to death. She accordingly orders the maid to pour her cup after cup of wine and downs them all at a gulp. She soon falls unconscious on the table, whereupon Ch'üeh bears her off to the bedchamber exulting.

12. Burning up Old Accounts (*Fen chüan*)

Ch'üeh Chung is about to start on his long journey to the frontier. The hundred thousand silver pieces are all stacked in travelling bags and the horses and men are all in readiness. Ch'üeh Chung's younger brother Ch'üeh I is to manage his master's financial affairs during his absence. In accordance with a scheme he has devised to win some local popularity for his master, Ch'üeh Chung instructs his younger brother to burn all the records of long outstanding debts owed to Ch'üeh Li-hou. He also instructs him to submit his report on the matter to Ch'üeh Li-hou after Ch'üeh Chung's departure. He is then joined by the road porters and begins the journey to the border region.

13. Soft Deceit (*Juan k'uang*)

Mistress Ho is bitter about having lost her virginity to such a clumsy, malodorous oaf as Ch'üeh Li-hou. She has heard that he has a first wife, Mistress Tsou, who has gone into religious seclusion in the library. She decides to trick Ch'üeh into allowing her to enter the library herself.

Ch'üeh Li-hou enters coughing and bent over from his amorous exertions. He complains to Mistress Ho that the effort of shaking hands with all the people who have come to congratulate him on his marriage has given him pains in his lower back. He asks her to massage it. The massage arouses his desire and he tries to induce Mistress Ho to make love with him on the spot. A tussle ensues during which he comes to orgasm spontaneously and falls back exhausted.

Mistress Ho then asks Ch'üeh Li-hou to confirm what she has heard about Mistress Tsou. She sympathizes with him over his mistreatment, praises his magnanimity in continuing to feed her, and blames Mistress Tsou for her coldheartedness. She offers to go the library to taunt and scold Mistress Tsou. Ch'üeh is delighted at this idea, as it gives him a means of demonstrating to Mistress Tsou that he has married a lady lovelier than she, just as he said he would. He promises to take Mistress Ho to the library the following morning with some incense to burn before Mother Mercy.

14. A Cunning Escape (*Ch'iao t'o*)

Mistress Tsou enters. She is mystified by what she has heard of the new bride's behavior. She had been sure there would be trouble on the wedding night and had asked the servants to observe and report to her. From them she has learned that Mistress Ho is strikingly beautiful, more so even than herself, that on the wedding night she appeared entirely free of shame or awkwardness and drank without restraint, and that afterwards she went docilely to bed and made not the slightest disturbance throughout the night. When I-ch'un (the maid) tells her that Mistress Ho is about to pay her a visit, she is therefore full of curiosity to discover what sort of person could possibly have so much forbearance.

Ch'üeh Li-hou triumphantly presents Mistress Ho to Mistress Tsou, but is first confused, then mortified, then angered, to find that instead of taunting Mistress Tsou as she promised, Mistress Ho addresses her as a devout disciple would address a great religious adept. She then professes a deep inner call to leave the world and live in seclusion with Mistress Tsou, saying she would rather die than return where she came.

Ch'üeh first threatens to beat Mistress Ho into returning, then charges Mistress Tsou with the task of persuading her to return, telling her that if she fails, she will have to return instead. He exits.

Mistress Tsou questions Mistress Ho further and finds she is entirely serious and wholehearted in her desire to pass the rest of her life in seclusion. She therefore agrees to have Mistress Ho stay in the library with her.

15. Creating Separate Disturbances (*Fen jao*)

The Black Lord of Heaven, a rebelling border general, enters and introduces himself. His father was general of that region before him and had many brilliant victories to his credit. Unhappily, he was wronged and slandered by a corrupt official at court and, though never sentenced to death, at length died of anxiety over the danger this placed him in. Enraged at this injustice, the Black Lord and his sister, the White Lord of Heaven, have resolved to avenge their father by overthrowing the dynasty. They have a hundred thousand troops, consisting of a male contingent trained and led by the Black Lord and a female contingent trained and led by the White Lord.

The brother and sister meet, exhort their troops and discuss strategy. The White Lord argues that since both the imperial troops and the populace at large are currently short of food provisions, they should surround the enemy's strongholds and wait for him to exhaust his supplies before attacking. The Black Lord objects that this will only lead the enemy to despise them and increase his will to fight. He at length decides that his and his sister's views on strategy are irreconcilably opposed and that it would therefore be best for them to campaign separately rather than in concert. He accordingly instructs his sister to attack in the east while he attacks in the west. Whoever enters the capital first will become emperor.

The two then review their troops. The male troops demonstrate an attack formation called "massed tigers chasing the sheep," and the female troops an attack formation called "myriad birds paying court to the phoenix." They then prepare to launch the campaign. The Black Lord urges on the male troops by telling them to "think of the women they'll meet." The White Lord similarly exhorts the female troops to "think of the men they'll meet."

This act concludes the first half of the play.

16. Driving Rivals Away (*Tu ch'ien*)

A servant of the house of Yüan (see act 5) enters. His master has left for a military assignment on the frontier less than half a year after taking two attractive concubines. Mme. Yüan is jealous of the concubines and has decided to take advantage of her husband's absence to get rid of them. She has instructed the servant to hire a matchmaker to find new households for them. The servant is reluctant to betray his master in this fashion and fears that the action will have unfortunate consequences, but he is too afraid of Mme. Yüan to disobey.

17. Chasing the Sheep (*Tsan yang*)

Yüan Cho-shui (see act 5) enters, attired as a general. He has arrived at the southwestern border with his troops, and has heard that the rebellious Black Lord is advancing on the region with his forces. His scouts report that these forces have until now been advancing very rapidly and observing strict discipline, but that due to a recent heavy snowfall that has rendered the road marks invisible, they have come to a halt nearby and have begun to drink and relax. Yüan reflects that after days of forced marching, the enemy will be dazed and exhausted; moreover, they will not expect an attack just after a heavy snowstorm. He therefore orders his forces to prepare white flags and don white armor so as to be inconspicuous against the snow, and then to march swiftly and silently to the site of the enemy camp. There they are to assemble in the snow and attack at the signal of a cannon blast. Yüan and his forces exit.

The Black Lord enters with his forces. He orders his men to post a strict guard against thieves during the night, but they object that no thief would venture out in such inclement weather. He then orders the captive women to be brought in and selects the most attractive to spend the night with him, leaving the rest for his followers. As there are not enough women to go around, the men double up, each pair taking one of the captives to bed with them. They exit.

Attired in white, Yüan and his troops enter as the Black Lord and his men snore offstage. Yüan mounts a hill and gives the cannon signal. They charge offstage.

The Black Lord and his men run onstage naked, unarmed, and shivering. They come upon the Black Lord's discarded sheepskin coat and start fo fight over it. The Black Lord claims it for himself so he can at least "make a warm ghost" when executed. His men sourly observe that their chief's capture by their tigerlike opponents will turn out to fit the name he invented for their battle formation: "massed tigers chasing the sheep." Yüan and his men enter and capture the Black Lord.

18. Switching to a New Strategy (*Kai t'u*)

Ch'üeh Li-hou enters. He is going to try marrying a third time. He can't imagine that the world could contain a third woman as crafty and wicked as his first two wives. This time, however, he is not going to seek talent or beauty in the bride. He has learned by now that these attributes only cause trouble.

The matchmaker Chang I-ma arrives and informs him that she has two excellent prospects for him to choose from. Both are concubines of the Yüan household whom the chief wife desires to sell. Ch'üeh inquires about their appearance and domestic skills. Chang I-ma replies that Mistress Chou, though no great beauty, has a good head for household management. Mistress Wu she describes as having superb literary ability and as being so beautiful that both of Ch'üeh's previous wives together could not compare with her. Ch'üeh replies that Mistress Wu is in that case definitely out of the question. By now the mere mention of the words *talent* and *beauty* is enough to give him a headache. Mistress Chou he is decidedly interested in, but he wants to get a look at her features to make sure she is not too beautiful. Chang I-ma rejoins that there is a gentleman from Szechwan coming to the Yüan household the next day to have a look at Mistress Wu. Ch'üeh can come at the same time to look at Mistress Chou. Ch'üeh agrees to this, and thanks her for all the trouble she has undergone seeking brides for him.

19. Coercion to Marry (*Pi chia*)

Han Meng-yang, the gentleman from Szechwan, comes to the Yüan household to look at Mistress Wu. Both parties are pleased with the other's appearance. Han tests her literary ability by having her compose a poem to go with a lady's portrait on a fan. Mistress Wu responds with a clever *chüeh-chü* or four-line poem. Entranced with the poem, Han agrees at once to the bride price of three hundred taels and arranges with Chang I-ma to have the marriage occur the following day.

As soon as Han has left, Ch'üeh Li-hou arrives to look at Mistress Chou. Ch'üeh is satisfied with her appearance, but Mistress Chou darts back behind the curtains in fright at her first glimpse of Ch'üeh. Chang I-ma assures him that this is due merely to her bashfulness. Ch'üeh agrees to a bride price of one hundred taels and, when he hears that Han is to be married the next day, arranges to be married himself at the same time, as he is sure that a scholar like Han must surely have chosen an auspicious date.

After Ch'üeh's departure, Mistress Chou reenters in a rage, asks Chang I-ma what she means by dragging ghosts up from hell to serve as husbands, demands that she break off the arrangement, and swears she will kill herself rather than live with Ch'üeh. She storms offstage.

Chang I-ma does not want to lose her matchmaker's fee, so she calls in Mme. Yüan and complains bitterly of Mistress Chou's behavior to her, adding the false accusation that Mistress Chou cursed Mme. Yüan. The latter tells her not to worry about a thing; she could force Mistress Chou to do her will even if the groom were a beggar. Chang I-ma praises her firmness and observes that such an ill-tempered concubine is lucky to have been tolerated in the household for so long.

20. Substituting One Beauty for Another (*Tiao mei*)

A servant of Han Meng-yang comes to the Yüan household at the time appointed for the wedding and informs Chang I-ma and Mme. Yüan that his master has just made the alarming discovery that Lord Yüan and Han's father took their metropolitan degrees in the same year. This means that Han's scholarly relationship to Lord Yüan is that of a nephew to an uncle. For a man to marry the concubine of his "degree uncle" (*nien po*) would be unthinkable. Han must, therefore, withdraw from his agreement to marry Mistress Wu. Mme. Yüan reluctantly returns Han's betrothal gift and the servant departs.

A few moments later, Ch'üeh Li-hou arrives at the gate in a palanquin to take Mistress Chou away to his house. Neither Chang I-ma nor Mme. Yüan receives any response when they call Mistress Chou, so they have a maid pry open her door. It is then discovered that Mistress Chou has hung herself.

Mme. Yüan is thrown into a panic at this intelligence, for she cannot imagine how she will ever explain the death to her husband. Chang I-ma advises her to tell him that she died of an illness. It is unlikely that he would have the corpse examined or that anyone would stir up trouble over the incident. Mme. Yüan objects that there will be no way of stopping up the mouth of the other concubine, Mistress Wu. Chang I-ma thinks intently for a moment and then has a brilliant idea. Mistress Wu, she tells Mme. Yüan, is still unaware that her husband-to-be has backed out of his marriage agreement. She is expecting to be called out at any moment to be taken away to his house. Why not call her out and tell her that the palanquin in front of the house belongs to Han Meng-yang? Ch'üeh will end up with a bride more beautiful than he bargained for, so naturally he won't complain. Mistress Wu will of course be shocked and upset, but she will be powerless to do anything but curse inwardly. Mme. Yüan exults over this plan and hastens to carry it out before Mistress Wu can learn what has happened.

21. Ingenious Intimidation (Ch'iao pu)

Mistress Wu is brought to Ch'üeh's household in his wedding palanquin. The ceremony is performed and the two sit down opposite each other. Ch'üeh is surprised at the beautiful and unfamiliar features of the bride and wonders if he is perversely fated to marry only lovely women. Mistress Wu is at first mystified to see a great oaf instead of a handsome scholar sitting before her, but then realizes that Chang I-ma and Mme. Yüan must have substituted her for Mistress Chou when they discovered the latter's death. She quickly thinks out a strategy to preserve her chastity and return to Lord Yüan; then, breaking the silence with a cold laugh, she asks the groom if he is Ch'üeh Li-hou. Ch'üeh answers affirmatively; who else should he be? Mistress Wu then asks what grudge the matchmaker bears him to play such a devilish trick. Ch'üeh denies any grudge and asks what she means. Mistress Wu replies that a great catastrophe is about to befall him. Ch'üeh begs to know what it is. Mistress Wu asks if he remembers the identity of the woman he looked at the previous day. Ch'üeh replies that he has noticed an alteration of appearance and asks if she was indeed a different person. Mistress Wu replies that the earlier lady was Mistress Chou and that her own surname is Wu, and adds, "Since you have driven Mistress Chou to suicide, I have come to take your life in return." Ch'üeh, now thoroughly alarmed, presses her to explain. Mistress Wu responds with the following story: When she and Mistress Chou knew they were to be sold, they made a secret agreement to maintain their fidelity to Lord Yüan by killing themselves the moment the bridal palanquins came to the gate. Mistress Chou, however, was overeager and killed herself before the palanquin's arrival, so their intentions were discovered prematurely. This was a fortunate thing for scholar Han. When he learned that his bride was bent on killing herself, he backed out of the agreement and took back his betrothal money. Then Ch'üeh's palanquin arrived and Mme. Yüan ordered her to go in Mistress Chou's place. She was unwilling to go and still determined to hang herself, when the matchmaker advised her that as long as she was bent on suicide, she might as well derive the maximum result from it by killing herself in Ch'üeh's household. Ch'üeh would then be responsible for the deaths of both concubines and would have to pay a great part of his fortune to Lord Yüan in compensation. Therefore, she concludes, she has come to Ch'üeh's house, first, to show her fidelity to Lord Yüan; second, to avenge the death of Mistress Chou; and last, to request that a sturdy coffin be prepared for her. She then removes the sash from her waist and begins at once to strangle herself with it.

Ch'üeh calls for help and orders the maid to fetch Mistresses Tsou and Ho from the library. He begs Mistress Wu to desist and offers to send her back to the Yüan household in the same palanquin in which she arrived. Mistress Wu declines the offer, saying that if she returns, Mme. Yüan will only sell her to someone else. Ch'üeh then falls on his knees, acknowledges himself to be at fault, and begs Mistress Wu to show him a way out of his predicament. She replies that if he wants to be saved, he must maintain her in separate quarters and not come near her until the return of Lord Yüan, whereupon he is to return her. Perhaps she can then speak a word or two in his behalf so he will not be held accountable for Mistress Chou's death. Ch'üeh kowtows and thanks her profusely, telling her she can live in the library where there are already two elegant ladies to keep her company. The maid then ushers in Mistresses Tsou and Ho. Ch'üeh turns Mistress Wu over to their care and exits.

Mistresses Tsou and Ho explain to Mistress Wu that they, like her, are wives of Ch'üeh. They take Mistress Wu to the library. They are amazed at Mistress Wu's swift escape and awed at her ingenuity and presence of mind. Mistress Wu observes to the other two that their place of seclusion should have a name. She suggests that they name it *Nai-ho t'ien* or "What Can You Do (About Heaven)?" since they all have been forced to live there by events beyond their control. The maid grinds some ink and Mistress Wu paints the three characters on a sign to be hung by the entrance to the library. As she is painting, Mistress Tsou remarks to Mistress Ho that if even women of such astounding brilliance and beauty as Mistress Wu can end up married to an oaf like Ch'üeh, perhaps they themselves have no cause to complain. Mistress Wu promises the other two that when she returns to Lord Yüan, she will try to think of a way to use her influence and his power to save them from their present mode of existence. The three women agree to stand by each other in this life and the next.

22. Planning Provisions (*Ch'ou hsiang*)

Ch'üeh Chung enters with his attendants and porters. He has been travelling several months, but has only covered half the distance to the border. They stop at an inn for refreshment. A courier and a military funds collector coming from the border also stop at the inn. From the courier Ch'üeh Chung learns that a band of women rebels (see act 15) have inflicted severe losses on the imperial forces. From the funds collector he learns that the price of rice and grain is sky-high at the border. "Money is like dirt and grain is like gold." Ch'üeh Chung then asks him if a person could make a profit buying grain at their present location and selling it at the border. The collector assures him that he would at least triple his investment.

Left alone in the tavern, Ch'üeh Chung decides he had better convert the cash he is carrying into provisions without further delay. The only problem is that his credentials authorize him only to deliver cash, not grain or rice. What if the receiving authorities notice this and refuse to accept the provisions? He then realizes that this is no real problem; he can always turn the provisions back into cash at the border if the need should arise. He and his men resume their journey northward.

23. A Good Scheme Goes Awry (*Chi tso*)

The servant of Lord Yüan enters. He informs us that his master has been given higher rank for routing the male rebels in the south and has now been ordered to subdue the female rebels in the north. His master is soon going to stop at home on his way to the northern frontier. The servant has already despatched a letter in secret informing him of the suicide of Mistress Chou and the sale of Mistress Wu. He has come out to meet his master at a nearby relay station so he can take advantage of Mme. Yüan's absence to put as much blame as possible on her.

At this point, Ch'üeh Li-hou comes hustling up to the relay station and tells Yüan's servant he has been looking all over for him. He wants to return Mistress Wu to Lord Yüan, and is counting on the servant to act as the middleman. He gives him twenty taels in advance and promises much more money if the business is successfully concluded. The servant advises Ch'üeh to bring Mistress Wu to the relay station, as she will have a better chance there to explain herself to Lord Yüan than she would if brought directly to the Yüan household. Ch'üeh agrees to this and hastens offstage to get Mistress Wu. The servant is very happy over this development, as it will allow him to please his master as well as make some money. He exits.

Lord Yüan and his retinue enter to the sound of drums marking the sculling rhythm of the boat they are on. He has been intending to stop at home, but is not sure how to deal with the domestic problem of which he has just learned. It is impossible simply to overlook such a matter, but if he shows his displeasure, it will inevitably lead to an open breach between himself and Mme. Yüan. This would cause a lot of gossip and severely injure his family's reputation. Suddenly, it occurs to him that illustrious statesmen of high antiquity were often so devoted to their public trusts that they would not pause to step inside their own homes even when they passed by their front gates. Why not use the urgency of the border situation as an excuse to continue on without stopping? He instructs the boatmen not to cast anchor after all.

Just then Yüan's servant, Ch'üeh Li-hou, and Mistress Wu enter, rowing a boat. The servant boards Yüan's boat and announces Mistress Wu's desire for an interview, but is sent back by Yüan with the message that there is no need for her to speak to him as she has already married someone else. Mistress Wu comes aboard anyway, falls at his feet, weeps, and tells the tale of her forced departure. She dwells on her misery and assures him that she has preserved her chastity. To her astonishment, Lord Yüan laughs coldly and ignores her. Thinking that his coldness may be due to embarrassment at showing affection before spectators, she walks toward the hold of the boat, hoping that Yüan will later come and speak to her alone. At this, Lord Yüan cries out, "Stop where you are! You are a literate person. Surely you must be familiar with the proverb 'spilt water cannot be regathered.' " He asks her why she didn't kill herself at once if she wanted to show her loyalty to him. How can a person show fidelity by marrying someone else? How can he verify her claim about her chastity? Besides, it is only because she was unexpectedly purchased by the ugly Ch'üeh instead of handsome scholar Han that she now wants to return. He orders his servant to call Ch'üeh Li-hou aboard to take Mistress Wu back.

Ch'üeh reluctantly comes aboard, bows to Lord Yüan and launches into a stream of nervous explanation, but Lord Yüan cuts him short, saying he is familiar with the facts in the case and that there is no need for Ch'üeh to apologize. It was all due to his wife's jealousy, his concubines' disloyalty, and the operation of destiny. That Ch'üeh and Mistress Wu came together unintentionally as they did shows that they must have a predestined affinity for each other. He urges Ch'üeh to take her back at once.

Ch'üeh thanks Yüan profusely but protests that he simply cannot take such a liberty. Even if he did so, Mistress Wu would only make a scene and try to kill herself as she did before. Lord Yüan assures him, however, that this time she will be more compliant, since he himself is ordering her to be Ch'üeh's wife.

He then calls Mistress Wu over to him and gives her a stern lecture on the futility of discontent and the advantages of resignation. It is perfectly fitting that she should marry a man like Ch'üeh, for it has been said of old that "lovely ladies have slender destinies." If she looks after his family contentedly, she may have a few children and enjoy some advantages in her declining years. But if she persists in making scenes, she will become a "ghost dangling from a rafter like Mistress Chou. He orders his servant to conduct Ch'üeh and Mistress Wu back to their rowboat.

In the rowboat, Lord Yüan's servant exhorts Mistress Wu never to forget any of the excellent advice she has just received from his master. He takes leave of them when they reach the shore.

Mistress Wu starts to exit, but Ch'üeh pulls her back, asking her where she is going. Mistress Wu replies, "To the retreat in the library." Ch'üeh says, "You can't go there anymore," and explains that he no longer has any reason to fear her anger. "The injured party and the murderer have met face to face and come to an agreement." Why should he fear a charge of homicide anymore? It is true they are not evenly matched in appearance, but as Lord Yüan has already explained, that only shows that their union is a suitable one. He therefore asks her to put a good face on the situation and finish getting married to him.

Mistress Wu wants to try another scheme, but feels that all her paths of escape have been blocked by Lord Yüan and so decides to comply with Ch'üeh's wishes. At this point, she turns to the audience and urges all the talented and lovely ladies among the spectators to learn from her example. Even if they have first-class minds or have dazzling beauty, it only means their case resembles her own, or that of Mistress Tsou or Mistress Ho. Even if their husbands are as ugly as they come, they still can't be as bad as Ch'üeh. She urges them to pass their lives contentedly, and sings an aria on the futility of brilliant schemes when opposed by the heavy weight of karmic destiny.

Ch'üeh tells the maid to make sure the wedding candles are good and bright and that not too much nuptial wine is poured. He is now an open, legitimate, authorized groom and has no intention of "stealing chickens in the dark" or "catching drunken thieves" as on the two earlier occasions. He embraces Mistress Wu and bears her offstage.

24. Taking Apollos Captive (*Lu chün*)

The White Lord of Heaven enters with four female generals. She is encountering no resistance in the central plain and is capturing city after city. She orders the generals henceforth to present all captured men to her for inspection so she can choose a consort. Those whom she does not select will be awarded to the generals for their private use. Any general who attempts to hide a man will suffer decapitation with subsequent exposure of the severed head. Four men come running onstage and are taken captive. None of them suits the fancy of the White Lord, so they are given to her generals. The horses are too few to go around, so each general has one of the captives sit facing her on the horse.

25. A Secret Plan (*Mi ch'ou*)

Lord Yüan enters attired as a general, followed by his subordinates. His position at the northern border is desperate, due to lack of provisions. The common people are coming in crowds to beg for food and his troops are threatening to desert. One of his generals then carries in a letter from the Hukuang pacification chief (see act 10) introducing Ch'üeh Chung and explaining his mission. Yüan is amazed to discover that Ch'üeh Li-hou (who of course is familiar to him as the man who married his concubine, Mistress Wu) is such a patriot and philanthropist. "Truly," he says to himself, "you can't judge people by their exteriors." He worries that the money won't altogether solve their problem, due to the inflated price of grain, and is delighted to discover that Ch'üeh Chung has already dealt with the problem by buying provisions elsewhere and transporting them to the border. Ch'üeh Chung also anticipates Yüan's thinking in suggesting that excess provisions be used to succor the starving common people.

Thoroughly impressed by Ch'üeh Chung's ability, General Yüan confers the rank of staff strategist on him at once. He then orders his other subordinates to leave, and proposes a secret plan to Ch'üeh Chung. He explains that the White Lord's forces are capturing good-looking men to use as military advisors and bedmates. He wants to infiltrate one of his own men into the enemy's camp. Ch'üeh Chung is an uncommonly handsome man, and Yüan asks him if he is willing to undertake the mission. Ch'üeh Chung agrees at once to attempt it. General Yüan tells him to mislead the enemy concerning the disposition and condition of their own forces. The act closes with jokes about Fu Ch'ai (a famous Warring States ruler who was toppled by a femme fatale) acting as a concubine and Hsi Shih (the femme fatale who toppled him) acting as the lord.

26. The Army is Victorious (Shih chieh)

Ch'üeh Chung is "captured" by the enemy and is selected by the White Lord to be her chief consort. Questioned about the state of General Yüan's forces, he replies that they are starving and on the point of dispersing.

Meanwhile, General Yüan and his men catch sight of a mountain in the distance, which they learn is called "Phoenix Mountain." General Yüan considers this a good omen, as the phoenix is the king of birds. He orders his men to set up camp on the mountain.

The White Lord's forces also come upon the mountain. Catching sight of General Yüan's imperial flags on the mountainside, they ask the White Lord if they should attack. The White Lord responds that they must send someone to reconnoiter before attacking, and asks Ch'üeh Chung if he will undertake the mission. He feigns great apprehension and reluctance to be parted from her before exiting. The

White Lord praises his depth of romantic feeling and orders her troops to dispose themselves in the assault formation called "myriad birds paying court to the phoenix" (see act 15).

Ch'üeh Chung hastens to the mountain campsite and informs General Yüan that the enemy is strong and fierce and must therefore be defeated by subterfuge rather than force. In the forthcoming engagement, Yüan's forces must pretend to lose, but they must also blockade the main paths to keep the enemy from ascending the mountain. He will persuade the White Lord to go to bed with him. At midnight they must fire a cannon signal and storm into the enemy camp. He will rejoin Yüan's forces after beheading the White Lord in bed. Finally, he requests Yüan to have some men pretend to pursue him down the mountain on his return so as to make the White Lord more inclined to trust him.

The White Lord learns that the mountain before them is called "Phoenix" and, thinking of the name of their assault formation, observes with displeasure that it is an auspicious omen for Yüan's side. Ch'üeh Chung comes running in, pursued by offstage cries of "Catch the spy!" The White Lord questions him about the enemy forces. He pantingly replies that they are totally disorganized and that their camp is scarcely even defended, but that they are presently attempting to make a show of force by charging down the mountainside. He advises her to counterattack in force. She gives the attack order, and a battle ensues in which Yüan's forces feign defeat and run away. The rebel forces are unwilling to pursue them up the mountain because of the late hour and the obstructed paths. The White Lord therefore orders them to close up camp and search the mountain in the morning. Ch'üeh Chung suggests to the White Lord that they can safely pass the night in bed together. She agrees, but orders her generals to establish night patrols and report any disturbances to her. Ch'üeh Chung puts his arm around the White Lord and exits with her.

As the rebel troops patrol the area, idly singing tunes, artillery and warcries suddenly erupt from offstage. Some troops face toward the White Lord's tent, report the disturbance, and request her to come out. Ch'üeh Chung's voice answers from within the tent, saying that the White Lord's orders are that the enemy is only making an empty show of strength and will almost certainly not attack. Even if they do attack, their strength is so reduced that there is no need for her to participate. The troops are to ward them off without her aid.

General Yüan and his forces charge onstage and fight with the rebels. Ch'üeh Chung suddenly comes onstage with the White Lord's head. He hangs up a lantern, stands in a high place, displays the head, and calls upon the rebels to surrender. Upon seeing their chief's head, they panic and flee in all directions.

General Yüan promises to compose a memorial announcing the victory as soon as they return to camp and asks Ch'üeh Chung to undertake its delivery. Ch'üeh Chung agrees and requests Yüan not to forget to mention his master's contribution to the victory. The act closes with the following four-line verse:

> Three thousand pink-cheeked beauties acted as yellow turbans [i.e., rebels];
> A hundred thousand blue-winged coins aided the purple ribbons [imperial forces].
> A hundred schemes, spread like a starry net, took the tigress captive;
> A night of clouds and rain [i.e., lovemaking] will be memorialized to the imperial unicorn [emperor].

27. A Magnanimous Petition (*Hsi ch'i*)

Three spirit ministers of the Jade Emperor, the fortune-bestowing minister of heaven, the crime-absolving minister of the earth, and the dilemma-resolving minister of the seas, enter accompanied by an other-worldly judge and other spirits. They have recently had to neglect their usual duties in order to wait on the Jade Emperor, but now have an opportunity to catch up on past business. The fortune-bestowing minister therefore requests the judge to present the various memorials sent them by earth spirits of different regions.

A memorial from the earth spirit of Hukuang province (modern Hupei and Hunan) reports Ch'üeh Chung's burning of debtor's accounts in his master's behalf (see act 12); and recommends that good fortune be bestowed on the master, Ch'üeh Li-hou. Another memorial from a committee of earth spirits in the northwest border region tells how Ch'üeh Li-hou, a rich commoner in the land of Ch'u (Hupei and Hunan), had his servant deliver three hundred thousand pecks of provisions to the area just when this was desperately needed, and begs that the act be brought to the attention of the Jade Emperor.

The fortune-bestowing minister is amazed at Ch'üeh's beneficence and resolves to memorialize the Jade Emperor at once. He requests the judge to report on Ch'üeh's fortunes, both good and bad, so he will know what recommendations to make in the memorial. The judge reports that the stars controlling Ch'üeh's enjoyment of wealth, wives, and servants are all extremely good and that he is destined to gain some children as well. The only blessing that he lacks is that of government office or hereditary rank. The fortune-bestowing minister resolves to remedy this.

The crime-absolving minister orders the judge to report all of Ch'üeh's offenses in his previous and present lives, so he can request that he be absolved of them. The only offense the judge can discover is that of having caused the death of a woman when seeking a bride. This was unintentional and can therefore be forgiven.

The dilemma-resolving minister orders the judge to report on all the problems suffered by Ch'üeh so he can mention them in the memorial. The judge replies that Ch'üeh has never suffered from flood, fire, bandits, or lawsuits. He has only two problems: physical deformity and beautiful women. The women have already retreated to his library and stopped harassing him, but the problem of his deformity still remains. The dilemma-resolving minister decides to request that an image-transforming spirit be sent down to change Ch'üeh into a handsome young man.

The crime-absolving minister objects that this proceeding would interfere with the process of punishment and repentance that Ch'üeh's wives are destined to undergo. The two other ministers agree, but maintain that Ch'üeh's merit is so great that an exception must be made in this one instance. They then write out the memorial and give it to the judge for delivery and presentation to the Jade Emperor.

28. A Change of Form (*Hsing pien*)

An image-transforming spirit enters carrying tools. He announces his mission to the Ch'üeh household, describes the role he plays in the world's affairs, and exits.

Ch'üeh Li-hou enters with Mistress Wu, who complains that Mistresses Tsou and Ho are still in seclusion while she alone suffers a wife's lot. Half a year has passed since Lord Yüan ordered her to return to Ch'üeh.

Two imperial messengers suddenly burst through the front gate.

Ch'üeh goes out to see what the trouble is and learns from the messengers that he has been given an exalted rank in recognition of his services, and that even his servant Ch'üeh Chung has been made an important official. Ch'üeh Li-hou's new title is *shang-i chün* (Lord of Righteousness). Hereafter, other men will be required to use the formula *ch'ien-sui* ("a thousand years of life") in greeting and address-ing him (this is analogous to *wan-sui*, "ten thousand years of life," used in addressing emperors). The messengers give Ch'üeh two cards that announce his own and his servant's elevation in status, and ex-plain that Ch'üeh Chung will arrive the next day with the official decree. Ch'üeh dismisses the messengers and calls excitedly to Mistress Wu.

When Mistress Wu learns the good news, she is suddenly glad she has been acting as Ch'üeh's wife for the past six months, as it prob-ably means that she will receive noble rank herself as Ch'üeh's wife. She advises Ch'üeh to fast and bathe so as to be in a fit state to hear the imperial decree on the following day. Ch'üeh readily agrees to this and Mistress Wu orders I-ch'un (the maid) to bring in some bath water. She exits.

Ch'üeh removes his clothing, and I-ch'un comes in with a pot of hot water which she pours into a tub. Ch'üeh climbs in and urges I-ch'un to scrub hard and thoroughly, causing pain if necessary. The image-transforming spirit enters unperceived and silently stands behind Ch'üeh. I-ch'un takes two or three swipes at Li-hou's hair, then gives up in disgust, saying, "Nothing I do can make him smell good. Let him do it." She exits.

The spirit then assumes the form of the maid and takes over the washing. He pours bathwater into Ch'üeh's mouth and hair and eyes. He uses a washcloth to wipe away his scars, warts, and freckles. He uses a plane to plane away his deformities, then pulls out his chest, pounds in his hunchback, and stretches and compresses his unequal legs. Ch'üeh then sends the spirit (whom he thinks is the maid) away, steps out of the tub, dries himself, and puts on his clothing. Glancing at the announcement cards the messengers gave him, he notices that whereas before he could only make out one or two characters on them, he can now read and understand both messages in their entirety. He wonders incredulously if the water he swallowed could have made him intelligent. He calls to Mistress Wu.

She enters with I-ch'un. At first she doesn't recognize Ch'üeh and asks where the lord of the house went. Ch'üeh indignantly denies that he is anyone but himself and Mistress Wu recognizes his voice, though all else is unfamiliar. She asks him to walk a few steps and observes to her astonishment that he is no longer lame or hunch-backed. I-ch'un comes up, sniffs him, and examines his hands. She calls to her mistress to observe that his skin has grown whiter and brighter and that his three odors (see act 4) have disappeared. Ch'üeh thanks I-ch'un for the vigorous scrubbing she gave him, saying that his improved appearance is all due to her efforts. She exclaims that he has been seeing ghosts and that she only made a couple of swipes before giving up and going elsewhere. Ch'üeh then realizes that something truly uncanny must have happened, looks in a mirror, and cries out, "What is the meaning of this?" Mistress Wu observes that it must surely have been the work of spirits, and Ch'üeh tells her that even his mind seems clearer than it was before.

Mistress Wu remarks that when she heard of Ch'üeh's new title she was only "thirty percent happy"; now, however, she is "one hundred percent happy." She decides to use some of her private savings to throw a little wine party that evening, to thank heaven and earth, and to congratulate Ch'üeh on his transformation. All she is afraid of is that the sutrachanters in the library may find out what has happened and return to the world again. That would be most inconvenient and unsuitable.

29. Conspiring in Jealousy (*Huo ts'u*)

Mistress Tsou and Mistress Ho are beginning to weary of the monotony of their existence. It has not escaped their attention that Mistress Wu has been living as Ch'üeh's wife for half a year and has not yet suffocated to death from the smell. Perhaps if they had put up with married life from the beginning, they would gradually have ceased to notice its inconveniences. As it is, they are locked up in their monastic retreat with no prospect whatsoever of regaining their freedom.

Mistress Tsou has heard of Ch'üeh's new title, and is furious beyond words at the thought of resigning her claim to be Ch'üeh's titled lady to Mistress Wu without a speck of compensation. She would like to have it out with her at once; the only problem is that she renounced her claims so emphatically in the past, she cannot imagine how she can now reassert them. Mistress Ho responds that they should go ahead and make a scene anyway. As the proverb says, "For each single day that you know no shame, you gain three days in which you get to eat your fill of rice."

I-ch'un comes in and tells them of Ch'üeh's transformation, but they refuse to believe a word of it. Ch'üeh himself then comes by to burn some incense before the Buddha's image in gratitude for his blessings. Seeing that he in fact looks different, the two ladies come out with smiling faces, offer congratulations, and invite him to sit down. Ch'üeh, however, leaves at once after barely acknowledging their attentions.

Mistresses Tsou and Ho resolve to wait until just before the imperial decree is due to arrive the following day, and then go before Ch'üeh and Mistress Wu to assert their rights. Even if they do not gain anything, it will be a first step in returning to the world.

30. A Quarrelsome Ennoblement (Nao feng)

Ch'üeh Chung enters dressed as an official, followed by attendants bearing the imperial decree and the ceremonial raiment to be bestowed on Ch'üeh and his wives. He announces that, from staff strategist, he has risen to imperial emissary and has been assigned the task of delivering the decree of ennoblement to his master. While in the capital he went to infinite pains, and endured terrible anxieties, in persuading the emperor to issue patents of nobility for all three of Ch'üeh's wives. Ordinarily, only the chief wife would be so honored. Ch'üeh Chung knew, however, that none of his master's three wives had settled positions in the family, and that if only one were made a great lady, there would be endless occasions for quarreling. Besides, he knew his master was not the sort who can easily face down rebellious women, so he took care to ensure that all three would be satisfied. He does not want them to take these titles too much for granted, however, and thinks it best to give them some moments of anxiety before they gain their rewards. He therefore decides to have the ladies' vestments delivered in successive intervals rather than all at once. He instructs his attendants and exits with them.

Mistress Wu enters. She has bathed, but has not, like Ch'üeh, been transformed. She feels it is crucial to keep the two "living Buddhas" in the library from emerging until after she has put on her vestments of nobility. She sends a maid to lock the door to the library, but the latter discovers that its occupants have already slipped out.

Mistresses Tsou and Ho enter in everyday attire rather than nun's robes. The three women begin at once to exchange sarcasms and to challenge each others claims. Ch'üeh Li-hou enters just as their quarrel is becoming loud, and is sarcastic on the subject of his first two wives' return. "Mine is just a common, vulgar household, much too cramped for people of high station. I have no idea what brought you two immortals here." They observe that as Mistress Wu has been just as rebellious in intent as they have, they should all be judged in a fair and evenhanded way. Ch'üeh objects that though all three were rebels, Mistresses Tsou and Ho were not as quick as Mistress Wu to "raise the flag of surrender."

An attendant brings in vestments for Ch'üeh and his chief wife. Ch'üeh dons his vestments as the ladies struggle over the single set of wife's vestments, one snatching the embroidered cap, a second the jade girdle, and the third the varicolored robe. When Ch'üeh demands that they cease quarreling and let one person have the vestments, they counter with the demand that he tell them to whom they should yield. Forced to make a decision, Ch'üeh takes Mistress Wu aside and asks her to yield to Mistress Tsou even though the title should by rights go to her. Now that he is one of the titled nobility, he can no longer conduct his household with the informality of an ordinary commoner. To have a concubine act as his titled wife would be a highly indecorous thing that might lead to criticism or even (if the court should hear of it) impeachment. Mistress Wu will have none of this, and a new round of quarreling and accusation begins. Ch'üeh cuts this short by restating his request to Mistres Wu: "My lady, the title cannot be given to you. Let me, therefore, bestow the substantial favors and attentions upon you and let the empty title be given to her." Mistress Wu tries to smash the jade girdle she is holding, but Ch'üeh rescues it and hands it to Mistress Tsou. Mistress Ho is relieved to see that the rules of precedence are now being observed and so resigns the robe to Mistress Tsou without objection. Mistress Tsou exults over her victory, singing, "You may think the substance is better than the empty title, but I'm pretty sure that once my title is high, substance will follow too."

The attendant enters and presents the second set of vestments. Mistresses Wu and Ho at once begin to fight over them. Ch'üeh separates them and tries to persuade Mistress Wu to follow the precedent just established and yield the title to Mistress Ho, as she is second in rank. She furiously refuses and Ch'üeh wavers. Mistress Ho points out to Ch'üeh that when Mistress Wu first arrived, she offered to help get herself and Mistress Tsou out of Ch'üeh's household once she returned to Lord Yüan. She asks if Mistress Wu is "such a loyal minister" that Ch'üeh wants to give her special protection. This convinces Ch'üeh that his wives are morally equal and that he should go by degrees of rank alone. He firmly presents the vestments to Mistress Ho.

Mistress Wu announces spitefully that there is nothing left for her to do but to return to religious seclusion in the library. Just as she is about to leave, the attendant enters and presents the third set of vestments. The rank is the same as the previous two, but the design is more resplendent. Ch'üeh puts the vestments on Mistress Wu, remarking that "she has earned some interest with her waiting." Mistresses Tsou and Ho grumble at their own stupidity in fighting over the two earlier titles.

Ch'üeh Chung then enters with the imperial decree ennobling Ch'üeh and his three wives. They kneel as he reads it and cry *wan-sui* ("ten thousand years of life") three times at its conclusion. Ch'üeh Li-hou thanks Ch'üeh Chung for all he has done, and asks to prostrate himself formally before his servant to express his sense of obligation. Ch'üeh Chung protests that he owes a far greater debt to his master for the favor of having been so trustfully employed and asks to prostrate himself formally before his master. Ch'üeh Li-hou proposes that they henceforth address each other as "nephew and uncle." Finally, they bow their thanks to each other simultaneously.

Glossary

The tones and characters for most of the Chinese names, titles, and expressions that appear in the text may be found by referring to this list. A few Japanese items are also included.

Aoki Masaru　青木正兒

Aoki Masaru zenshu　青木正兒全集

"Ch'à lǎo"　詫老

"Ch'à měi"　詫美

Chān Ài-chüān　詹愛娟

Chān huā-k'uéi　占花魁

Chān Shú-chüān　詹淑娟

Chān Wǔ-ch'éng　詹武承

Chāng Ch'í-yún　張其昀

Chāng Chìng　張敬

Chāng Hsiéh chuàng-yüán　張協狀元

Chāng Ì-mā　張一媽

Chǎng shēng chǔ hǎi　張生煮海

Ch'áng shēng tièn　長生殿

chǎng shǐh　長史

Ch'áo chì shū chuāng　朝記書莊

Chào Fēi-yèn　趙飛燕

Ché-fán　謫凡

ché hsiēn　謫仙

ch'éng　誠

"Chēng chì"　爭繼

"Chēng kòu"　爭購

"Chēng lì"　征利

Ch'éng Pú-shìh　程不識

Ch'éng wén ch'ū-pǎn shè　成文出版社

chí　集

245

"Chì chiāng" 祭江

"Ch'ī-ch'ièh pào p'í-p'á méi hsiāng shǒu chiéh" 妻妾抱琵琶梅香守節

Ch'í Jú-shān 齊如山

Ch'ī kūng-tzǔ 戚公子

ch'ī kūng-tzǔ 七公子

Ch'ī Pǔ-ch'én 戚補臣

"Chì tsǒ" 計左

Ch'ī Yǔ-hsiēn 戚友先

"Chiǎ shén" 假神

Chiǎ Ssū-wén 賈斯文

"Chiāng hsüěh" 江雪

Ch'iáo 喬

"Chiāo chièn" 郊餞

"Ch'iǎo chǜ" 巧聚

"Ch'iáo Fù-shēng Wáng Tsài-lái èrh chī hó chuàn" 喬復生王再來二
姬合傳

"Ch'iǎo huì" 巧會

Chiāo p'à chì 蕉帕記

"Ch'iǎo pù" 巧怖

"Chiǎo t'o 狡脫

Ch'iǎo t'uán-yüán 巧團圓

"Ch'ièh fā" 竊發

"Chiěh fēn" 解分

"Chièh huāng-t'áng" 戒荒唐

Chièh-tzǔ yüán 芥子園

Chièh-tzǔ yüán huà chuàn 芥子園畫傳

"Chiēh wáng" 偕亡

"Chiēn ch'á" 煎茶

"Chiěn fā" 剪髮

Ch'ien lǎo-yéh 錢老爺

"Chiēn lěi" 堅壘

Ch'ién Nán-yáng 錢南揚

"Chiēn p'èi" 艱配

"Ch'iěn shìh" 遣試

Ch'ién Wàn-kuàn 錢萬貫

Ch'ién yéh 錢爺

Ch'ién Yǜ-lién 錢玉蓮

Chīh kāo 雉皋

Chīn ch'üèh chì 金雀記

Chīn huá 金華

"Ch'ín-huái chièn-érh chuàn" 秦淮健兒傳

Ch'ín lóu yüèh 秦樓月

Chīn Yún Ch'iáo chuàn 金雲翹傳

chìng 淨

Chīng ch'āi chì 荊釵記

"Chīng ch'ǒu" 驚醜

"Chīng hsiěn" 驚變

Ch'īng-hsīn Ts'ái-jén 青心才人

"Ch'íng pīng" 請兵

"Ch'ìng yū" 倩優

ch'ǒu 醜

ch'ǒu 丑

"Ch'óu hsiàng" 籌餉

"Ch'ǒu láng chūn p'à chiāo p'iēn té yèn" 醜郎君怕嬌偏得艷

ch'ǒu-t'ài 醜態

ch'ū 齣

"Chù chiēn" 拒姦

Ch'ǔ hǎi 曲海

chǔ nǎo 主腦

"Chù piēn" 助邊

Ch'ǔ p'ǐn 曲品

Chū Sù-ch'én 朱素臣

Chū Tsǒ-ch'áo 朱左朝

"Chǔ yáo" 囑鷂

Ch'ū Yüán 屈原

chüàn 卷

ch'uán-ch'í 傳奇

"Ch'üán chiéh" 全節

"Ch'üàn núng" 勸農

"Ch'uǎng fēn" 闖氛

chuàng-yüán 狀元

"Chüéh chì" 決計

"Chüéh chì" 議計

Ch'üēh Chūng 闕忠

Ch'üēh Ì 闕義

Ch'üēh Lǐ-hóu 闕里侯

Chüéh-shìh Pài-kuān 覺世稗官

Chüéh-tào jén 覺道人

"Chuī tsūng" 追踪

"Chūka bunjin no seikatsu" 中華文人の生活

Ch'ūn tēng mì　春燈謎

Chūn t'iēn lè　鈞天樂

Ch'ún wén-hsüéh ch'ū-păn shè　純文學出版社

Chūng-huá shū chú　中華書局

Chūng-huá wén-huà ch'ū-păn shìh-yèh wěi-yüán huì　中華文化出版
事業委員會

Chūng-kuó chìn shìh hsì-ch'ǔ shǐh　中國近世戲曲史

Chūng-kuó wén-hsüéh fā tá shǐh　中國文學發達史

Chūng-kuó wén-hsüéh shǐh lùn chí　中國文學史論集

Chūng-lí Ch'ūn　鍾離春

Chūng yúng　中庸

è chá　惡札

"Ěrh jèh"　耳熱

Èrh-láng shén　二郎神

"Fā tuān"　發端

"Fáng jù"　防辱

"Féi tùn"　肥遯

"Fén chüàn"　焚券

"Fēn jăo"　分擾

Fēng chēng wù　風箏誤

Féng Huān　馮驩

Fèng huán ch'áo　鳳還巢

"Hài chǔ"　駭聚

Hàn hsüéh　漢學

Hán-huáng　寒簧

Hán Mèng-yáng　韓孟陽

Hán Shìh-hsǔn　韓世勳

Hǎo ch'iú chuàn　好逑傳

"Hò kuēi lóu"　鶴歸樓

"Hò suì"　賀歲

"Hò yáo"　和鷂

"Hsí chàn"　習戰

"Hsí ch'í"　錫棋

hsǐ chù　喜劇

Hsī hsiāng chì　西廂記

Hsī Shīh　西施

"Hsià chì hsíng lè chīh fǎ"　夏季行樂之法

Hsià lǐ　下李

Hsiāng yáng　襄陽偶寄

Hsiàng Yǔ 項羽

Hsiǎo Sūn t'ú 小孫屠

Hsién ch'íng ǒu chì 閒情

hsién jén pù té chìh 賢人 不得志

Hsién níng 咸寧

Hsīn-t'íng K'ò-chiāo 新亭客樵

"Hsíng pièn" 形變

"Hsüán piāo" 懸標

hú chiǎ hǔ wēi 狐假虎威

Hú-shàng Lì-wēng 湖上笠翁

"Hú wēi" 狐威

"Hú yáo" 糊鷂

huá chī 滑稽

"Huá ssù" 譁詞

Huáng ch'iú fèng 凰求鳳

Huáng Lì-chēn 黃麗貞

Huáng Wén-yáng 黃文暘

"Huī chīn" 揮金

huī-hsiéh 詼諧

"Huí shēng" 囘生

"Hūn nào" 婚鬧

Húng lóu mèng 紅樓夢

Húng Shēng 洪昇

húng yén pó mìng 紅顏薄命

húng yén pó mìng, kǔ chīn ch'áng chièn 紅顏薄命,古今常見

"Huǒ ts'ù" 夥醋

Ì chiā yén 一家言

"Ì chuì" 議贅

Í-ch'ūn 宜春

Ì-chūng yüán 意中緣

Ì hsiá chì 義俠記

"Ì hūn" 議婚

Ì p'ěng hsüěh 一棒雪

"Í ts'è" 貽冊

ǐ wèi 乙未

"Ǐ wù" 掎杌

Jén-mín wén-hsüéh ch'ū-pǎn shè 人民文學出版社

"Jèn mǔ" 認母

Jòu p'ú-t'uán 肉蒲團

Jú kāo　如皋
Jú lin wài shih　儒林外史
"Jù pān"　入班
"Juǎn k'uáng"　軟誆
Juǎn Tà-ch'éng　阮大鋮
"Júng fā"　榮發
K'āi-míng shū tièn　開明書店
"Kǎi shēng"　改生
"Kǎi t'ú"　改圖
"K'ǎi yèn"　凱宴
　k'ǎo chèng　考證
Kāo Míng　高明
"K'òu fā"　寇發
kǔ-chī　滑稽
kǔ-chiǎo　鼓角
kū chōu suō lì wēng　孤舟蓑笠翁
Kù Yén-wǔ　顧炎武
Kuān ch'ǎng hsièn hsíng chì　官場現形記
Kuǎng chìh shū chú　廣智書局
"Kuèi hsiěn ch'iěn"　貴顯淺
"Kuēi hùng"　閨閧
K'ǔng Chìh-kuēi　孔稚珪
K'ǔng Shàng-jèn　孔尚任
Kuó-lì Pěi-p'íng t'ú-shū kuǎn kuǎn-k'ān　國立北平圖書館館刊
"Lā yǐn"　拉引
Lán ch'ī　蘭谿
Lán ch'ī hsièn chìh　蘭谿縣志
Lǐ Ch'áo-wēi　李朝威
"Lì chǔ-nǎo"　立主腦
Lǐ Hào-kǔ　李好古
Lì-húng　笠鴻
Lǐ Jìh-huá　李日華
"Lǐ Li-wēng chù Wú shēng hsì chí Lién ch'éng pì chiěh t'í"　李笠翁
著無聲戲即連城璧解題
Lǐ Li-wēng shíh chǔng ch'ǔ　李笠翁十種曲
Lǐ Pǎo-chiā　李寶嘉
"Lì pī"　利逼
Lì Tào-jén　笠道人
Lǐ Tzù-ch'éng　李自成

Lì-wēng 笠翁

Lì-wēng ì chiā yén ch'üan chí 笠翁一家言全集

Lǐ Yú 李漁

Lǐ Yù 李玉

"Lǐ Yú chuàn" 李漁傳

Lǐ Yú ch'üán chí 李漁全集

Lǐ Yú yén-chiù 李漁研究

Liáo tù kāo 療妒羹

Lién ch'éng pì 連城壁

Lién hsiāng pàn 憐香伴

"Lién pān" 聯班

Liú Chiàng-hsiēn 劉絳仙

Liú Ch'ièn-ch'ièn 劉倩倩

"Liǔ Ì chuàn" 柳毅傳

Liǔ Ì ch'uán shū 柳毅傳書

Liú Miǎo-kū 劉藐姑

Liú Pāng 劉邦

Liù-shíh chǔng ch'ǔ 六十種曲

Liú Tà-chiéh 劉大傑

Liú T'íng-chī 劉廷璣

Liǔ Tsūng-yüán 柳宗元

Liú Wén-ch'īng 劉文卿

Liǔ Wú-chì 柳無忌

"Lǔ chǔn" 擄俊

"Lǔ hūn" 慮婚

Lǚ T'iēn-ch'éng 呂天成

Lù Ts'ǎi 陸采

"Lüèh yǜ" 掠嫗

Mǎ T'à-t'iēn 馬踏天

Madame Hó (Hó fū-jén) 何夫人

Madame Yüán (Yüán fū-jén) 袁夫人

"Mǎi fù" 買父

mài wén 賣文

"Mán chēng" 蠻征

Mǎn t'iěh 滿鐵

màn yěn fá chiéh 漫衍之節

Mào Hsiāng 冒襄

"Mào měi" 冒美

"Méi chēng" 媒爭

"Méi ch'ĭ" 媒欺

mèi-t'ài 媚態

"Mèng hài" 夢駭

"Mèng hsùn" 夢訊

Mèng Yáo 孟瑤

"Mì ch'óu" 密籌

míng 名

Míng chū chì 明珠記

Míng fēng chì 鳴鳳記

Míng Wǔ-tsūng 明武宗

Mistress Chōu (Chōu shìh) 周氏

Mistress Hó (Hó shìh) 何氏

Mistress Plum (Méi shìh) 梅氏

Mistress Tsōu (Tsōu shih) 鄒氏

Mistress Willow (Liǔ shìh) 柳氏

Mistress Wú (Wú shìh) 吳氏

Mò-líng ch'ūn 秣陵春

"Mò tìng" 默訂

Mò Yú-wēng 莫漁翁

Mù-júng Chièh 慕容介

Mǔ-tān t'íng 牡丹亭

mù-t'úng 牧童

Nà shū yíng ch'ǔ p'ǔ hsù-chí 納書楹曲譜續集

Nài hó t'iēn 奈何天

"Naò fēng" 鬧封

"Nǔ Ch'én P'íng chì shēng ch'ī ch'ū" 女陳平計生七出

"Pài hsiàng" 敗象

Pái t'ù chì 白兔記

Pǎn ch'iáo tsá chì 板橋雜記

Pàn mǒu yüán 半畝園

"Pàn tséi" 辦賊

"P'ān yüán" 攀轅

pǎo chiǎ 保甲

Pào-ch'ín 抱琴

"Pěi shān í-wén" 北山移文

pěn sè p'ài 本色派

"Pī chià" 逼嫁

"Pī hūn" 逼婚

Pǐ mù yǘ 比目魚

P'i-p'á chì 琵琶記

"Piéh shǎng" 別賞

"Pièn hsiàng" 變餉

P'íng-làng hóu 平浪侯

P'íng Shān Lěng Yèn 平山冷燕

Pó hsiào chì 博笑記

Pó-tào 伯道

"P'ǒu ssū" 剖私

P'ú chāi chǔ-jén 樸齋主人

p'ú-hsüéh 樸學

pù jén 不仁

Sān ch'ú 三衢

"Sān yǔ lóu" 三與樓

Sān yüán chì 三元記

Shā kǒu chì 殺狗記

Shān Tà-wáng 山大王

Shàng Chùng-hsién 尚仲賢

shàng-ì chūn 尚義君

"Shāng lí" 傷離

Shāng-wù yìn-shū kuǎn 商務印書館

Shè yüán huì yìn ch'uán-ch'í 涉園彙印傳奇

shéi 誰

Shěn Chīng 沈鯨

Shěn Chǐng 沈璟

Shèn chūng lóu 蜃中樓

"Shén hù" 神護

Shèn luán chiāo 慎鸞交

Shěn Pó 沈白

Shěn Shòu-hsiēn 沈受先

"Shēng wǒ lóu" 生我樓

shíh 實

"Shīh chiéh" 師揲

"Shìh chiēn" 試艱

Shíh chǔng ch'ǔ 十種曲

Shíh-èrh lóu 十二樓

Shīh hǒu chì 獅吼記

"Shìh í" 釋疑

Shíh-láng 十郎

Shǐh lùn 史論

Shìh shàng chǐh yǔ í kò p'ién-ì, pèi Wáng Hūa érh mǎi ch'ǜ lě
世上只有一個便宜,被王花兒買去了
"Shíh ssù" 時祀
Shíh ts'ò jèn 十錯認
"Shū p'à" 書帕
Shuāng chū chì 雙珠記
Shuǐ hǔ chuàn 水滸傳
Shunjūsha 春秋社
Suí-ān chǔ-jén 隨菴主人
Sūn Jǔ-ch'üán 孫汝權
Sūn K'ǎi-tì 孫楷第
Tà Chūng-kuó t'ú-shū kūng-ssū 大中國圖書公司
Tà hsüéh 大學
tà huā-mièn 大花面
"T'ài-tù" 態度
Taiwan shíh-tài shū chú 臺灣時代書局
T'án Ch'ǔ-yǜ 譚楚玉
"T'án Ch'ǔ-yǜ hsì-lǐ ch'uán ch'íng, Liú Miǎo-kū ch'ǔ-chūng ssǔ
  chiéh" 譚楚玉戲裏傳情,劉藐姑曲終死節
T'án huā chì 曇花記
Tān Pěn 單本
T'āng Hsiěn-tsǔ 湯顯祖
T'āng Hsiěn-tsǔ chí 湯顯祖集
"T'áo ch'án" 逃禪
T'áo huā shàn 桃花扇
"Tào yín" 導淫
"Té ch'ī" 得妻
Tēng Huì-chüān 登蕙娟
Tèng Yū 鄧攸
"T'í yáo" 題鷂
"Tiào měi" 調美
"Tiéh hài" 疊駭
"Tiēn mò" 巔末
T'īng chōu 汀州
Tīng Lán 丁蘭
"Tìng yū" 定優
"T'ō k'ò-chiù" 脫窠臼
"T'óu chiāng" 投江
tsá-chǚ 雜劇

ts'ái-tsǔ chiā-jén　才子佳人

Tsài yüán tsá chìh　在園雜志

"Tsǎn yáng"　攢羊

Tsāng Chìn-shū　臧晉叔

"Ts'ǎo chá"　草札

Ts'áo Hsüěh-ch'ín　曹雪芹

tsào-huà　造化

Ts'áo shìh　曹氏

Ts'áo Yù-yǔ　曹玉宇

"Tsèng hsíng"　贈行

Ts'éng yüán　層園

"Tsòu chiéh"　奏捷

Tsōu Wú-huái　鄒無懷

"Tsui chǐn"　醉爸

"Ts'uì yǎ lóu"　萃雅樓

"Ts'ūn chǐn"　村爸

ts'úng liáng　從良

tsǔng lùn　總論

"Tù ch'iěn"　妒遣

"T'ú ch'iúng"　途窮

Tù Chùn　杜濬

"T'ú fēn"　途分

tú tiào hán chiāng hsüěh　獨釣寒江雪

t'uán-yüán　團圓

Tūng kuó chì　東郭記

Tzǔ-chìh hsīn shū　資治新書

Tz'ú-ch'ǔ chú　詞曲局

"Tz'ú-ch'ǔ pù"　詞曲部

tzù-ján　自然

Tzǔ-líng　子陵

Tzǔ pù yǔ, kuài, lì, luàn, shén　子不語, 怪, 力, 亂, 神

"Tz'ú yüán"　詞源

Wáng　王

Wáng Chāo-chūn　王昭君

Wáng Kài　王槩

Wáng Kǔ-lǔ　王古魯

Wáng Shìh-chēn　王士禛

Wáng Shìh-chēn　王世貞

Wáng Shíh-p'éng　王十朋

Wáng Tào-k'ūn　鶯啼序

Wáng T'íng-nà　憂嫁

Wáng Yáng-míng　王陽明

Wáng Yù-ch'iáng　王又牆

wéi　維

Wèi Wú-chīh　魏無知

"Wèi yǐn"　僞隱

"Wén chào"　聞詔

"Wén chiéh"　聞捷

"Wén háo"　聞耗

Wén hsüǎn　文選

"Wén-hsüéh mén"　文學門

wén-tz'ú p'ài　文辭派

Wǒ yù jén, ssū jén chìh ǐ　我欲仁，斯仁至矣

"Wù ch'ín"　誤擒

Wǔ chìn　武進

Wú Chìng-tzǔ　吳敬梓

"Wù hsiàng"　誤相

Wú Pǐng　吳炳

Wú shēng hsì　無聲戲

Wú Wěi-yèh　吳偉業

"Yái lüèh"　崖畧

yámén　衙門

Yáng Tsūng-chēn　楊宗真

Yáng Yù-huán　楊玉環

Yáng Yǔn　楊雲

Yáo K'ò-ch'éng　姚克承

Yáo Tūng-shān　姚東山

"Yáo wù"　鷂誤

Yèh T'áng　葉堂

Yén Kuāng　嚴光

"Yén kuēi"　言歸

Yén Shìh-fān　嚴世蕃

Yén Sūng　嚴嵩

Yèn-tzǔ chiēn　燕子箋

Yī Hsiǎo-lóu　伊小樓

Yǐn Hsiǎo-lóu　尹小樓

"Yǐn tù"　隱妬

yǐn-tzǔ　引子

"Yīng t'í hsù" 汪道昆
"Yū chià"   汪廷訥
Yù Chiāo Li 玉嬌梨
Yú Huái 余懷
Yù Sāo-t'óu   玉搔頭
Yú T'úng 尤侗
yǔ-t'úng   漁童
Yüán Chó-shuǐ 袁濯水
Yüán ch'ǔ hsüǎn   元曲選
"Yüán mèng" 原夢
yüàn-tzǔ   院子
Yüán Yǔ-ling 袁于令
"Yǔn ch'óu" 運籌
Yǔn yáng 鄖陽

Key to Shortened References

Shortened Reference	*Full Reference*
Aoki Masaru	Aoki Masaru. *Chung-kuo chin-shih hsi-ch'ü shih*. Translated by Wang Ku-lu. Hongkong: Chung-hua shu-chü, 1975.
Hsien ch'ing ou chi	Li Yü. *Hsien ch'ing ou chi*. Taipei: Taiwan shih-tai shu-chü, 1975.
Huang Li-chen	Huang Li-chen. *Li Yü yen-chiu*. Taipei: Ch'un wen-hsüeh ch'u-pan she, 1974.
I chia yen	Li Yü. *Li-weng i chia yen ch'üan-chi*. Nanking: Chieh-tzu yüan, 1730.
Li Yü ch'üan-chi	Helmut Martin, ed., *Li Yü ch'üan-chi*. 15 vols. Taipei: Ch'eng wen ch'u-pan she, 1969.
Mao and Liu	Nathan K. Mao and Liu Ts'un-yan. *Li Yü*. Twayne's World Authors Series, no. 448. Boston: G. K. Hall and Co., 1977.
Shih chung ch'ü	Li Yü. *Li Li-weng shih chung ch'ü*. 10 *chüan*. Shanghai: Ch'ao-chi shu-chuang, 1918.

Notes to the Biographical Introduction

1. Li Yü's most commonly used courtesy-name is Li-weng. Some of his other names were Li-hung, Shih-lang, Che-fan, and Sui-an chu-jen. When living in Hangchow he called himself Hu-shang Li-weng, and in Nanking Hsin-t'ing K'o-chiao. As a short-story writer, he employed the pseudonyms Chüeh-tao jen, Li tao-jen, and Chüeh-shih Pai-kuan.

   Li Yü does not have a biography in the Ch'ing-shih and the accounts of his con-temporaries are rare and brief. For details concerning his life I rely on Huang Li-chen, pp. 4–46, where the available material is presented in a painstakingly documented fashion. For a much fuller English-language account of Li Yü's life than I present here, see Mao and Liu, pp. 11–30.

2. A high percentage of existing notices, articles, and studies on Li Yü are concerned with some aspect of Hsien ch'ing ou chi, especially the dramaturgical chapters. These chapters probably constitute the most thorough discussion of the principles of drama ever undertaken by a pre-Republican Chinese writer. Hsien ch'ing ou chi is included in the comprehensive edition of Li Yü's collection I chia yen, chüan 11 through chüan 16, and appears also in many separate editions. Because of its more general accessibility, I shall refer in these notes to the 1975 edition, which has oc-casional mistakes that can be corrected through reference to the I chia yen text.

   The drama chapters in Hsien ch'ing ou chi are discussed and translated in Helmut Martin, "Li Li-weng über das Theater, Eine Chinesische Dramaturgie des Siebzehnten Jahrhunderts" (Ph.D. diss., Ruprecht-Karl Universität, 1966).

3. There are ten extant plays by Li Yü. Their titles are listed below in the order in which they are usually published. Dates are supplied in the five instances where they are known.
   (1) Lien-hsiang pan (The Fragrance-adoring Companion)
   (2) Feng cheng wu (The Kite's Mistake)
   (3) I-chung yüan (An Ideal Marriage Destiny)
   (4) Shen-chung lou (The Mirage Tower)
   (5) Huang ch'iu feng (The Hen Seeks the Rooster), c. 1655–56
   (6) Nai-ho t'ien (What Can You Do?)
   (7) Pi-mu yü (The Paired Shoes), preface 1661
   (8) Yü Sao-t'ou (The Jade Scratcher), 1655; preface 1658
   (9) Ch'iao t'uan-yüan (The Amazing Reunion), 1668
   (10) Shen luan-chiao (The Careful Couple), preface c. 1667
   The edition of Li Yü's plays upon which I chiefly relied and to which these notes will refer is Shih chung ch'ü. This edition of the plays has the advantage of being clearly and attractively printed, and the disadvantage of containing occasional. misprints. In order to identify and correct the latter, I compared the Shih chung ch'ü texts with the older wood-block texts that appear in facsimile in Helmut Mar-tin's edition of the complete works of Li Yü, Li Yü ch'üan chi, vols. 7–11.

4. These are both included in Li Yü ch'üan-chi, vols. 12-15. Shih erh lou has been much the better known of the two collections.

5. James Hightower examines the evidence for this attribution in "Franz Kuhn and His Translation of Jou p'u-t'uan," Oriens Extremus 8 (1961): 252–257. He is inclined to doubt Li Yü's authorship, since (1) he knows only one dateable early passage that ascribes the book to him (in Tsai yüan tsa-chih by Liu T'ing-chi, preface 1715)

and (2) Li Yü would have had to have been only twenty-two years old at the time the preface to *Jou p'u-t'uan* was written if it was written in his lifetime.

On the other hand, Nathan Mao and Liu Ts'un-yan argue persuasively that *Jou p'u-t'uan* is probably by Li Yü, pointing out many conceptual and stylistic resemblances between the novel and the stories in *Shih erh lou* and *Wu-sheng hsi* (see Mao and Liu, pp. 90–95). Many resemblances of the same kind exist between *Jou p'u-t'uan* and the plays of Li Yü, but I shall refrain from engaging here in the lengthy process of pointing them out, for the question of *Jou p'u-t'uan's* authorship is only tangentially related to an appreciation of the plays and cannot in any case be conclusively determined by noting resemblances. The novel as a whole does suggest Li Yü's manner in its ingeniously symmetrical, many-layered plot and in its use of symbolic objects and situations.

6. This is a book of essays on painting accompanied by engraved reproductions. It was prepared by Wang Kai, Li Yü's son-in-law, and was first published in 1679 by Li Yü's own printing establishment, the "Mustard-seed Garden" *(Chieh-tzu yüan)*. The book proved popular and went through a number of subsequent expansions and continuations (see Huang Li-chen, p. 24). Selections from it, including Li Yü's preface, are translated in Mai-mai Sze, *The Way of Chinese Painting* (New York: Vintage Books, 1959), pp. 125–424.

7. See J. L. Van Hecken and W. A. Grootaers, "The Half-acre Garden, Pan-mou Yuan" *Monumenta Serica* 18 (1959):360–87.

8. Li Yü's admirers included the playwright Yu T'ung (1618–1704) and the memoirist Yü Huai (1616–96). His detractors included the playwright Yüan Yü-ling (d. 1674) and a variety of others whose comments are quoted in Huang Li-chen, pp. 1–3. Yüan Yü-ling's comment on Li Yü appears in translation at the beginning of chapter 2 in this book.

9. Li Yü's family seat was in Hsia-li village, Lan-ch'i district, Chin-hua prefecture, Chekiang, but he was born and partly raised in Chih-kao. Huang Li-chen says that Chih-kao was an old name for Ju-kao in Kiangsu (Huang Li-chen, p. 4). According to Nathan Mao and Liu Ts'un-yan, however, Chih-kao was part of a Hsia-chih district (characters not supplied) in Hupeh (see Mao and Liu, p. 151).

10. See the section "Hsia chi hsing-le chih fa" ("how to enjoy the summer season") in *Hsien ch'ing ou chi*, pp. 332–33.

11. See Huang Li-chen, pp. 4–7.

12. This probably refers to the famous *chüeh-chü* or four-line poem "River Snow" ("*Chiang hsüeh*") by Liu Tsung-yüan (773–819), the closing couplet of which goes, "In a solitary boat, a thatch-clothed old man [*ku chou suo li weng*] angles alone in the cold river snow [*tu tiao han chiang hsüeh*]." His adoption of the name was perhaps an offhand expression of a wish to be regarded as having abandoned all worldly ambition.

13. For a discussion of this practice (known as *mai-wen*) and its relation to the overall life-style of the traditional Chinese literatus, see Aoki Masaru, "Chuka bunjin no seikatsu," in *Aoki Masaru zenshu*, 12 vols. Tokyo: Shunjusha, 1969–70), 218–38.

14. The preface to *The Jade Scratcher (Shih chung chu'ü, chüan 8)*, dated 1658, mentions that Li Yü wrote the play in the winter of the year *i-wei* or 1655, while the preface to *The Careful Couple (Shih chung ch-ü, chüan 10)*, written c. 1667, implies that by that time Li Yü had already written sixteen plays.

15. The preface to *Twelve Mansions* is dated 1658, the year just following Li Yü's move to Nanking. The date of *Plays Without Sound* is uncertain, but Sun K'ai-ti believes on stylistic grounds that the stories in it are earlier than the stories in *Twelve Man-*

sions. See Sun K'ai-ti, *"Li Li-weng chu Wu-sheng hsi chi Lien ch'eng pi chieh t'i,"* *Bulletin of the National Library of Peiping* (*Kuo-li Pei-p'ing t'u-shu kuan kuan-k'an*) (1932): 9–25 (reprinted in *Li Yü ch'üan-chi,* vol. 15, pp. 6599–614.

16. *The Paired Soles* has a preface dated 1661. As for *The Hen Seeks the Rooster*, an autobiographical short story in classical prose by Li Yü mentions that at the time of a journey taken in 1666, the play had been completed "not quite several months ago" (see Li Yü, *"Ch'iao Fu-sheng Wang Tsai-lai erh chi ho chuan,"* *I chia yen, chüan* 2, pp. 28a–28b). *The Careful Couple* has a preface by a district counsellor of Hsien-ning (present-day Hsi-an, Shensi) whom Li Yü met during his western tour of 1667–68 (see Huang Li-chen, p. 11). *The Amazing Reunion* has a preface dated 1668.

17. See Huang Li-chen, p. 17. Two of Li Yü's revisions, *"Chien fa"* (act 29 of *P'i-p'a chi*) and *"Chien ch'a"* (act 25 of *Ming chu chi*) by Lu Ts'ai (1497–1537) are included in *Hsien ch'ing ou chi* at the end of chapter 1, *"Tz'u-ch'ü pu."*

18. See Huang Li-chen, p. 15.

19. Ibid., p. 24.

20. Ibid., pp. 22–23.

21. Ibid., p. 25.

Notes to Chapter One

1. The same concerns are expressed by Oliver Goldsmith in "An Essay on the Theatre or a Comparison Between Laughing and Sentimental Comedy" (1773) and in his preface to *The Good-natured Man* (1768). These pieces and Walpole's essay are all reprinted in W. K. Wimsatt, ed., *The Idea of Comedy* (Englewood Cliffs, New Jersey: Prentice Hall, 1969).

2. These definitions are derived from L. J. Potts, *Comedy* (1948; reprint ed., New York: Capricorn Books, 1966), p. 120.

3. For a recent expression of this attitude, see Walter Sorell, *Facets of Comedy,* (New York: Grosset and Dunlap, 1972), pp. 192–218.

4. The relation of comedy to the portrayal of social foibles has been acknowledged in some form by most theoreticians of comedy since Aristotle, who said that comedy portrays relatively base men whose vices belong to "the ridiculous" (*to geloion*), defined as harmless error, deficiency, or ugliness (see Aristotle, *Poetics,* trans. Leon Golden, commentary by O. B. Hardison, Jr. (Englewood Cliffs, New Jersey: Prentice Hall, 1968), chapter 5, p. 9. Two millenia later, the idea is confidently and succinctly expressed (in Venetian dialect) by Carlo Goldoni (1707–93): "La commedia lè stada inventada per corregger i vizi e metter in ridicolo i cattivi costumi" (comedy was invented to chastise faults of behavior and to ridicule disagreeable habits). See Goldoni, *Il Teatro Comico* (1751), reprinted in Goldoni, *Opere,* ed. Gianfranco Folena and Nicola Mangini (Milan: printed for Ugo Mursia, 1969), act 2, scene 1. p. 353.

5. Cf. Henry Fielding, preface to *Joseph Andrews:* "life every where furnishes an accurate observer with the Ridiculous" ([New York: Penguin Books, 1977] p. 26).

6. Molière seems to have regarded the faculty of reason as the primary means of comic perception. In "Lettre sur *L'Imposteur*" (1667), a pamphlet written in defence of

Tartuffe, Molière or a close associate defines the comic as "la forme extérieure et sensible que la providence de la nature a attachée à tout ce qui est déraisonnable," and goes on to say, "nous estimons ridicule ce manque extrêmement de raison . . . il s'ensuit que tout mensonge, déguisement, fourberie, dissimulation, toute apparence différente du fond, enfin toute contrariété entre actions qui procèdent du même principe, est essentiellement ridicule." See W. G. Moore, *Molière* (1949; reprint ed., Oxford: Clarendon Press, 1962), pp. 143–44.

7. Some examples of *ch'uan-ch'i* plays other than ones by Li Yü that could be considered comic in their totality are *The Tale of the Lion's Roar (Shih hou chi)* by Wang T'ing-na, *The Tale of the Eastern Wall (Tung-kuo chi)* attributed to Wang Tao-k'un, *The Tale of the Gold Sparrow Clasp (Chin ch'üeh chi*; authorship unknown), and *The Tale of the Plantain-leaf Scarf (Chiao p'a chi)* by Tan Pen. There are doubtless others as well. See Eric Henry, "Varieties of Comedy in Chinese Ch'uan-ch'i Drama" (unpublished paper), in which *Lion's Roar* and *Eastern Wall* are discussed.

8. *Hsi-chü*, the term for comedy now current in China and elsewhere in the Far East, was coined in modern times to provide an equivalent for the western word. In traditional times, Chinese literati used terms like *hua-chi* (pronounced *ku-chi* by sticklers for historical correctness), "comical, buffoonlike;" *hui-hsieh*, "funny, humorous;" and *ch'ou-t'ai*, "comically inappropriate or indecent behavior;" when discussing comic material. Thus Lü T'ien-ch'eng in his *Ch'ü-p'in* (1610) says of *The Tale of the Lion's Roar* that "it is replete with comical misbehavior [*ch'ou-t'ai*] and is enough to make you hold your belly with laughter. The concluding portion in which [the heroine] repents can be used to improve the habits of womenfolk." See Aoki Masaru, p. 254.

9. See Northrop Frye, *Anatomy of Criticism* (Princeton: Princeton University Press, 1957), pp. 43–44, and George E. Duckworth, *The Nature of Roman Comedy* (Princeton: Princeton University Press, 1952), pp. 20–33.

10. See Eric Henry, "On the Nature, Structure, and Evolution of the *Chin Yün Ch'iao chuan*, a Popular Novel of the Early Ch'ing" (unpublished paper).

11. See L. J. Potts, *Comedy* (New York: Capricorn Books, 1966), pp. 16–22 and passim.

12. Contemporary references to *ch'uan-ch'i* performances often make it clear that only isolated acts were performed. Li Yü's *Paired Soles*, for example, has two episodes in which an itinerant troupe of actors give *ch'uan-ch'i* performances on the occasion of a local religious festival. In both cases they perform one act only (from *The Thorn Hairpin, Ching-ch'ai chi*). On the first occasion, the leading actress invites the patron to choose additional acts if he wishes. See *Shih chung ch'ü, chüan* 7 (*Pi-mu yü*), act 15, pp. 21a–23a, and act 28, pp. 39b–41b.

13. See Birch's preface to K'ung Shang-jen, *The Peach Blossom Fan*, trans. Ch'en Shih-hsiang, Harold Acton, and Cyril Birch (Berkeley: University of California Press, 1976).

14. In act 9 of the *ch'uan-ch'i* play *A Medicine for Jealousy (Liao tu kao)* by Wu Ping, for example, the heroine stays up throughout the night reading *The Peony Pavilion (Mu-tan t'ing)* by T'ang Hsien-tsu.

15. The principal anthology of Yüan dynasty *tsa-chü (Yüan ch'u hsüan*, edited by Tsang Chin-shu) was published c. 1616, some three hundred years after the peak period of Yüan drama. It remained the only known collection of *tsa-chü* texts for several centuries until recent discoveries (c. 1918 and 1940) of Yüan dynasty wood-block editions and manuscripts of *tsa-chü* (see James I. Crump, "The Elements of Yuan Opera," *Journal of Asian Studies* 17 [1957–58]: 417–34).

16. In adopting this term, I follow the usage of Richard Strassberg in his dissertation "The Peach Blossom Fan: Personal Cultivation in a Chinese Drama" (Princeton University, 1975).

17. The overwhelming predominance of the romantic pattern makes it easy to forget that not all *ch'uan-ch'i* plays are concerned with love stories. Of those that are not, perhaps the most well known is *Tale of the Singing Phoenix (Ming-feng chi)*, a political protest play attributed to Wang Shih-chen concerning the wicked minister Yen Sung and his son Yen Shih-fan. It is somewhat loosely organized, in the manner of a chronicle play such as Shakespeare's *Henry the Sixth*. The play *Snow Bearer (I p'eng hsüeh)* by Li Yü (not to be confused with the subject of this study, Li Yü), a political protest play on the same topic, is also without a love story, but is closer to the romantic pattern in that it focusses on the tribulations of a single family and is centered upon an emblematic object.

   Other *ch'uan-ch'i* plays that do not conform to the romantic pattern are *Tale of a Dog Killing (Sha kou chi)*, concerned with the resolution of family dissension and injustice; *Tale of Three First-Places (San-yüan chi)* by Shen Shou-hsien, which deals with the rewards of secret philanthropy; *Tale of the Eastern Wall (Tung-kuo chi)*, which is concerned with the humorous adventures of three eccentric characters of the Warring States period; and *Limitless Laughs (Po hsiao chi)* by Shen Ching, which is composed of ten unrelated funny stories. There are also *ch'uan-ch'i* plays devoted to crime-solving stories (the early *nan-hsi* or "southern play" *Butcher Sun* [Hsiao Sun t'u] is an example), and *ch'uan-ch'i* plays devoted to heroic outlaws from the novel *Shui hu chuan*, such as Shen Ching's *Tale of a Chivalrous Hero (I-hsia chi)*.

18. This is a feature found in all *ch'uan-ch'i* plays; it is not limited to romantic comedy.

19. The chief exception to this situation are plays in which the male protagonist is an emperor yearning for an ideal consort, as in *The Palace of Eternal Life (Ch'ang-sheng tien)* by Hung Sheng. One of Li Yü's plays, *The Jade Scratcher (Yü Sao-t'ou; 1655)* is of this type. It is a fanciful treatment of a romance between the Ming Cheng-te emperor (Ming Wu-tsung; reigned 1506–22) and the courtesan Liu Ch'ien-ch'ien. It is the earliest of Li Yü's dateable plays.

   Another subtype concerns a romance between a man who is married but without heirs and the woman he desires to gain as a concubine, as in *A Medicine for Jealousy* (see note 14) by Wu Ping and *The Careful Couple* by Li Yü.

20. An important subtype explores what happens when the protagonist, already married, forsakes the wife of his years of obscurity and accepts the advantageous new alliance. Examples of this are the *nan-hsi Top Graduate Chang Hsieh (Chang Hsieh chuang-yüan)* and the famous *Tale of the Lute (P'i-p'a chi)* by Kao Ming.

21. Li Yü himself happens to have been the only notable exception to this rule. He discusses drama structure at length in the opening chapter of *Hsien ch'ing ou chi*.

22. C. S. Lewis, *The Allegory of Love* (Oxford: Oxford University Press, 1936), p. 141.

23. *The Tale of the Udumbara Blossom (T'an hua chi)* is thus described in *Ch'ü-p'in* by Lü T'ien-ch'eng (fl. late sixteenth early seventeenth century). See Aoki Masaru, p. 209.

24. Li Yü, *Hsien-ch'ing ou chi*, p. 11 under the heading "T'o k'o-chiu."

25. Examples are act 6 in *The Paired Soles*, in which T'an Ch'u-yü soliloquizes on his reluctance to join an actor's troupe, and act 6 in *The Amazing Reunion*, in which Miss Ts'ao decides to send a love message to Yao K'o-ch'eng.

26. This suggests a distinction that Auden makes between primitive poetry and modern poetry: "Primitive poetry says simple things in a roundabout way where modern poetry tries to say complicated things straightforwardly." See W. H.

Auden, "The Greeks and Us" in his *Forewords and Afterwords* [New York: Vintage Books, 1943], pp. 3–32), p. 6.

27. The example is taken from a *ch'ü* (aria) sung by Mu-jung Chieh in act 25 of *The Paired Soles* (*Shih chung ch'ü, chüan* 7, pp. 36b–37a).

28. See act 4 of *The Amazing Reunion.*

29. See act 19 of *The Paired Soles.*

30. See act 3 of *The Kite's Mistake.*

31. Li Yü, *Hsien ch'ing ou chi*, pp. 14–15 under the heading "Chieh huang-t'ang."

32. See act 5 of *The Amazing Reunion.*

33. *Pi-mu yü, Shih chung ch'ü, chüan* 7, act 14, p. 19b.

Notes to Chapter Two

1. It appears probable that the idea for *The Paired Soles* first occurred to Li Yü in the form of a vernacular short story. Sun K'ai-ti describes an early edition of Li Yü's short story collection *Plays Without Sound (Wu sheng hsi)* that he found in the Man t'ieh Library of Dairen, China. This edition bears the title *Lien ch'eng pi* and contains several stories that do not occur in other early editions of *Plays Without Sound*. One of these "extra" stories concerns the same subject matter as *The Paired Soles*, as may be seen from its title: "T'an Ch'u-yü conveys his love within a play; Liu Miao-ku concludes her performance by dying to preserve her fidelity" ("T'an Ch'u-yü hsi li ch'uan ch'ing, Liu Miao-ku ch'ü chung szu chieh"). See Sun K'ai-ti, "Li Li weng chu Wu-sheng hsi chi Lien ch'eng pi chieh t'i," in *Li Yü ch'üan-chi*, vol. 15, pp. 6599–619.

   Unfortunately, copies of the Dairen library edition are not readily obtainable and I have not seen the story. Judging from the title of the story and the nature of the two genres (play and story), it appears likely that the story ends with the lovers' suicides and contains nothing of their transformation and return to life.

2. *Pi Mu Yü, Shih chung ch'ü, chüan* 7, act 1, p. 1a.

3. The expression *ts'ung liang* does not mean "to follow honesty" but (of a prostitute or actress) "to become properly married," "to become an honest woman," etc. Here I was forced to resort to the literal "following honesty" in order to preserve the parallelism of this line with the other three.

4. *Shih chung ch'ü, chüan* 7, act 1, p. 1a.

5. Ibid., act 8, p. 8b.

6. Ibid., act 2, p. 1b.

7. Ibid., p. 2a.

8. Ibid., act 3, p. 3a.

9. Ibid., p. 3b.

10. Examples occur in the *ch'uan-ch'i* play *Chan hua-k'uei* by Li Yü (to be distinguished from Li Yü, the subject of this study) and the novel *Chin Yün Ch'iao chuan* by Ch'ing-hsin Ts'ai-jen (pseudonym).

11. *Shih chung ch'ü, chüan* 7, act 3, p. 3b.

12. Ibid., pp. 3b–4a.

13. Ibid., p. 4a.

14. Ibid., p. 4b.

15. Ibid., act 6, pp. 6b–7a.

16. Ibid., act 7, pp. 7b–8a.
17. Ibid., act 3, p. 4a.
18. Ibid., p. 4a.
19. Ibid., act 7, pp. 7b–8a.
20. Ibid., act 2, p. 2a.
21. Ibid., act 7, p. 7a.
22. Ibid., p. 7b.
23. Ibid.
24. Ibid., p. 8a.
25. Ibid., act 9, p. 10a.
26. Ibid., act 10, p. 10b.
27. Ibid., p. 11b.
28. Ibid., p. 12a.
29. Ibid.
30. Ibid., pp. 12a–12b.
31. Ibid., p. 12a.
32. Ibid., p. 12b.
33. Ibid., p. 13a.
34. Ibid., p. 13b.
35. Ibid.
36. Rendered literally, the title of this act would be "The Imposing Air of a Fox." The two-character title is a condensation of the proverb *hu chia hu wei* (a fox assumes the imposing air of a tiger). The idea it conveys is that of intimidation through an empty display of fierceness.
37. *Shih chung ch'ü, chüan* 7, act 11, pp. 13b–14a.
38. Ibid., p. 14b.
39. Ibid.
40. Ibid., p. 15a.
41. Ibid., pp. 14b–15a.
42. Ibid., p. 14b.
43. Ibid., p. 15a.
44. Ibid.
45. Ibid., p. 15b.
46. Ibid., p. 15a.
47. Ibid., act 5, pp. 5b–6b.
48. Ibid., act 8, pp. 9b–10a.
49. Ibid., act 12, p. 15b.
50. Ibid.
51. Ibid., p. 16a.
52. Ibid., pp. 16a–16b.
53. Ibid., p. 16b.
54. Ibid., pp. 16b–17a.
55. Ibid., p. 17a.
56. Ibid., p. 16b.
57. Ibid., p. 17b.
58. Ibid., p. 17a.
59. The pastoralism in act 8 of *The Peony Pavilion* (*Mu-tan t'ing*), "Encouraging Agriculture" (*Ch'üan nung*), is, for example, much more restrained. The situations, of course, are not parallel; prefect Tu goes to the countryside, not as a settler, but as an official with a function to perform. His distantly appreciative response to his rustic entertainers accords both with his character and his situation. See Ch'ien

Nan-yang, ed., *T'ang Hsien-tsu chi* (Shanghai: Chung-hua shu-chü, 1962), vol. 3, pp. 1836–40.

60. *Shih chung ch'ü*, *chüan* 7, act 12, p. 17b.
61. Ibid., act 16, pp. 24b–25a.
62. Ibid., act 18, p. 29b.
63. Ibid., act 13, p. 18b.
64. Ibid., pp. 18b–19a.
65. Ibid., p. 19a.
66. Ibid., act 14, p. 19b.
67. Ibid.
68. Ibid., p. 20a.
69. Ibid., p. 20b.
70. Ibid.
71. In *Hsien ch'ing ou chi* Li Yü states that however many characters there are in a play, all must exist for the sake of a single character and that however many events involve this character, all must exist for the sake of a single event. See *Hsien ch'ing ou chi*, p. 10 under the heading "Li chu-nao."
72. *Shih chung ch'ü*, *chüan* 7, act 15, p. 22a.
73. Ibid.
74. Ibid.
75. Edition consulted: *Liu shih chung ch'ü* (Shanghai: K'ai-ming shu-tien, 1935), *chüan* 6, pp. 80–81.
76. *Shih chung ch'ü*, *chüan* 7, act 15, p. 23a.
77. Ibid.
78. Ibid.
79. Ibid., act 16, p. 23b.
80. Ibid., p. 24a.
81. Ibid., p. 24b.
82. Ibid.
83. Ibid., p. 25a.
84. Ibid., act 17, p. 25b.
85. Ibid., p. 26a.
86. Ibid., pp. 26b–27a.
87. Ibid., pp. 27a–28a.
88. Ibid., p. 28a.
89. Ibid., p. 28b. A similar effect of combined shock and inevitability, as in the springing of a prepared mechanism, occurs near the close of Chaucer's "Miller's Tale" when the cuckolded carpenter hears Nicholas (who has just been burned in a sensitive place) crying for water, concludes therefrom that the flood predicted by Novalis has come, and axes the rope from which his bucket is suspended.
90. Ibid., act 10, p. 12a.
91. Ibid., act 18, p. 29a. "With the milky way between us" is an allusion to a traditional tale concerning two Chinese constellations on either side of the milky way, "the herdboy" and "the weaving girl." These two heavenly lovers are said to be able to meet only on the seventh day of the seventh month of each year, when a flock of magpies forms a bridge across the sky.
92. Ibid., p. 29b.
93. Ibid., act 19, pp. 30a–30b.
94. Ibid., act 27, p. 39a. Actors are sometimes associated with ghosts or spirits, since their performances make the famous dead come to life again on the stage—hence the reference to "the underworld."

95. Ibid., act 19, p. 31a.

96. Ibid., p. 32a.

97. Ibid.

98. Ibid., act 28, pp. 39b–41a. In *The Paired Soles*, this borrowed act is identified as *Chi chiang* ("Sacrificing by the River"), which is the title of act 30 in *The Thorn Hairpin*, an act in which the heroine is mourned only by her mother-in-law. The borrowed material (comprising five arias) is not, however, taken from this act, but from act 35, "*Shih ssu*," in which both husband and mother-in-law offer sacrifices to the heroine. The mother-in-law's part is suppressed in the adaptation. See *Ching ch'ai chi* (cf. note 75), pp. 106–8.

99. *Shih chung ch'ü*, *chüan* 7, act 25, pp. 35a–37b.

100. Ibid., act 23, pp. 34a–35b.

101. Ibid., act 30, p. 43b.

102. Ibid., act 32, pp. 47b–48a.

103. Ibid., act 25, p. 37b.

104. Ibid., act 26, p. 38b.

105. The earliest well-known example of this satiric theme is "Proclamation on North Mountain" *(Pei-shan i-wen)* by K'ung Chih-kuei (447–501), in *Wen-hsüan* (1936; reprint ed., Hongkong: Shang-wu yin-shu kuan, 1973), *chüan* 43, pp. 957–60). One of the marginal comments accompanying this act refers to the piece: "This Proclamation-on-North-Mountain kind of thing is surely enough to make scholars die of shame." See *Shih chung ch'ü*, *chüan* 7, act 23, p. 34b.

106. Ibid., p. 34a.

107. Ibid., p. 34b.

108. Ibid., p. 35a.

109. Ibid., act 32, p. 47b.

110. Ibid., pp. 48a–48b.

111. Ibid., p. 48b.

112. Ibid.

113. Cf. *Confucian Analects, The Great Learning, and the Doctrine of the Mean*, Chinese text with translation, exegetical notes, and character index by James Legge (1893; reprint ed., New York: Dover Publications, 1971), book 7, chapter 20: "*Tzu pu yü, kuai, li, luan, shen*," "The master never talked of prodigies, feats of strength, natural disorders, or spirits." (p. 201).

114. *Shih chung ch'ü*, *chüan* 7, act 32, p. 48b.

Notes to Chapter Three

1. Li Yü, "Sheng-wo lou," story number 11 in *Shih erh lou, Li Yü ch'üan-chi*, vol. 15, pp. 6481–82.

The quotation "Wealth nourishes the house" is from chapter 6, section 4 of the commentary to the *Ta-hsueh*; see *Confucian Analects, The Great Learning, and the Doctrine of the Mean*, Chinese text with translation, exegetical notes, and character index by James Legge (1893; reprint ed., New York: Dover Publications, 1971), p. 367.

The plot of *The Amazing Reunion* seems in the main to be original with Li Yü; however it is highly probable that its central idea was borrowed from a popular tradition concerning the Ming Cheng-te emperor (reigned 1506–22). According to this tradition, the heirless emperor disguised himself as a beggar and went among the people, offering himself for sale as a father to any orphan who wished to purchase him. Everyone heaped ridicule upon the disguised emperor until a young man named Wang Hua came forward and took him at his word. The emperor put Wang to countless tests of patience and constancy. When Wang proved adequate to them all, the emperor took him to the palace and made him the successor to the throne, with the result that he later became the Ming Chia-ching emperor (1522–67). From this story a proverb is derived: "There is only one stroke of luck in the world, and that was bought up long ago by Wang Hua" (*Shih shang chih yu i ko p'ien-i, pei Wang Hua erh mai ch'ü le*). See Arthur H. Smith, *Proverbs and Common Sayings from the Chinese* (1914; reprint ed., New York, Paragon Book Reprint Corp. and Dover Publications Inc., 1965), pp. 117–18.

I am indebted to Clara Park for pointing out to me that a version of the emperor Cheng-te story outlined above appears in a book of Chinese stories for children by Arthur Bowie Chrisman, *Shen of the Sea* (New York: E. P. Dutton and Co., 1925), "Buy a Father," pp. 65–78 (1968 edition, pp. 70–80).

2. Li Yü, "Sheng-wo lou," *Li Yü ch'üan-chi*, pp. 6527–28.
3. Li Yü, *Ch'iao t'uan-yüan*, *Shih chung ch'ü*, *chüan* 9, p. 43b.
4. Fyodor Dostoyevsky, *The Brothers Karamazov* (1880), trans. Constance Garnett (New York: New American Library, 1957), p. 89 (part 1, book 2, chapter 8).
5. The Compact Edition of the Oxford English Dictionary, s.v. "sincere."
6. *Analects*, *Ta-hsüeh*, sections 4 and 5, pp. 357–59.
7. *Analects*, *Chung-yung*, chapter 20, section 17, pp. 412–13.
8. Ibid., 25, 1, p. 418.
9. Ibid., 20, 19–20, pp. 413–14.
10. Ibid., 20, 18, p. 413.
11. Ibid., 25, 3, pp. 418–19.
12. Ibid., 26, 2–3, p. 419.
13. Ibid., 24, pp. 417–418.
14. This device is used to excellent effect in *Tale of the Eastern Wall* (*Tung-kuo chi*), attributed to Wang Tao-k'un. See *Liu shih chung ch'ü* (Shanghai: K'ai-ming shu tien, 1935), *chüan* 3.
15. *Shih chung ch'ü*, *chüan* 9, p. 44a.
16. Ibid., act 2, pp. 1b and 2b respectively.
17. Ibid., act 8, pp. 10a–11a.
18. Ibid., pp. 11b–13a.
19. Ibid., act 24, p. 30a.
20. Ibid., act 31, p. 38b.
21. Ibid., act 19, p. 23b.
22. "Sheng wo lou" (see note 1), conclusion to chapter 3, p. 6523.
23. *Shih chung ch'ü*, *chüan* 9, act 13, pp. 16a–16b and act 15, pp. 18a–19b.
24. Ibid., act 33, p. 43b.
25. Ibid., p. 43b. Yao and Shun are two legendary sage-kings of high antiquity whose reigns are held up as ideal patterns of enlightened government.
26. Ibid., act 32, p. 41b.
27. Ibid., act 10, p. 13b. Po-tao was the courtesy name of Teng Yu, a great official of the Western and Eastern Chin dynasties. Once, while escaping from Hsiung-nu invaders, he sacrificed his only son in order to save the only son of his deceased younger brother. He was later unable to have another son in spite of exemplary conduct of his official duties under the Eastern Chin. After his death, his friends

made a punning proverb about him that went, "the way of heaven [*t'ien-tao*] is without wisdom, for it caused Teng Po-tao to be without a son."

Ting Lan was a filial son of the Han dynasty. Having lost his parents when young, he carved wooden images of them that he served as if they were alive. When a neighbor got drunk and insulted the wooden images, Ting Lan killed him. "A Po-tao and a Ting Lan" therefore signifies "a father without a son and a son without a father."

28. Ibid., act 14, p. 18a.
29. Ibid., act 24, p. 29b.
30. Ibid., act 11, pp. 14a–14b.
31. Ibid., p. 15a.
32. Ibid., act 23, pp. 28b–29a. "To face perpetually to the left" appears to mean "to have a predisposition to commit blunders." For another example of this use of the word *left* (*tso*), see the title of act 23 in *What Can You Do?*
33. See Note 3 to the Biographical Introduction
34. C. S. Lewis, *A Preface to Paradise Lost* (Oxford: Oxford University Press, 1942), p. 3.
35. *Shih chung ch'ü*, *chüan* 9, act 17, pp. 21a–21b.
36. Ibid., act 31, p. 39b.
37. Ibid., p. 39b.
38. Ibid., act 33, p. 43b.
39. Ibid., 44a.
40. Ibid., act 8, p. 10a.
41. Ibid., p. 10b.
42. Ibid. This is a slightly altered version of poem 64 in the *Shih-ching*. The translation is based on Arthur Waley's rendering of that poem in his *Book of Songs* (1937; reprint ed., New York: Grove Press, 1960), in which poem 64 appears as Poem 18, p. 31.
43. Ibid.
44. Ibid., p. 11a.
45. Ibid.
46. Ibid., act 5, p. 7a.
47. Ibid., act 6, p. 8a.
48. Ibid., act 33, p. 43a.
49. Ibid., act 9, p. 11b.
50. Ibid.
51. Ibid., act 10, p. 13b.
52. "Sheng wo lou" (see note 1), chapter 1, p. 6487; heading to chapter 2, p. 6491.
53. *Shih chung ch'ü*, *chüan* 9, act 10, p. 13a.
54. Ibid., p. 13b.
55. Ibid., act 18, p. 23a.
56. Ibid., act 24, p. 30a. "Golden planets" and "silver jellyfish" are slang names for varieties of coins.
57. Ibid., act 16, p. 21a.
58. Ibid., act 9, p. 11b.
59. Ibid., act 17, p. 21a.
60. "Sheng wo lou" (see note 1), p. 6477.
61. Ibid., pp. 6479–80.
62. Ibid., pp. 6530–31.
63. *Shih chung ch'ü*, *chüan* 9, act 2, p. 1a.
64. Ibid., act 31, p. 39b.

65. Ibid., act 32, p. 40a.
66. Ibid., p. 40a.

Notes to Chapter Four

1. Of the four plays discussed in this volume, *The Kite's Mistake* is the only one that does not appear to have been sketched previously in the form of a short story. Also, there appears to be no obvious way of dating the play, though its excellence naturally inclines one to assign it to the author's maturity.

2. That Li Yü could distinguish between moral and physical beauty even while using the latter to represent the former is evident not only in this play, but in his treatment of the ugly protagonist of *What Can You Do?* (who is deformed but not wicked), and in his conception of "charm" in women, which he thought resided more in certain indefinable emanations of personality than in details of appearance. See *Hsien ch'ing ou chi*, pp. 121–24 under the heading *t'ai-tu*.

3. *Every Man in His Humor* perhaps comes closest to supplying the type of title whose absence we have observed (*Cosi Fan Tutte* would be another possibility), but the word *humor* is inseparably bound to the notion of a particular foible.

4. *Feng cheng wu, Shih chung ch'ü, chüan* 2, act 13, p. 15a.

5. Ibid., act 16, p. 19b.

6. Ch'i Yu-hsien is the son and heir of the head of the household in which his romantic double, the orphaned Han Shih-hsün, is raised out of his host's loyalty to the memory of Han's deceased father. The ugly Ai-chüan and the refined Shu-chüan are both daughters of a general's concubine, but Ai-chüan's mother has more seniority than Shu-chüan's.

7. *Shih chung ch'ü, chüan* 2, act 13, pp. 14a–16a.

8. Ibid., act 16, p. 19a.

9. Ibid., act 11, p. 12a.

10. Ibid., act 9, pp. 10a–10b and act 11, p. 13a.

11. Ibid., act 28, p. 33b and act 21, p. 25b.

12. Ibid., act 30, p. 38a.

13. Ibid., act 28, p. 33b.

14. See Northrop Frye, *Anatomy of Criticism* (Princeton: Princeton University Press, 1957), p. 172.

15. *Shih chung ch'ü, chüan* 2, act 13, pp. 14b–15a.

16. Ibid., act 22 and 23, pp. 16a–17b.

17. Ibid., act 28, p. 33a.

18. Ibid., act 29, pp. 34a–34b.

19. Ibid., pp. 36b–37a.

20. Ibid., act 17, pp. 20a–20b.

21. Ibid., act 3, p. 4b and acts 21–22, pp. 25b–26a.

22. Ibid., act 15, pp. 17b–18b and act 13, p. 15b.

23. Ibid., act 16, p. 20a.

24. Ibid., act 30, p. 38a.

25. Ibid., p. 40a.

26. *Confucian Analects, The Great Learning, and the Doctrine of the Mean*, Chinese text

with translation, exegetical notes, and character index by James Legge (1893, reprint ed., New York: Dover Publications, 1971), book 7, chapter 3, pp. 195–96.

27. Ch'ü Yüan was a nobleman of the state of Ch'u during the Warring States period (403–221 B. C.). At first he was a trusted advisor in the court of King Huai of Ch'u, but due to the slanders of a rival he became estranged from favor and was eventually banished. After suffering this punishment he committed suicide by throwing himself into the Mi-lo River. "Encountering Sorrow" is the name of a poem by Ch'ü Yüan that gives extended lyrical expression to the author's sense of grief and outrage at his unjust treatment. "The common run of men" is a slightly misquoted version of the forty-fifth couplet of this poem. For an English translation of "Encountering Sorrow" together with an excellent discussion of the poem and its author, see David Hawkes, trans., Ch'u Tz'u: The Songs of the South, An Ancient Chinese Anthology (Oxford, Clarendon Press, 1959), pp. 1–34.

28. Hsi Shih was a famous beauty said to have been responsible for the fall of the state of Wu to the state of Yueh in 473 B.C. She was especially beautiful when she frowned; other women therefore tried to imitate her beauty by frowning, but only succeeded in emphasizing their own ordinariness.

29. Wang Chao-chün was a lady in the harem of the emperor Han Yüan-ti (reigned 48–32 B.C.). She is said to have refused to bribe a court painter, who therefore made her portrait ugly. Assuming the portrait to be veracious, the emperor never chose to have her admitted to his presence and only discovered her beauty after he had already promised her to a king of the Hsiung-nu, a nomadic people to the northwest of China. He regretted losing her, but it was then too late to prevent it. Her tomb was said to have remained green, though surrounded by desert.

30. Yang Yü-huan and Chao Fei-yen were both imperial concubines whose names have become proverbially associated with beauty. The former was the favorite of T'ang Hsüan-ti (reigned 713–56), and the latter of Han Ch'eng-ti (reigned 32–6 B.C.). The "witch from Wu-yen" is a reference to Chung-li Ch'un, a woman proverbial for ugliness whose wise advice made her a favorite of King Hsüan of Ch'i (Warring States period).

31. Shih chung ch'ü, chüan 2, the two unnumbered pages directly preceding the table of contents. I am indebted to Cheng Kuang-yüan for the suggestion (which I have adopted) that the character shei occurring near the close of this preface both in this edition and in Li Yü ch'üan-chi is probably an error for wei, as the word shei does not properly belong in a piece of classical prose.

32. Yu T'ung wrote one ch'uan-ch'i play and five tsa-chü. The ch'uan-ch'i play, Chün t'ien le (Joy Vast as Heaven), is a perfect example of a play with a hsien-jen pu te chih theme. The story is as follows: two talented young scholars, Shen Po and Yang Yün, travel to the capital together to take the metropolitan examination. They complain bitterly to each other of the corruption then prevalent in the examination system and try to submerge their sorrows in wine and song. They then go to a fortune-teller to try to learn if they will be successful or not. Just then, three stupid and ignorant sons of great officials appear at the fortune-tellers' as well. Their names are Chia Ssu-wen ("Feigned Culture"), Ch'eng Pu-shih ("Utter Blockhead"), and Wei Wu-chih ("Ignorant Imposter"). These three tell the fortune-tellers to predict their success by studying their features. The different fortune tellers all agree that Shen and Yang are likely to gain first place, but that no such good fortune is in store for Chia, Ch'eng, and Wei. The three lose their tempers upon hearing this prediction and beat the fortune-tellers to a pulp. As it turns out, Chia Ssu-wen gains first place because the chief examiner happens to

have been his father's student. Ch'eng and Wei are awarded second and third place in return for bribes. Shen and Yang both fail the examination. Shen has long been engaged to Wei's younger sister Han-huang, but has been unable to marry her because of his proverty. When Han-huang hears of her brother's wicked behavior and its results, she falls ill from vexation. Shortly afterwards, a letter from her brother arrives instructing the family to annual Han-huang's engagement to Shen and marry her to his friend Ch'eng instead. Han-huang cannot withstand this sudden blow, and dies of sorrow and resentment. When Shen returns home, he hears of Han-huang's death and sets out to make sacrifices at her grave. Shen is captured by a group of rebelling bandits and the bandit leader Ma T'a-t'ien tries to force Shen to join his staff. When it becomes apparent that Shen is prepared to die rather than accept, Ma, moved by his courage and rectitude, sets him free. Shen then learns that his friend Yang has fallen ill and died while running from the disorders. He mourns for his dead friend. Shortly afterwards he hears that Han-huang's older brother Wei Wu-chih has become governor of Fu-feng. Since he has been connected with Wei's family through marital engagement in the past, he stops in Fu-feng to pay him a visit, but is turned away at the door. He departs in anger. Shen sends a memorial to the throne, criticizing the corruption prevalent in the examination system. He is in consequence accused of insolence, given a beating, and expelled from the capital. He then wanders aimlessly about the countryside, at a loss as to how to give vent to his burning indignation. Coming across a temple to Hsiang Yü, he goes inside and tells the story of the injustices he has suffered to a statue of the warrior. He then embraces the statue, weeps, and says, "Great king, you were unable to gain the world in spite of your matchless heroism, and I have been unable to pass the metropolitan examination in spite of my literary mastery. Have there ever been greater injustices than these?" At this, the statue weeps, and a statue of Hsiang Yü's favorite concubine Mme. Yü weeps as well. Shen then falls asleep from exhaustion and has a dream in which Hsiang Yü appears to him and says, "After you have returned home, the heavenly emperor will give you employment." Shen wakes up, bids farewell to the statue, and departs. Shen's soul then takes leave of his body and rises to heaven. In heaven, the Han dynasty emperor Wen-ch'ang is moved by his indignation at the corruption of the examinations on earth to hold a scholarly examination in heaven. Shen, his friend Yang, and the T'ang poet Li Ho gain the three highest places, and are given a banquet honoring their success. The banquet is presided over by the famous Sung poet Su Shih and the banquet musicians perform the piece "Joy Vast as Heaven," from which the play derives its title. In the meantime the soul of Shen's fiancée Han-huang has drifted to the palace of the Queen Mother of the West. Not knowing where she is, Shen and Yang search for her in the earth and in the ocean but do not find her. They then travel to the Queen Mother's palace, but find on their arrival that Han-huang has already gone with the Western Mother to the Palace of the Moon. Yang's wife then travels to the moon and tells Han-huang what has happened to Shen Po. The Queen Mother then sends a memorial to the Emperor of Heaven announcing the marital intentions of Shen Po and Han-huang. The Emperor issues an official directive giving assent to the marriage, and the play ends with the wedding celebration. See Aoki Masaru, pp. 343–44.

It is worth noticing that this play, which unquestionably belongs to the *hsien-jen pu te chih* category, adheres quite closely to the pattern set by Ch'ü Yüan. It even includes the journey through heaven to the palace of the Queen Mother of the

West, a detail that the development of the story by no means demands. *The Kite's Mistake*, on the other hand, has no otherworldly episodes at all, let alone a journey through heaven.

33. See Huang Li-chen, p. 5. See also Mao and Liu, pp. 11–22.

34. For all of these biographical details, see Huang Li-chen, pp. 4–25 and Mao and Liu, pp. 11–22.

35. *Mo-ling ch'un (Spring in Nanking)* by Wu Wei-yeh (a friend of Li Yü's), and *T'ao-hua shan (The Peach-blossom Fan)* by K'ung Shang-jen are both examples of early Ch'ing *ch'uan-ch'i* plays that *do* have themes of dynastic collapse. See Aoki Masaru, pp. 328–33 and pp. 383–90.

36. See *Shih chung ch'ü, chüan 10 (Shen luan chiao)*, the two unnumbered pages directly preceding the table of contents.

37. See Ts'ao Hsueh-ch'in, *Hung-lou meng* (Peking: Jen-min wen-hsüeh ch'u-pan she, 1957), chapter 23, pp. 268–71.

38. *Shih-chung ch'ü, chüan* 10, p. 3a.

39. Ibid., act 36, p. 49b.

40. The Peking opera version is by Ch'i Ju-shan (I am indebted to Hans Frankel for this information) and is entitled *Feng huan ch'ao* ("A Phoenix Returns to its Nest"). I have not had an opportunity to look at the Chinese text. There is an English rendering of the play by Elizabeth Te-chen Wang entitled *Snow Elegant* (Taipei: Meiya Publications, 1971).

41. *Shih chung ch'ü, chüan* 2 *(Feng-cheng wu)*, act 2, p. 1a.

42. Ibid.

43. Ibid., p. 1b.

44. Ibid.

45. Ibid., act 26, pp. 30a–31b.

46. Ibid., act 2, p. 2a.

47. Ibid. The quotation is from the *Analects*, book 7, chapter 29.

48. *Shih chung ch'ü, chüan* 2, act 2, p. 2a.

49. Ibid.

50. Ibid., act 13, p. 16a.

51. See the notice in Liu T'ing-chi, *Tsai-yüan tsa-chih* (preface dated 1715), *chüan* 1 (quoted in Huang Li-chen, p. 2), in which Li is described as "more clever than erudite." See also the section on Li Yü in Meng Yao (pseudonym of Yang Tsung-chen), *Chung-kuo wen-hsüeh shih* (Taipei: Ta Chung-kuo tu-shu kung ssu, 1974), p. 746, which refers to his "vulgarity of style." See also Josephine Hung, *Ming Drama* (Taipei: Heritage Press, 1966), pp. 207–8.

52. See *Hsien ch'ing ou chi*, the section entitled "Kuei Hsien-ch'ien" ("Treasuring the Obvious and the Shallow") pp. 18–20.

53. In a letter to *The Christian Century* reprinted in Walter Hooper, ed., *God in the Dock* (Grand Rapids: William B. Ferdmans Publishing Co., 1970), p. 338, Lewis remarks apropos of the promulgation of Christian doctrine, "Any fool can write *learned* language. The vernacular is the real test. If you can't turn your faith into it, then either you don't understand it or you don't believe it." Elsewhere in the same volume of essays (p. 98) he remarks, "if you cannot translate your thoughts into uneducated language, then your thoughts were confused. Power to translate is the test of having really understood one's own meaning."

54. *Li Yü ch'üan-chi*, vol. 1, pp. 19–20.

55. Ibid., pp. 21–22.

56. *Shih chung ch'ü, chüan* 2, act 6, p. 6a.

57. Ibid., act 3, p. 4a.

58. Ibid.
59. Ibid., act 2, p. 2b.
60. Ibid., act 11, p. 12b.
61. Ibid., act 6, pp. 6a–6b.
62. *Hsien-ch'ing ou chi*, the subsection "I wu" ("Chairs and Stools"), pp. 220–23. This passage also appears in English translation in Cyril Birch, ed., *Anthology of Chinese Literature* (New York: Grove Press, 1972), vol. 2, pp. 154–57.
63. "Li Yü chuan," *Lan-ch'i hsien chih* (1888), *chüan* 5, Wen-hsüeh men, quoted in Huang Li-chen, pp. 1–2.
64. See *Shih chung ch'ü*, *chüan* 9, act 13, pp. 16a–16b and act 15, pp. 18a–19b. The device is also used in the fifth of the *Wu sheng hsi* stories, "Nü Ch'en P'ing chi sheng ch'i ch'u." See *Li Yü ch'üan-chi*, vol. 12, pp. 5341–80.
65. See Aoki Masaru, p. 341.
66. See *Shih chung ch'ü*, *chüan* 7, act 15, pp. 22b–23a.
67. See Ibid., *chüan* 10, act 4, the clown's entrance poem in the last two lines of p. 3b.
68. See Ibid., *chüan* 7, act 18, p. 29b and act 19, p. 31b and 32a.
69. Ibid., *chüan* 2, act 3, pp. 3b–4a.
70. Ibid., act 6, p. 6b.
71. Ibid., pp. 6a–6b.
72. Ibid., act 7, p. 7a.
73. Ibid.
74. Ibid., pp. 7a–7b.
75. Ibid., p. 7b.
76. Ibid.
77. Ibid., act 8, p. 7b.
78. Ibid.
79. Ibid., pp. 7b–8a.
80. Ibid., p. 8a.
81. Ibid., p. 8b.
82. Ibid., p. 9a.

Notes to Chapter Five

1. *Nai-ho t'ien*, *Shih chung ch'ü*, *chüan* 6, act 30, p. 46b.
2. Ibid., act 1, p. 1a.
3. The earliest locus classicus I can discover for this proverb is the mid-Ming dynasty *ch'uan-ch'i* play *Shuang-chu chi* by Shen Ching (not the well-known Ming playwright Shen Ching), which contains the line *hung-yen po ming, ku-chin ch'ang chien*.
4. *Shih chung ch'ü*, *chüan* 6, act 2, p. 1a.
5. Ibid., pp. 1a–1b.
6. Ibid., p. 1b.
7. Ibid.
8. Ibid.
9. Ibid., p. 2a.
10. See Szu-ma Ch'ien, *Shih-chi* (Peking: Chung hua shu chü, 1959), *chüan* 7 and 8, pp. 295–394. These two chapters are translated in Burton Watson, *Records of the Grand Historian of China* (New York: Columbia University Press, 1961), pp. 37–119.

11. Quoted in Edgar Johnson, *Charles Dickens, His Tragedy and Triumph* (New York: Simon and Schuster, 1952), 2:1129.
12. *Shih chung ch'ü, chüan* 6, act 2, p. 2a.
13. Ibid., act 5, p. 7a.
14. Ibid., act 2, p. 2a.
15. Ibid., p. 2b.
16. Ibid., act 10, p. 14b.
17. Ibid.
18. Ibid., act 28, pp. 40a–40b.
19. Ibid., act 12, pp. 16a–17a.
20. Ibid., p. 16b. This is loosely paraphrased from the second part of a two-part proposition: "People realize that in order to enjoy this kind of wealth, it is necessary to have had virtue-accumulating ancestors; but they do not realize that the same condition must be fulfilled before one can hope to enjoy the services of such a loyal and intelligent servant."
21. Li Yü, "Ch'ou lang chün p'a chiao p'ien te yen," story number 1 in *Wu sheng hsi, Li Yü ch'üan chi*, vol. 12, pp. 5075–164.
22. *Shih chung ch'ü, chüan* 6, act 28, pp. 39b–40a.
23. Ibid., p. 42a.
24. Ibid., act 27, p. 39b.
25. Ibid., subsequent to act 30, p. 47a.
26. Ibid., act 23, p. 33a.
27. Ibid., p. 34a.
28. Ibid.
29. See Aoki Masaru, pp. 251–54. The play is included in the collection *Liu-shih chung ch'ü*, 60 vols. (1935; reprint ed., Taipei: K'ai-ming shu tien, 1970), vol. 49.

Notes to Chapter Six

1. See Eric Henry, "On the Nature, Structure, and Evolution of the *Chin Yün Ch'iao chuan*, a Popular Novel of the Early Ch'ing" (unpublished paper). The first Chinese novels to be translated into European languages were all of the *ts'ai-tzu chia-jen* (dashing young genius and exquisite beauty) variety. *Hao ch'iu chuan* appeared in English in 1761 (this version was based on a manuscript translation dated 1719), in German in 1766, again in English in 1829, and in French in 1842. French translations of *Yü Chiao Li* and *P'ing Shan Leng Yen* appeared in 1826 and 1860 respectively. *The Dream of the Red Chamber*, on the other hand, did not appear in a western language until a partial English rendering by Bancroft-Joly was published in 1892–93.
2. The three stories appeared in John Francis Davis, F.R.S., *Chinese Novels Translated from the Originals; to which are added Proverbs and Moral Maxims, collected from their Classical Books and Other Sources. The Whole Prefaced by Observations on the Language and Literature of China* (London: John Murray, 1822), pp. 53–224. The third of these stories, "San-Yu-Low; or, The Three Dedicated Rooms," had appeared previously in the opening numbers of *The Asiatic Journal and Monthly Register* 1 (1816): 34–41, 132–34, 243–49, 338–42.
3. The three stories translated by Davis were rendered in French by Abel Rémusat in

Contes Chinois, 3 vols. (Paris: 1827). A German translation, *Chinesische Erzäh-lungen,* appeared the same year in Leipzig. (See Helmut Martin, "Li Li-weng über das Theater, Eine Chinesische Dramaturgie des Siebzehnten Jahrhunderts," (Ph. D. diss., Ruprecht-Karl Universität, 1966). Bibliography, pp. 316–17). An abridged version of the eleventh story in *Twelve Mansions, Sheng wo lou,* appeared in *The Asiatic Journal and Monthly Register* 35 (1841): 33–38, signed with the single initial "B." Martin gives the translator's name as "S. B(irch)." (See Martin, p. 318.) A précis of the plot of *The Paired Soles* prepared by Camille Imbault-Huart appeared in *Journal Asiatique,* 8th ser. 15 (1890): 483–92. Excerpts from *The Careful Couple, The Kite's Mistake,* and *What Can You Do?* appeared in Latin translations accompanying the Chinese texts in A. Zottoli's *Cursus Litteraturae Sinicae* (Shanghai: Typographia Missionis Catholicae, 1882), vol. 1, pp. 397–99, 400–407, 407–11. A French translation of *Cursus Litteraturae Sinicae* by P. C. deBussy appeared in Shanghai in 1891, also published by the Catholic Mission Printers.

4. Quoted from Huang Wen-yang, *Ch'ü-hai* (c. 1782) in Huang Li-chen, p. 2. Huang Wen-yang was in charge of the *Tz'u-ch'ü chü,* a temporary bureau established c. 1777 in order to censor dramatic works. The project was completed in four years and resulted in the publication of *Ch'ü-hai,* which is an annotated catalogue of dramatic works in twenty *chüan.* (See Tu Lien-che's article on Ling T'ing-k'an in Arthur Hummel, ed., *Eminent Chinese of the Ch'ing Dynasty* [Washington: U.S. Government Printing Office, 1943], pp. 514–15.)

5. See Liu Ta-chieh, *Chung kuo wen hsüeh fa ta shih* (1941; reprint ed., Taipei: Chung-hua shu chü, 1973), pp. 1049–50; and Liu Wu-chi, *An Introduction to Chinese Literature* (Bloomington: Indiana University Press, 1966), pp. 257–59.

6. See for example Aoki Masaru, pp. 333–42 and the article "Li Yü" by Chang Ching in *Chung-kuo wen hsüeh shih lun-chi* ed., (Taipei: Chung-hua wen-hua ch'u-pan shih-yeh wei-yüan hui, 1958), pp. 1009–15.

7. Yü Huai (1616–96) contributed a preface dated 1671 to Li Yü's essay book *Hsien ch'ing ou chi.* He is best known for his reminiscences of singing girls in the pleasure quarters of Nanking before the fall of the Ming: *Pan ch'iao tsa chi* (1697).

Tu Chün (1611–87) contributed a preface dated 1658 to Li Yü's vernacular story collection *Shih erh lou.* He was the editor of a selection of the works of Mao Hsiang (1611–93). (See Fang chao-ying's article on Mao Hsiang in Hummel, *Eminent Chinese of the Ch'ing Dynasty,* p. 566.)

Many of Li Yü's preface contributors and commentators are not readily iden-tifiable, as they use obscure pseudonyms. Among his other friends were the historian and dramatist Yu T'ung (1618–1704), the poet and dramatist Wu Wei-yeh (1609–72), and the poet Wang Shih-chen (1634–1711). See Mao and Liu, pp. 14–15.

8. See William Dolby, *A History of Chinese Drama* (New York: Harper and Row, 1976), passim.

9. *Shen luan chiao, Shih chung ch'u,* chuan 10, act 17, p. 22a.

10. Chu Su-ch'en's play with Li Yü's commentary may be found in *She-yüan hui yin ch'uan ch'i* (Wu chin: She yüan, 1927), vols. 7 and 8. There are several shared elements between the plot of this play and that of *Shen Luan-chiao (The Careful Couple)* by Li Yü.

11. See James Cahill, "Confucian Elements in the Theory of Painting," in *The Confu-cian Persuasion* ed. Arthur Wright (Stanford: Stanford University Press, 1960), pp. 115–40.

12. In *A Random Lodge for My Idle Feelings,* Li Yü extensively discusses *The Tale of the Lute, The Peony Pavilion, The Southern Romance of the Western Chamber* (by Li Jih-

hua), and a number of other well-known plays.

13. *Shih chung ch'ü, chüan* 2 *(Feng-cheng wu)*, p. 40a.

14. This appears in a commentary by Yü Huai on a *tz'u* poem by Li Yü "Ying t'i hsü." See *I chia yen, chüan* 2, pp. 28a–28b.

15. Northrop Frye, *A Natural Perspective: The Development of Shakespearean Comedy and Romance* (New York: Columbia University Press, 1965), p. 6. *The Return from Parnassus* is a comedy in two parts (Frye quotes from part II, act I, scene 2) comprising the second and third parts of a Parnassus trilogy performed at St. John's College, Cambridge during the years 1597–1601. See W. D. Macray, ed., *The Pilgrimage to Parnassus with the Two Parts of the Return from Parnassus* (Oxford: Clarendon Press, 1886), p. 87.

16. The word is used here in its old sense of "charlatan"; but that meaning derives from the etymological sense of the word as a person whose knowledge comes from experience rather than instruction.

17. See John Dennis (1657–1734), "A Defence of Sir Fopling Flutter" (1722), included in W. K. Wimsatt, ed., *The Idea of Comedy* (Englewood Cliffs, New Jersey: Prentice-Hall, 1969), p. 138. Rapin's dictum was (perhaps unconsciously) restated by Horace Walpole in his essay on comedy published in 1728. See Wimsatt, p. 199.

18. The grammar is slightly altered in the translation for the sake of smoothness. The original wording is as follows: "Questo e la grand' Arte del Comico Poeta, di attaccarsi in tutto alla Natura, e non iscostarsene giammai." See Carlo Goldoni, "Prefazione dell' Autore alla Prima Raccolta delle Comedie" (1750), reprinted in *Tutte le Opere di Carlo Goldoni*, ed. Giuseppe Ortolani (Milan: Mondadori, 1935), p. 773. Goldoni has a good deal more to say in the same vein, and quotes some of the same passages from Rapin used by Dennis in his "Defence."

19. In the case of England, for example, it is possible to think of important eighteenth-century comic dramatists, such as Goldsmith and Sheridan, as well as comic novelists, such as Fielding and Sterne; but in the following century the important comic artists such as Austen, Dickens, Thackeray, and Meredith tend to be novelists, while the stage is practically taken over by farce, sentiment, and melodrama.

20. This novel is often loosely characterized as a satire, but it is actually free from the destructive intent that is the mark of satire proper. The late Ch'ing "exposure" novelists felt they were working in the novelistic tradition of *The Scholars*, but they looked only to its satiric aspects as a guide in their own writings and thus failed to create novels of similar scope. *The Scholars* and *Exposure of the Officials* (*Kuan ch'ang hsien hsing chi*) by Li Pao-chia (1867–1906) could be taken as textbook examples of the distinction between comedy and satire. The first is written from a detached and amused perspective that allows one's feelings of sympathy or antagonism to assume a natural equilibrium that adjusts delicately to each slight change in the moral climate of the action. The second is written from the penetrating but unbalanced standpoint of anger and disgust.

21. The first European comedies were fifteenth and sixteenth century imitations of Plautus and Terence composed in Latin. The first Italian-language comedy, *La Cassaria*, was produced by Ariosto in 1508; the first English-language comedy, *Ralph Roister Doister*, by Nicholas Udall c. 1552 (see George E. Duckworth, *The Nature of Roman Comedy: A Study in Popular Entertainment* [Princeton: Princeton University Press, 1952], pp. 396–412).

22. By "the greatest development of the Chinese novel of manners," I mean *The Scholars* and *The Dream of the Red Chamber*. While these two novels differ

drastically from each other in countless respects, both are remarkable for steady, clear, and minute attention to peculiarities of everyday behavior.

23. See chapter 4, pp. 101–5.
24. See Aoki Masaru, pp. 341–42.
25. See chapter 1, pp. 15–16.
26. See *Hsien ch'ing ou chi*, "T'o k'o-chiu," pp. 11–12 and "Kuei hsien-ch'ien," pp. 18–20.
27. Ibid., p. 11.
28. *Shen chung lou* (*Shih chung ch'ü*, *chüan* 4) combines the plots of two Yüan dramas: *Liu I ch'uan-shu* (*Liu I transmits the letter*) by Shang Chung-hsien (this is in turn based on the T'ang *ch'uan-ch'i* tale "Liu I chuan" by Li Ch'ao-wei) and *Chang sheng chu hai* (Chang Boils the Sea) by Li Hao-ku. See Huang Li-chen, p. 157.
29. See Aoki Masaru, p. 310.
30. Ibid., p. 308. Aoki quotes this from Yeh T'ang, *Na-shu ying ch'ü p'u* (1792) *hsü-chi*, *chüan* 3. Aoki also thinks the two playwrights are related in style and temperament.
31. See Juan Ta-ch'eng, *Yen tzu chien* (c. 1630–40) (Hongkong: Kuang-chih shu-chü, n.d.).
32. See *Hsien ch'ing ou chi*, "Li chu-nao," pp. 10–¡1.
33. See *Shih chung ch'ü*, *chüan* 2 (*Feng cheng wu*) act 13, pp. 14a–16a.
34. See *I chia yen*, *chüan* 2, pp. 18b–22b. This story has been translated into English by Conrad Lung in *Traditional Chinese Stories*, ed. Y. W. M. and Joseph S. M. Lau (New York: Columbia University Press, 1978), pp. 110–14.
35. For a discussion of this aspect of comedy see L. J. Potts, *Comedy* (1948; reprint ed., New York: Capricorn Books, 1966), p. 124.

Index